UNCANNY REST

TRANSLATED FROM SPANISH BY **CAMILA MOREIRAS**

DUKE UNIVERSITY PRESS   DURHAM AND LONDON   2022

ALBERTO MOREIRAS

UNCANNY REST

FOR ANTIPHILOSOPHY

© 2022 DUKE UNIVERSITY PRESS
All rights reserved
Uncanny Rest: For Antiphilosophy, published by
Duke University Press, is an expanded translation
of *Sosiego siniestro*, originally published in
Spanish in 2020 by Guillermo Escolar Editor.
Project editor: Lisa Lawley
Designed by Matthew Tauch
Typeset in Chaparral Pro and Bahnschrift
by Copperline Book Services

Library of Congress Cataloging-in-Publication Data
Names: Moreiras, Alberto, author. | Moreiras, Camila, translator.
Title: Uncanny rest : for antiphilosophy / Alberto Moreiras ;
translated from Spanish by Camila Moreiras.
Other titles: Sosiego siniestro. English.
Description: Durham : Duke University Press, 2022. | Includes
bibliographical references and index.
Identifiers: LCCN 2022026528 (print)
LCCN 2022026529 (ebook)
ISBN 9781478016380 (hardcover)
ISBN 9781478019022 (paperback)
ISBN 9781478023654 (ebook)
Subjects: LCSH: COVID-19 Pandemic, 2020—Social aspects. |
COVID-19 | Pandemic, 2020-—Philosophy. | COVID -19 Pandemic,
2020—Political aspects. | Epidemics—Philosophy. | BISAC:
LITERARY CRITICISM / Semiotics & Theory | PHILOSOPHY /
Movements / Critical Theory
Classification: LCC RA644.C67 M6713 2022 (print) |
LCC RA644. C67 (ebook)
DDC 362.1962/414—DC23/eng/20220715
LC record available at https://lccn.loc.gov/2022026528
LC ebook record available at https://lccn.loc.gov/2022026529

TO TERESA

If one were only an Indian, instantly alert, and on a racing horse, leaning against the wind, kept on quivering jerkily over the quivering ground, until one shed one's spurs, for there needed no spurs, threw away the reins, for there needed no reins, and hardly saw that the land before one was smoothly shorn heath when horse's neck and head would be already gone.
—FRANZ KAFKA, "The Wish to Be a Red Indian" (1913)

PREFACE ix

CONTENTS

UNCANNY REST FOR ANTIPHILOSOPHY

MARCH 20, 2020 3
Remark 1: The Path of the Goddess

MARCH 27, 2020 7

MARCH 29, 2020 7

APRIL 1, 2020 A.M. 8
Remark 2. The Pandemic and the Event

APRIL 1, 2020 P.M. 15

APRIL 3, 2020 17

APRIL 4, 2020 18

APRIL 9, 2020 21

APRIL 12, 2020 23
Remark 3: Self-precursion

APRIL 15, 2020 26

APRIL 16, 2020 30

APRIL 18, 2020 32

APRIL 24, 2020 35

APRIL 25, 2020 38

APRIL 28, 2020 39

MAY 2, 2020 39

MAY 5, 2020 41

MAY 6, 2020 43

MAY 7, 2020 47

MAY 9, 2020 48

MAY 10, 2020 50
Remark 4: Fools and Free Spirits

MAY 11, 2020 57

MAY 12, 2020 A.M. 59

MAY 12, 2020 P.M. 61

MAY 13, 2020 A.M. 62

MAY 13, 2020 P.M. 64

MAY 14, 2020 68

MAY 15, 2020 72

MAY 16, 2020 A.M. 73

MAY 16, 2020 P.M. 78

MAY 17, 2020 84

MAY 18, 2020 88

MAY 19, 2020 88

Remark 5: The Fourth Position

MAY 20, 2020 A.M. 98

Remark 6: An Invitation to Social Death

MAY 20, 2020 P.M. 106

Remark 7: Infracendence: Unpublished Fragments from Fernando Pessoa's (Posthumous?) Milieu Notebook of Alberto Moreira, Heteronym

APPENDIX 1 123

More Questions for Jorge Alemán: A Presentation for 17 Instituto de Estudios Críticos, Ciudad de México, May 25, 2020

APPENDIX 2 127

From a Conversation with Jaime

APPENDIX 3 131

From a Conversation with Gerardo

APPENDIX 4 139

Alain Badiou's Age of the Poets

NOTES 165

BIBLIOGRAPHY 183

INDEX 189

PREFACE

Most of the following texts were written in Spanish between March 20 and May 20, 2020, during the first period of confinement mandated by the Texas civil authorities in response to the pandemic caused by COVID-19. I include several appendixes from weeks following, and a few texts I have called remarks. The appendixes attempt to clarify threads or elaborate on implications derived from themes in the main text, and the remarks provide, I hope, consistency to the set of arguments in the diary entries, but mostly they develop issues in the book I came to consider crucial from my own perspective. Initially thought of as private notes, or posts for a blog that I sometimes use (infraphilosophy.com), they ended up conditioning each other and tending on their own toward the form of a book, even if an unusual one. I wanted to respect the sequence in which they came to mind, on occasion developing from scribblings and materials I already had in my computer that now seemed to take on new personal importance. They are presented without modifications. They are not any kind of diary of life in the initial months of the pandemic; they are rather meant to be a meditation on the experience of suspension of everyday time in conditions of confinement, and on its consequences, both existential and political. Several were composed as contributions to conversations in virtual spaces where I was invited to participate. I am grateful to Joseba Buj and Angel Octavio Alvarez Solís, to Jon Beasley-Murray, and to Gerardo Muñoz for those invitations, and to Benjamin Mayer. And I am especially grateful to Teresa Vilarós for reading most of these notes, as well as for her specific comments. I also want to thank Jaime Rodríguez Matos, Maddalena Cerrato, and Gerardo Muñoz for their ongoing observations on the blog posts. José Luis Villacañas asked me to send him some of the entries for a book he was editing, *Pandemia: La comunidad de los vivientes* [*Pandemic: The community of the living*], now published by Biblioteca Nueva (Madrid). I would also like to thank Matías Bascuñán for his letter, which I include in these pages. And Gareth Williams, Brett Levinson, Yoandy Cabrera, and Miguel Morey for reading the draft of the final manuscript, minus the appended texts, which were added after May 2020.

The pandemic did not end in May, and a continued confinement was the consequence. During the summer of 2020, when I was finalizing corrections to the version of the book that was published at the end of it, *Sosiego siniestro*, a second wave arose and would last into the early fall. Eventually, a third wave developed in December through February 2021, and at the time of my writing this preface, it seems to be receding. In the meantime, in spite of the not yet quite available vaccines, new virus variants keep appearing, and the truth is that nobody knows what the future will bring. The Texas governor has just announced the end of the statewide mask mandate and is authorizing the full reopening of all businesses as usual, but there are ample reasons to mistrust the Texas governor's judgment, and we continue our isolation, interrupted only by trips to get household supplies and provisions. Our human contacts are mostly digital, through Zoom, including our classes and working group meetings. There is very little else: our handyman, Mario, when something needs to be fixed, a casual chat with a neighbor encountered on a walk. Last fall, as the confinement was becoming a heavy burden, brought the great political perplexity of the Republican reaction to the North American elections, which continues to this day and presages nothing good for the future. My daughter Camila finished her translation of the book into English, and my revisions included some additional materials from notes I had been taking through the summer. But at the time of preparing to send the finished typescript to my editor, Kenneth Wissoker, who provided me with keen and opportune suggestions for improvement, I knew that my book was essentially finished, and that there was no question of attempting to extend it in order to give it an expanded chronology that would match the first year of the pandemic. Somehow only the first two months of it were decisive for me, as, I suppose, a kind of habituation to the situation crept in. But it was a transfigured habituation: those two months changed me in significant ways, or changed something in me, and it is not for me to decide whether the change was the consequence of the trend of thought, certainly somewhat capricious and unsystematic, fragmented, perhaps untotalizable, that I attempted to register in the pages that follow, or whether it was the other way around: the change motivated the thoughts. I could probably say the change was liberating. But, as these things go, things are never just liberating, and other problems cropped up and continue to do so.

In January, as I was transferring a few books and papers from my garage library to my study in the house, one of our cats tripped me, and I fell on the driveway concrete and was unable to catch my fall. I fractured the proximal humerus of my left arm. It hurt, and I saw no choice but to go reluctantly to the emergency room of the local hospital. As I was exiting their X-ray room, the nurse told me to keep going straight and not turn left, as the COVID ward was on the left. I had a funny feeling in that instant that something bad had just happened. Three or four days later I started feeling ill, and so did my wife, Teresa. Camila, who had come to visit with us for a few days, had just returned to North Carolina, and that was fortunate because it prevented her becoming infected. Four awful weeks followed, tinged with apprehension that the infection might develop into long-haul COVID or pneumonia or what not. Needless to say, no medical care was available. We were lucky that both of us pulled out of it without catastrophe, none the wiser and considerably weakened. It was then that the huge winter storm called Uri hit Texas. Toward the end of that dismal week, a flock of white pelicans, accompanied by many cormorant comrades, visited the lake by our house. Our neighbor Kristi Sweet took the picture that you will see at the end of the book. Since I am writing this note almost exactly one year after we started our confinement, I trust the renewal of the annual cycle promised by the pelicans will bring good and joyful times. For me, with these words, the diary of the plague year, such as it is, will have come to an end.

The reader will find in the pages that follow a number of references to things and issues that I have been working on for some time: those include the notions of infrapolitics, exodus, decision of existence, posthegemony, and antiphilosophy. Although I have tried to make this text self-sufficient, that is, capable of being understood on its own merits or demerits, those topics have been the object of much discussion among friends and a considerable amount of already published writing. So it would have been absurd to pretend to summarize all of them here, which was not my interest in the book, preferring it to move forward rather than present or describe work from the past. I trust that patient readers, if they truly must interrupt their reading in order to get a clearer idea of, say, infrapolitics, might check out *Infrapolítica: Instrucciones de uso* (2020) (*Infrapolitics: A Handbook*, in English translation, published by Fordham University Press). The dialogic tone to the book is a direct consequence of the fact that a sustained interlocution with distant friends is at its origin, but let me add that there is no esoteric message to be found between the lines. What you see is what you get, and you must not become disoriented by the references to conversations had by email or Zoom or by mentions of Facebook or blog discussions on this or that topic. Everything relevant, as far as I am concerned, is in these pages. I have left Facebook anyway—one of the positive changes the confinement has brought about in my personal life. I could summarize it all by saying that *Uncanny Rest* is an attempt to continue the thought of infrapolitics in the direction of exploring and making a "decision of existence" through the untimely temporality of the pandemic.

—March 5, 2021

UNCANNY REST

MARCH 20, 2020   My attempt at mowing the lawn was interrupted by today's rain. I am almost certain my tractor is about to break down, and I don't know if I will be able to get it fixed. Time vanished over the last week between preparing for the online classes that will start on Monday and bewilderment. My attention was both distracted and given over to the news, to impatient curiosity about what is being said on Facebook or WhatsApp, and to some anxiety for our children, who live elsewhere. I have to flip this around and find another way. I will need to do something other than teach my classes, which are more or less prepared. There are no routines since normal conditions for daily work and for everything else are now in question. I can no longer go to the gym, for instance; it did shape my days. The habitual has been put on hold and there is an unchosen leisure, an anxious lack of occupation, and anxiety increases from my attempts at taking advantage of it, of capitalizing on it. I want to be able to use this strange lapse as a possible entry into my own life, from which I seem to have been uncannily separated; to realize what is this halted time, which nevertheless continues onward. Two of Francisco de Quevedo's verses come to mind: *You seek Rome in Rome, o Pilgrim / and in Rome itself Rome you cannot find.*[1] Underneath is the sensation that all of this is nothing more than a precarious project that will wither as soon as someone close to me falls sick. I feel a sense of urgency for quietude, a pressing need for quietness, but quietness and urgency do not mesh. This is the beginning of what will continue for a while in one form or another—everything indicates as much—and that duration, imagined, produces a slight anguish that I cannot deny or hide.

"In the meantime it was folly to grieve, or to think." This is a line from Edgar Allan Poe's "The Masque of the Red Death."[2] Now is not a time of affliction, not for me or for my loved ones; nothing has happened to us, and I hope nothing will. But thinking also feels like an excessive effort. What is there to think about? Only the inane, inanely. My condition has, also, elements of Prince Prospero's: I too am taking refuge in my "magnificent structure," and I too have invited a thousand ladies and gentlemen found every night on Netflix or Amazon Prime to join me. We have supplies. The only thing that remains is for the masquerade to be organized. In the story, the prince's castle includes a strange interior room, with its contrasting black and purple, where there is a "gigantic clock of ebony" whose chimes interrupt the orchestra's music and stop the ladies' and gentlemen's waltz. When they feel these chimes tremble, they turn pale without understanding why the sonic disturbance is affecting them. At the stroke of midnight, a "new presence" appears, masked like all others at the ball. It is the Red Death, which came like "a thief in the night . . . And the life of the ebony clock went out with that of the last of the gay. And the flames of the tripods expired. And Darkness and Decay and the Red Death held illimitable dominion over all."[3] But this doesn't occur, according to the story, until the fifth or sixth month of confinement. In the meantime, it is not about finding a measure of rest in uncanny times but, instead, about seeking it out and grasping it. This search will be imposed on us as an essential task over the coming months. Or am I just imagining it? And it will mark these months. It will change my life only if something else doesn't change it more harshly first. One cannot grieve or think, but grieving and thinking—thinking their hidden rapport—are for the time being all that seems possible, the only open track.

Remark 1. The Path of the Goddess

In my copy of Mario Untersteiner's edition of the Parmenidean texts (*Parmenide: Testimonianze e frammenti*) I wrote "Catania, August 1978." Today, while reading the transcription of Alain Badiou's 1985–86 seminar on Parmenides, I recover, somewhat tumultuously, images and memories from that trip. I almost missed my train in the immense railroad junction at Messina, because I became distracted while sitting at the station cafeteria. I had to run through the tracks and jump into an already moving train, where Teresa was waiting for me. In Sicily our first destination was Catania, and there I bought Untersteiner's edition. But before Catania and before Messina, the train had left us at Velia, in the middle of a dusty hot afternoon. We wanted to go from Velia to the Elea archaeological site. I think we took a cab or perhaps we hitchhiked. But it was almost 6:00 p.m. when we arrived, and the site was closed for the day. What could we do? It was unthinkable for me to miss seeing the site, probably in my mind the main attraction of the whole trip. In Barcelona I had been reading Antonio Capizzi's book on Parmenides and Elea—for Capizzi the poem told the story of an initiatic, shamanic trip around the town.[4] It was imperative to see the gate to the city, the founding site of philosophy through which the path of the goddess goes. Also the poplar trees, the maidens in the poem, and the fountain or spring of the goddess. And the acropolis from which the contemplation of the well-rounded sphere of truth could take place. If thinking and being are the same, if being is the same as that which being calls for, it was necessary for me to imprint on my retina, and to wager then on the revelation that might never come, the impression of that without which, or that is what I felt, my own life was a waste of time, a waste of life. But the gate to the site was locked, and we could not see anybody who might help. Disheartened and fatigued by the heat, we sat on some stone, we made some noise, we yelled, just in case somebody could hear us, and to our surprise a guard showed up on the other side of the wall and asked us what we wanted, what we sought, since the site was closed and we could not come in. In my rucksack I had a leaflet on the Elea site that I had found at a Naples bookstore, authored by a Mario Napoli. I had to lie (I almost never lie) and identify myself falsely as Professor Napoli's student, hoping there was indeed a Professor Napoli that had something to do with the site and was known there. I alleged some important errand; *il professore* had sent me there, we needed to enter the place, just a short while, a few minutes, please. And then, behind the guard, somebody else showed up, a thin gentleman, with white hair and a goatee, who addressed us in French, a language I was not so comfortable in. We responded in English and we seemed to impress him enough, since he instructed the guard to let us in with a hand movement. We entered, and we saw the pink gate, the spring (from which we drank), and the trees. There was also a splendid red Mercedes roadster with a woman inside with whom the gentleman with the goatee spoke in German. He asked us in English about our real interest in the site, and I said I wanted to look out at the sea from the acropolis. He had in his hand a ridiculous black plastic handbag with some Badajoz insurance company branding. So he might also speak Spanish, which we confirmed, and in Spanish he said that all visions from any acropolis were only ever the vision of the Styx, as I should know or learn. I had the impression, fleeting though strong, that the man was Charon the Polyglot. All of this happened. Teresa and I continued with our visit, and when passing a rudimentary wooden hut the guard asked us to stop. He opened the door and extracted from the inside what he told us was the latest find: a bust of Parmenides with the inscription *iatrós, physikós, sophós*. I held it in my hands. He told me to speak of it to Professore Napoli.

It was, of course, impossible not to see the Styx, river or lagoon, from the acropolis at twilight. The sun was low on the horizon, and there was a dark light cast among yellow rays. I remembered that dark light today as I was reading in Badiou: "It is the impossibility of non-being . . . as a creation of the possibility of the thinking of being. Thinking cannot be thought . . . except at the price of an interdiction: there must be an interdiction so that there may be thinking as thinking of being. But the interdiction . . . is thought itself."[5]

In Catania we had a friend, a friend of friends, rather, and we had dinner with her: sea urchins and pizza, as I remember. We never saw the gentleman with the goatee again, or his German companion, but on returning to the hotel, in the great Catania piazza, a dog crossed our path and looked at us. The warning in his gaze alerted me. How can I not understand it now as a reference to the Parmenidean interdiction? Not to follow the path of non-being, since non-being *is* not, is a condition of thought, hence a condition of being. But, Badiou says, "a point of non-submission to the interdiction is necessary."[6] How to live the non-submission? Today's memories revealed to me that the last forty-two years could be summed up as its tattered experience, for better or for worse: an errancy sometimes ecstatic and joyful, other times dense and obscure, of which no account can be rendered, far from the path of the goddess, to which I cannot know whether there is a return. I never did read Untersteiner's edition, but I still have that book, miraculously, since most of my things from that time in my life ended up in the hands of some junkman in the Encants fleamarket in Barcelona, who bought them as a bargain and probably sold them at a better price.

MARCH 27, 2020

Our inability, on the left as well as on the right, to deal with this pandemic implies the need for new thought, or perhaps just for thought. Nobody knows how to think this, its arrival, its implications. It becomes necessary to renounce conventional ideologies and commitments, which, despite their indigence, have not only held out, but are also hardening in an increasingly dogmatic and harebrained way. Old forms of rhetoric are applauded with mounting ferocity while the incipient or possible is immediately disqualified, condemned to the hell of irresponsibility. If this continues, anything can happen. There is no telling how people will react.

MARCH 29, 2020

A feeling, perhaps mistaken, that the world will change in such a way that our known coordinates and parameters, and everything that we spend our lives trying to know and understand, are going to stop being relevant; to this extent, that everything we are currently saying or thinking is merely provisional and uncertain, but also that everything we read, written by those who lived before this uncanny incursion, is not more than false hope or compensation: not necessarily irrelevant, but of indeterminable relevancy. Either that is the case or it is a warped excuse for my sluggishness. And so, second uncanny blow, the notion pops up that the felt indeterminability of history should not be constrained to our understanding in times of crisis, but rather that it extends to our entire temporality. In every case, everything changes always in such a way that how one thought and lived ceases to be relevant and does not deliver anything other than a provisional and treasonous truth, a lie. And what one reads is always, in every instance, false guidance and compensation. And that moment of vision that risks disorder reminds me of old thoughts: how the expression *ho autontimoroumenos*, which was an example used in my old Greek textbook of a participial substantive, from which we could translate from the verb *timeo* as "he who honors himself," can also be read from the verb *timao*, which would then have to be translated as "he who destroys (or torments) himself." Friedrich Nietzsche remits *circulus vitiosus deus* to this structure of the double blow of the uncanny. But Nietzsche was not able to avoid radicalizing his idea toward the participial construction of *timao*.

APRIL 1, 2020 A.M. When Badiou, whom I am reading with a certain intensity these months, in a specific moment in his seminar on the essence of politics, mentions the "political-ecstatic style of the 1930s," he says that "its seriousness and depth" were inevitably tied to the production of a disaster. The disaster would have been the "theatricalization, found under the sign of a staging of place, of a singular knot between politics, state and philosophy."[7] The surging of the sacred name of the leader and the production of political space as a space of terror, in which a part of what is is prohibited from being, are direct consequences of the ecstasy of place. One would tend to think of fascism as being the most obvious manifestation of that ecstatic theatricalization. Badiou, who excludes Nazism from the notion of disaster insomuch as Nazism never proposed itself as a politics of emancipation, offers another precise name: Stalinism. It is no good to think that such a name will not recur again in our history. The right will radicalize. Where is the left moving toward today? Where, in the height of the coronavirus crisis, or of this first crisis, are the incipient emancipatory proposals? And in what place are we to find the politics that never claimed to be emancipatory but still mean to be democratic?

The politico-ecstatic style of the 1930s was not separate from the economic crisis of the '20s. Given present economic predictions and political conditions, we run the not so remote risk of a new ecstatic territorialization. Carlo Galli, in a short text entitled "Epidemic and Sovereignty," identifies it as an incipient exacerbation of sovereignty, in a situation that

PHOTO BY AUTHOR

calls, from a democratic point of view, for "two equal and opposite demands": first, that the reclaimed sovereignty be effective, that it work, for example, to handle the public health problem and to promote economic reconstruction; and, second, "that the emergency not be institutionalized into a state of exception." But, if overcoming the crisis supposes "inventing a new normality, re-founding the pact of our democracy," for Galli "we will have a need for sovereignty."[8] And that is the danger: that in this new need for sovereignty, under the pretext of a refounding of the democratic pact, political practice be rebuilt as a will to found a new ecstatic place in terror, out of an affirmation of sovereignty in an identitarian formulation. This is bound to come from the right.

In a confinement that is necessary to minimize the risk of contagion, communitarian whims and voluntarisms appear. But the generous applause, from Spanish balconies at 7:00 p.m., for instance, for the frontline health and public order professionals who are working to contain or mitigate the viral intrusion, has on its dark side the denunciation of those who dare break the prohibition of confinement and the aggressive fear of possible carriers of the virus. The community ban that is implicit in confinement is an unstable counter-communitarian sign. That the community is, today, murderous, becomes inverted into an imprecise communitarian nostalgia. That contradiction could lean toward resolving itself—there are still weeks of confinement ahead of us, weeks of communitarian nostalgia, perhaps more than weeks—into a new epochal equivalence of ecstatic character that would force an identification, a sameness of the good and the necessary. The political (or economic) good would be constituted from the postulation of a new communitarian suturing. We know what this can implicate. We know that there are sectors of the population already predisposed to it. On the right, and on the left.

In the early 1990s Badiou references the three great books that closed philosophically the communitarian (communist) sequence that would have started with the French Revolution: the books by Jean-Luc Nancy, Maurice Blanchot, and Giorgio Agamben on community.[9] From these, Badiou asks for a reconstitution of the thinking of community that would dwell on the impossibility and unnameability of community itself, in other words, on that which, in the history of community, or of communism itself, constituted absolute disaster: its suture to the place, its suture to ecstatic leadership, and its suture to terror as a liquidation of everything the suture excludes. Is there a residue today for an emancipatory politics that would allow us to avoid those risks? Or is what is exacerbated within the new communitarian voluntarism, from the left and from the right, which is the other side of the state-administrative management that will reclaim, or has already reclaimed, a vaster and more infinite sovereignty, nothing more than an insistence on a new hegemonic community whose achievement would force a return, as farce, to the politico-ecstatic style of the 1930s? In the words of Badiou, to a new Stalinism; but also, perhaps primarily, to the ghost of that which Badiou excludes from disaster. Or a mixture of the two.

Remark 2: The Pandemic and the Event

In the best of possible worlds, there is no event, everything is linked to the principle of sufficient reason, which is either a warranty that God exists or God itself. If everything is preordered, if there are no indiscernibles, then there is no event, there are only happenings. The event, insofar as it can be conceptualized as a supplement to a given situation, as its point of excess, as that which happens indiscernibly to undo the situation such as it is and to open another history and another truth, does not take place. For Badiou it is not easy, it might even prove impossible, to refute Leibniz's theory of the indiscernibles and their negation. It is finally a matter of belief. If for you the world is finished as the best of all possible worlds, you will always find reasons to establish your faith in the principle of sufficient reason. But for Badiou to posit the emergence of an event as a point of excess and overflow of a given situation is also a matter of belief. And it is equally irrefutable, to the extent that it can only be posited as a truth process from the future anterior. The pandemic will have been an event if the pandemic becomes an indiscernible starting from which we can unleash a process of fidelity, and if the world changes as a result of fidelity to what the indiscernible brings to the world. We can only ascertain this from the future anterior, which makes it irrefutable at any given point in time.

In the June 2 session of his 1986–87 seminar on Heidegger, Badiou says:

Le savoir en situation, que j'ai convenu d'appeler 'encyclopédie,' distingue et classe toute une série de parties de la situation et les subsume sous *des concepts, des désignations, des opérateurs de différenciation. Par principe, un indiscernable est évidemment soustrait à ces opérations, donc il est comme tel exclu du savoir structurel. À vrai dire, c'est bien parce que Leibniz considère que la pensée c'est le savoir structurel que, pour lui, il n'y a pas d'indiscernable. Du moment où l'on identifie pensée et savoir structurel, on est amené à dire qu'il n'y a pas de pensée de l'indiscernable, que penser l'indiscernable c'est penser rien, ce qui revient à ne rien penser.*

(Knowledge in situation, which I have arranged to call "encyclopedia," distinguishes and classifies a whole series of parts of the situation and subsumes them under concepts, designations, operators of differentiation. In principle, an indiscernible is evidently subtracted from these operations, which means it is excluded as such from structural knowledge. In truth, there is no indiscernible for Leibniz because he considers thought structural knowledge. From the moment thought and structural knowledge are identified one is brought to say that there is no thinking of the indiscernible, that thinking the indiscernible is thinking nothing, which comes to not thinking at all.)[10]

There is a knowledge, which is always the knowledge of a situation, and there are truth processes that for Badiou become organized on the basis of the irruption of an undecidable. But the undecidable prompts a decision. The event is an undecidable supplement to a given situation. To decide on the undecidable of the event is an intervention that organizes a truth procedure in the time or tense of the future anterior.

Somewhere else in the seminar on Heidegger, Badiou speaks about a "third stage," which is his version of the Heideggerian theme of an "other beginning." If, for Badiou, the first stage is the stage of the age of God, that is, the time of the ontotheological conception of the world (in Leibniz, for instance), the second stage is the age of the human, which perhaps the Nietzschean word on "the last man" in *Thus Spoke Zarathustra* begins to close. For Badiou, Heidegger—who sutures philosophy to art and particularly to poetry—is still a character from the age of the human. The third stage would have commenced with the liquidation of the notion of the age of man in the renunciation of the metaphysics of presence. The abandonment of the subjective position of the age of the human implies the dissolution of the suture of thought to poetry, or to science, or to politics. There will be poetry, and politics, and science, but thought breaks its suture to any one of those conditions of its very possibility and is no longer chained to them. What remains is, in the words of Bernard Stiegler, the need to think a "a new system of *cure*," where cure not only refers to its therapeutic meaning but also absorbs the connotations of *care* in the English sense, or of the German word *Sorge*. Such would be the responsibility of thought at the time of the third stage, which is our time.[11]

It is a matter of belief or of a decision. To understand the pandemic as an indiscernible, that is, as the point of excess of a situation, which Heidegger could have interpreted as an irruption of Being, organizes a truth procedure whose *potentia* is to change our lives. But we may reject the idea and return to the consoling Leibniz theme: we are already in the best of all possible worlds. We prefer not to exit the age of the human or, if we cannot avoid it, we choose to leave it looking backward, and attempting some new suture of thought to its conditions, which is of course what the encyclopedia tried to do in the last couple of centuries. Badiou calls that option "regressive humanism." At the time of the sixth extinction, which the pandemic should remind us of, no regressive humanism is sustainable. A virus can make us a part of that massive species extinction. That would certainly be an event that might generate, for those who keep on surviving for a time, a fidelity to truth and a change of life. The regressive compensation in the face of the movement of historical time is not a figure of thought. It is only a return to the unthought, which we are nevertheless irrefutably free to choose if we so desire.

My friend Benjamín Mayer has been known to ask: "What fictions can we give ourselves over to in order to recover desire?" It is not an innocent question at the time of the pandemic. To recover desire is not the same as to feel the need to purchase a Woobie Doobie that will then justify the pleasure of going to the mountains to try it out. And it is not the same as to wake up from our confined dormition and march toward some site where the presence of bodies can generate sexual stimulation. To recover desire, in Mayer's terms, has to do with generating a new experience of the Thing, that is, that elusive or supremely elusive entity that became the warranty of humanity after the death of God in the Freudian revolution. The Thing does not exist, but it replaces God through its consistency to the very precise extent that it itself has not been lost. If Stiegler is right in his positing of a third limit of capitalism— the first would have been the tendency of the rate of profit to fall and the second the consumerist saturation that saved the rate of profit but destroyed the very possibility of experience—then we live today in a thoroughly automated world: "A world of reticulation is being implemented, and it constitutes a new stage of the grammatization process. In this stage, it is the mechanisms of transindividuation itself that are grammatized, that is, formalized and made reproducible, and therefore capable of being calculated and automated."[12] But this implies a general hyperproletarianization of humanity at the service of the machine. Industrial reproduction has saturated our world to the point of accomplishing a reduction and general domestication of libidinal energy that capitalism will seek to continue to intensify until the point of total entropy that will destroy the planet, if that nonexistent God is unable to stop it. Unless, that is, the Thing comes back, unless the Thing accomplishes a reactivation and recovery of desire. Mayer calls for new fictions, but those new fictions have as their very condition a general defictionalization of existence if they are to provoke the Thing's rescue. When nothing is left to sustain the symbolic edifice, not even as regressive compensation, then perhaps the Thing will begin again to gleam in the shadow.

In that context the notion of political emancipation is subject to question. There will be no political emancipation without a previous, and deeper, recovery of an existential energy that must today be exodic, not vis-à-vis the world, but from the apparatuses of techno-industrial reproduction that have saturated the planet at the limit of productionist calculation. The pandemic fosters the thoughtless reproduction of inane desires, redemptive wishes, which on their reverse side hide a hatred for those supposedly given over to the neutralization of politics from a presumed death anxiety that rejects the commonality of community. But what is needed is, rather, an exodic withdrawal from the emancipatory pretensions of those whose postulation of community remains blind to the fact that community has fallen into the nihilism of the absence of desire, the void of desire, and is only expressive of an ecstasy of place in coexistent subjugation. An alternative gaze is indispensable and necessary in order to move past a social world where factical hyperproletarianization means an expropriation all the more insidious for being concealed. If we ever want the Thing to come back from the shadows.

APRIL 1, 2020 P.M.   Last week, Jaime Rodríguez Matos, Gerardo Muñoz, and I wrote to Jorge Alemán over Facebook to ask him the question that appears in the letter below. Jorge has yet to respond formally, but he gave a second interview in *Punto de emancipación* (*Point of Emancipation*) wherein he seemed to propose an answer under the notion that "the transformation of the subject is a condition of political transformation."[13] It should perhaps be said—in full assumption that, when a Lacanian speaks of the "transformation of the subject," he or she is not saying the same thing self-help gurus or the false prophets of happiness are saying—that this answer does not seem sufficient, in the sense that it can promote misunderstandings. We are not particularly interested in the transformation of the subject from any ideal of meditative introspection; we are not particularly interested in self-care, in the traditions that Michel Foucault mentions, or therefore in any aesthetics of existence; and we are least interested in propositions for a mending of one's ways so dear to the Christian tradition. Instead, our question peeked into the possibility of recovery, in confinement, of an existential exteriority, an *ex-scription* neither directly communitarian nor directly political. This is what we called "facticity," which is, in our judgment, what has been immensely lost in contemporary thought. And in facticity, and therefore also in the possibility of a transfigured facticity, we were also referring to what Jean-Luc Nancy, to give an example, called at some point a "decision of existence,"[14] and what Jacques Derrida toward the end of his own life, to give a different example, tended to label a "learning how to live."[15] We do not want, of course, to force Jorge into saying what he does not wish to say, or into agreeing with something he rejects. We simply find it useful to note that, if it is indeed necessary to speak of a "transformation of the subject" in order to instrumentalize some novel operation of political reinvention, it would also be necessary to speak of a transformation of the "object," that is, of the outside that today has been so drastically reduced to the search for a "commons," which is as unlikely as it is unnamable in our epoch and, we fear, would have no generative capacity. Or it would only have one, perversely. It would not be possible to have political invention—only farcical repetition—without a fundamental revision of the definition of the subject of existence that would implicate as well the destructive revision of the subject-world difference in contemporary coordinates. The latter are still the modern coordinates, though now in an agonic state.

This is the initial letter we wrote to Jorge:

DEAR JORGE:

Jaime, Gerardo, and I have been speaking informally about your interview with Papo Kling in *Punto de emancipación* and we agreed that it was crucial we asked you something. We're hoping you'll have the time to respond. We understand, firstly, that in the interview, you establish four points that could be summarized as follows: 1. Capitalism today has gone off the rails, producing—and it will continue to produce—effects that go beyond the control of any human agents. 2. It is necessary to reinvent the left, which continues to contemplate the situation from inadequate parameters. 3. The only semi-visible possibility is a strong statalization without totalitarianism, a non-authoritarian statalization. 4. In short, in the face of a failure of civilization, another beginning becomes necessary—one which is still to be thought. Those are your points. But there is another, less obvious, proposal in your text, one that we link with what you say at the beginning of the interview about how this global viral intrusion represents an irruption of the real, through which reality is tinged with anguish. You speak, as the second point notes above, of the need for a reinvention of the left and a reinvention of the social link. And, in response to the question of confinement, you again use the word "reinvention," only this time as a "reinvention of oneself," associated with the opportunity that confinement offers in its reverse side, which you describe as a "separation of the world that allows for the world to be thought." A strangeness, distance, or remoteness, you say, "that could give something other than anguish and loss." You call it a "meditative experience," and it is here where you cipher the possibility for "reinventing oneself." Jaime, Gerardo, and I were wondering whether it was perhaps necessary to think of that double reinvention—political and personal—as not two but one singular necessary reinvention. And whether for thinking them together your old theme of solitude: common becomes crucial.[16] Toward the beginning of your interview, you link the pandemic's intrusion in the real to the catastrophe of disinhibited capitalism and to the culmination of metaphysics in that will-to-power now beyond the control of the human. Your allusion to meditative experience cannot but evoke Heidegger's existential analytics and his mandate to make one's own facticity explicit. Could that be what, with respect to existence, this step back makes possible, as an opportunity in the experience of confinement, in its general connection to the solitude: common of the human, the political reinvention that you are calling for, which is also a reinvention of the social bond? A new analytics of existence would become an absolute precondition for political reinvention. What do you make of this?

Hugs,

Alberto (and Jaime and Gerardo)

APRIL 3, 2020 A.M. We are in the world as factical exteriority, and the shutting down of experience alludes to a wish for not having that exteriority manifest itself. We insist that the world should be no more than a political colony of human subjectivity. But the world excedes and sub-cedes. To exist, not insist, goes through a retraction toward the exteriority of the world, against its subjective closure. The notion of the "transformation of the subject" is insufficient, it backslides into mere insistence. Think of this retraction toward exteriority as a condition of possibility for politics itself. Without which politics will collapse into a theater of closed-off subjectivities.

APRIL 3, 2020 P.M. In relation to contemporary thought, and for writing in Spanish, some of my friends are in the position of the indigenous to whom the Spanish *compañías* would read the Requirement of Juan López de Palacios Rubios. In the name of God and the King, submit yourself or be killed, and everything you say henceforth must be said in our tongue or not at all. And when you die, if you do not submit, it shall be your own fault. And my friends, who do not understand or do not wish to understand the Requirement of submission and who wipe their backsides with the folios of Pánfilo de Narváez or Hernando de Soto, are the indigenous who have to go up the mountain in order to avoid extermination. But it is always better to head toward the mountain, anyway.

APRIL 4, 2020

It has been three weeks. I talk to the trees that surround our house and I mow the lawn (I was able to get my tractor fixed; mine was the last they worked on before the lockdown), and I wait for the next time the roadrunner that lives around here, who is capable of outrunning my lazy cats, makes an appearance. I haven't stopped being busy, but I'm realizing that my work is not work, only an occupation that fills the time, even if laboriously. I read, perhaps obsessively. I look at the news, try and stay current on what is happening on social media, but only to a certain extent (social media is becoming as unbearable as committee meetings; it means nothing to have 1,000 friends). I grade the work my students send me, or I come up with more assignments for them to do. I try to read without continually getting distracted by text or WhatsApp messages, and head out for obligatory walks, which are themselves becoming a burden. I make dinner, frustratingly look for some movie or television series that could hold my attention, but I'm almost never successful (even if two hours will have gone by). If ever I have had the secret temptation to celebrate confinement as a form of regaining time, and therefore pleasure, that temptation has already proved to be a useless delusion. Distended time produces dull boredom, although also only minor. As all meetings and workshops have been canceled for the next few months, and since this crisis has, in general, ineluctably extended all deadlines and reduced professional emergencies, there is nothing urgent I must write (well, there is one thing I was supposed to have sent in a couple of months ago—but I don't feel that urgency, I won't do it).

I don't feel that this emptiness is particularly generative for writing other, longer-term, things. I begin to think, faintly, that this note or the whole series of notes is an attempt to give these incipient thoughts a push; that this very situation, whose psychic tonality I cannot yet name, demands that I take critical stock of my life—a general critique of life, or rather, of the conditions that I have come to put up with as a way of life, as habit. Hobbes used to say that his fundamental passion in life would have been fear. Mine, I think, is boredom: trying to elude it, in whatever form it has taken. This has been my vital strategy, the one I have sustained the longest, forever really, from the time when I was a student in Barcelona and had to deal with those concave Sundays up until the present, where I now try to secure interlocution via Slack groups with students or friends, usually with diminishing returns. I have passed through so many working groups, I have organized seminars, proposed conversations, accepted in-person commitments or calls for articles, book chapters, conference papers that in reality, for me, did not lead to anything, or not to much, and have never led to much except perhaps filling in that vacant time. I have to accept this harsh truth, which has been the merely compensatory quality of almost all of my professional activities of the last forty years. Perhaps that is why I have written relatively little: my stimuli have always been cut short, condemned to a specific lack of liquidity, a receptive occlusion. In the self-generated haze of my compensatory strategies, I have always been able to see the horror of the question "what for," even while never being able to answer it outright except in punctual and therefore unsatisfactory ways. (I exclude from all of this my conversations with my friends, which have been crucial for me and still are.)

And better not to say any more about this, because it would only get me in trouble. The real question involves understanding whether taking critical stock of my life can turn into some regenerative something over the next number of years; to know whether it is possible to pick up where those false starts left off, to pick up the real or authentic aspects of my life and give them free rein; to know whether I could live in and for a time that is something other than a time of symbolic compensation. At this point I have come to understand the totality of my professional life as failed symbolic compensation. I wonder whether that happens to others. Is it possible to renounce all of that which is more boring than the boredom that it ostensibly seeks to reduce or eliminate? Why not? But the idea of even entertaining this terrifies me. My life would change in such a way that I am not sure I have the resources for it. But I can obviously pretend that the lockdown means nothing, that it will and even should be continued by business as usual. Is that what I must do? And the horror only increases.

I came across some words by Jean-Luc Nancy that have haunted me all day today: "To leave behind all our determining, identifying, destin-

PHOTO BY AUTHOR

ing thoughts. That is, to leave behind what 'thinking' usually means. But, first of all, to think this, that there is something to think, and to think the some of this thing at the heart of thought. This would be completely the opposite of 'whatever' thought. This would be the thought—itself undetermined, included as it is in all thought—of what determines us to think: neither concept nor project, but rather thought brought up short against the heart of things. Our history today is concentrated, suspended, at the point where this exigency piles up."[17]

APRIL 9, 2020

As I look for a book, I see and look at a specific photograph, propped up on a bookshelf in my study. It's a photograph we took of the four cousins on a beach in Connecticut. The memory comes rushing back as a perturbingly intimate sensation, an involuntary memory. Or maybe it's not a memory, not a remembrance at all, but rather something that pertains to the materiality of the photograph itself, and it's only now that I am registering it—like a shadow lurking somewhere within the photograph. This sensation speaks to me of an internal hurriedness. Or perhaps it is only the disjointedness or a disequilibrium between being there, in that place, at that moment, and simultaneously feeling displaced into another, pressing, time from which the time of the photograph could only be remembered with grief. As though, in that brief instant of the photograph, an obligation that would obliterate the reality of that very moment were weighing down on me, something that would un-realize it, returning it to a place of loss.

But yes, this rushes back to me as a memory. It is not in the photograph; it is not what I read into it now but what I felt then. And that I am only now identifying and naming. As though some previous pact would have already consummated the impossibility of being there, then. As though my soul verified its previous sale—who bought it?—for a future that was never to come, but which has nevertheless ordered my life. As though everything that was done or every place I had to be was always in relation to a subtraction of time to which I would have consented immemorially, a disguise. Some form of trickery, of error. As though I was not able to be there even while being there, by virtue of being or having to be in some other place that does not exist.

PHOTO BY AUTHOR

APRIL 12, 2020

The configuration of styles generated through confinement across social media confirms a special kind of division, one that to me feels ultimately decisive. We try, sometimes, to establish typologies of the intellectual in relation to diverse sets of problems or themes. These typologies always end up being murky, with multiple gray zones and overlapping areas. Perhaps the one I am about to risk is just another one of those typologies, and nothing more. But it seems to me that it might be possible, and even necessary, to divide the field of scribblers into preachers and *marranos*. Erin Graff Zivin speaks of a typology of writing from the notions of the inquisitorial or identitarian register and the marrano register.[18] The first has to do with the extraction of some concealed truth, whereas the second problematizes its ethico-political relationship to the secret, on the one hand, and, on the other, its entry into a dimension of the incalculable, that is to say, of what rejects calculation. To these two registers, the inquisitional, or inquisitorial, and the marrano, I can link the two Kierkegaardian knights of *Fear and Trembling*: the knight of resignation and the knight of faith. It is perhaps paradoxical that the intellectual of infinite resignation can be described as a scribe of the inquisitorial register, while the knight of faith appeals to the marrano register. One would think it would be the opposite—that infinite resignation corresponds to the marrano and faith to the inquisitor. But no, and that is what is interesting. For me, infinite resignation leads to preaching, whereas Kierkegaardian faith, and in this I do not differ from Kierkegaard, leads to the acknowledgment of an extreme singularity that he calls an "absolute relation to the absolute."[19]

There is much preaching out there, which can only lead us to Nietzsche's critique of priestly thought. It goes without saying that the thought of the marrano register abhors that of the priestly one. Its function is to witness, not to teach or to preach. It renounces all forms of heroism, including the generous version that Kierkegaard presents through his knight of infinite resignation, who is the tragic hero. For Kierkegaard, this last one

> drains in infinite resignation the deep sorrow of existence, he knows the bliss of infinity, he has felt the pain of renouncing everything, whatever is most precious in the world, and yet to him finitude tastes just as good

as to one who has never known anything higher, for his remaining in the finite bore no trace of a stunted, anxious training, and still he has this sense of being secure to take pleasure in it, as though it were the most certain thing of all. And yet, and yet the whole earthly form he presents is a new creation on the strength of the absurd. He resigned everything infinitely, and then took everything back on the strength of the absurd.[20]

Is this not the priest in his best typological configuration? The priest or the tragic hero, reconciled with existence via his pleasant sermons, which link him with the universal. He preaches for all; he speaks for all. Like Socrates. He is a political man. Most intellectuals are like that, particularly today.

It is not that the marrano claims any kind of exceptionality, even though he or she speaks for no one. It is true, Kierkegaard says, that all can give the preacher, during his rough sojourn on earth, advice, and that is exactly how the preacher is in permanent contact with everyone. In contrast, nobody gives the marrano advice, and nobody understands him or her either. This is a radically singular position, and yet for Kierkegaard there is no human being that is excluded from it. Perhaps the decisive factor is that the tragic hero of unconditionally verbose predication considers the universal higher than the particular, superior to the particular. But the marrano has long been, forever really, subordinate to the universal, whether he or she wishes it or not, since the destiny of the marrano is to break with the universal in rebelliousness and, in doing so, to position himself or herself "in an absolute relation to the absolute." But what does such a strange and untimely phrase mean today, when, without a doubt, there is no longer an enlightened ear to hear it?

The marrano is no figure of Enlightenment, not primarily. Those are the preachers. The marrano walks on paths devoid of travelers, where there are only shadows of strangers. The absolute relation to the absolute is an Abrahamic sign, and what it says is that ethics is not the highest. Neither a tragic hero, a preacher, nor an aesthetic hero, a hero of style. The marrano cannot offer anything. Only to be a witness and to take on the responsibility of his or her solitude, which is shared by all.

Remark 3: Self-precursion

There is a bad movie circulating through Amazon Prime: *The Mercenary*. In it a particularly brutal soldier, capable of triumphing over many enemies all by himself, is wounded and comes to be saved from death by a Colombian priest. At some point in the movie, the priest tells the soldier that "there is a reason for everything." That is perhaps the final truth of the religious structuration of existence, or at least the site where the religious structuration of existence identifies itself with the metaphysical structuration of existence, which Gottfried Wilhelm Leibniz summed up in his principle of sufficient reason: *nihil est sine ratione*. Let us suppose that the destruction of such a principle is the task of the antimetaphysical or postmetaphysical thinker, Nietzsche for instance. His most intimate struggle would have been that of liberating life from any hermeneutical priesthood. He appealed to "the philosopher Dionysus," no longer a god, only a radically anti-Socratic philosopher. To want to be Dionysus, Dionysus against the Crucified, means a sort of self-positing as precursor: as self-precursor. I, Nietzsche, will become my own precursor. The postmetaphysical philosopher is perhaps always obligatorily a self-precursor. The task is to seek or to chase the moment when metaphysical temporality—the temporality that has fallen into the reluctant facticity of an excessively hermeneutic *hic et nunc*—be canceled out in favor of the absolute liberation of chance, *beyond* any interpretative caesura. That would be the name of the *matheme*, the properly philosophical act if it were true that philosophy has always sought to supplement and not to identify with the metaphysico-religious structuration of existence. From that moment on, the antiphilosopher, that is, the true philosopher, could no longer tell themselves stories, which would not be a limitation or an impossibility, but rather a proof of emancipation from slave narratives that, in each and every case, are responses to a life-denying hermeneutic drive. Antiphilosophy is the absolute affirmation of life as hazardous and uninterpretable—the moment after which it could perhaps be possible to say again, and anew, "for the same are thinking and being," to quote old Parmenides, the torsion of whose words generated the historical totality of metaphysics such as it has come down to us.

Hence antiphilosophy appears as the most intimate gesture of philosophy, not its contrary: in antiphilosophy philosophy finds its power as mere self-precursor. Everything is preparation, the labor of thought is the advancement, from metaphysical temporality, of its ultimate suspension. Is that not the secret of the works that Nietzsche wrote in the months before his mental collapse? *Twilight of the Idols* and *Ecce Homo* and *Nietzsche contra Wagner* and *The Antichrist* would be, would have been, prolegomena, acts of cleansing and of preparing a clearing from which to launch that last work that would have broken the history of the world in two and that was never written (even if *The Antichrist* is perhaps a first draft of a first part of it). Nietzsche's mental collapse was the interruption and not the culmination, never the culmination, of such a process. Nietzsche's collapse interrupted the antiphilosophical suspension of philosophical or metaphysico-religious temporality. The collapse, caused by terminal syphilis, could not be conjured away by the "great health" that Nietzsche may have thought the labor of thinking could bring about. We will never know the quality of Nietzsche's great antiphilosophical act, since it never took place, and it is an imposture to claim that the mental collapse was such an act. At the same time: to conceive of the labor of thought as the self-deliverance into a process of preparation, of a cleansing of any metaphysico-religious residue, of a destructuration of the metaphysical structuration of existence, is that not in itself the deepest and most proper metaphysical structuration of time? As a destructuring structuration, the self-precursive process is still fundamentally the legitimation of a beyond that would supremely interpret the factical and existential *hic et nunc*. Self-precursion is still counterfeit money. It still secretly depends on the principle of sufficient reason.

What is the alternative? How is it possible to think outside the hermeneutical trap? How can we distort the torsioned Parmenidean word without precursively falling into an end of times that would restore a religious philosophy of history? Is that not the task of what I have been calling infrapolitics? This weird confinement, the common solitude, gives us perhaps an entry into the needed untimely temporality, its condition. There is no infrapolitics without antiphilosophy. There is no antiphilosophy without infrapolitics.

APRIL 15, 2020

The story of Tobias, his magical fish, and his angelic companion has always fascinated me, ever since it was told to me in my Sacred History class in grade school. In its wake I eventually read Juan Benet's abstruse book *El ángel del Señor abandona a Tobías* (*God's Angel Abandons Tobias*), and I got to know Rembrandt's engravings on the subject. The Book of Tobit is one of the books deemed deuterocanonical, which means that it cannot be read in the Protestant Bibles. My Spanish Bible in Casiodoro de Reina and Cipriano de Valera's translation does not include this text, and neither is it in my King James version, even though Reina and Valera and the wise men who worked for the English King produced versions of it. Mysteriously, however, it is considered an apocryphal book and therefore censurable and censored by the pious publishers publishing most of the world's Bibles nowadays. Anyway, I have it available in my copy of *The New Oxford Annotated Bible*. It is also found in the translation of the Vulgate by Félix Torres Amat (that is, in the version he produced on the basis of José Petisco's translation).

The young Tobias is the son of Tobit, a pious man in exile who never forgot to bury the dead or care for the widows and orphans of his town but who nevertheless was brought to ruin by those in political power. For his father's benefit, Tobias must go somewhere remote to collect a debt. In order to do so, he finds help from a companion, the Angel Raphael, who advises him on how to defend himself against an unusual fish that attacks Tobias when he goes into a river. Raphael shows him how to extract from that fish some indispensable tools for his own life. Thus Tobias learns how, by using matter from the fish, he can exorcise the demon plaguing the life of Sarah, his future wife, and how he can cure his father's blindness, which was caused by a swallow's droppings. But also, remarkably, the angel teaches Tobias how to find his way through the desert without getting lost. When Tobias returns to his paternal place, with wife and fortune, his father asks him to pay his companion. At that point the companion reveals his angelic status and then departs. Tobias lives on for many more years, and one cannot help but think that the rest of his life, the non-narrated life, the life that remains, is sustained and enabled by a time of waiting. Life is now the wait for the angel's return; it is the only time that remains and must be lived through until it happens. A pandemic time? A sort of pandemic time. And perhaps there is no hope in that wait; there is only desire.

This life in waiting, the life of the one abandoned by the angel who at some point accompanied them, is infrapolitical life. In *Survival of the Fireflies*, Georges Didi-Huberman invokes the figure of the firefly understood as the splendor of a body in the night, and as such a place of desire. Those are the fireflies in Pier Paolo Pasolini's childhood, an experience that Pasolini darkly rejected in 1975, shortly before his actual death and as a premonition of it. There are, also, the fireflies of Giorgio Agamben's childhood—the fireflies of which Agamben would say that they have been burned by the blinding light of the society of the spectacle or, alternatively or complementarily, by the headlights of neofascist cars. Didi-Huberman rejects the idea of the death of the fireflies. He appeals to Walter Benjamin's weak messianism so as to insist that the destruction of experience is never total, even under ruinous conditions, and that in the very fall one may still—and this *still* is perpetual—find beams of desire, given the plausible final indestructibility of the eminently destructible. The destruction of experience can never eliminate the residue of the wait, or at least not until death. But we are not dead. We survive, and as such we live; and survival, if it is anything at all, is a production of brightness in the night. The image—all gleams in the shadow are gleams of images—survives the apocalyptic horizon and demonstrates the illusion of all apocalypse, and the illusion of all horizons. That is why, for Didi-Huberman, all manners of imagining are manners of doing politics. The firefly ultimately stands in for the survival of politics, paradoxically understood as the survival of desire or of thought. The firefly is a "diagonal force" that impedes the liquidation of politics and in that way still promises a redemption, or an irreducibly political faith in redemption. From this point of view the survival of the fireflies encodes a voluntarism or a decisionism—Georges Bataille's exodus toward "inner experience" may have a similar key. I should look into this.

But why call it politics? The Book of Tobit allows us to wonder whether the wait for the return of an angel whose mission is not to redeem, but only to accompany and to endow our days with an anxious confidence, is truly a political wait; whether it makes sense to adjectivize as political that action without action that marks the rhythm of the wait in the time of the fall of experience. Are fireflies—gleams in the night—not, rather, the involuntary result of an attentive wait for the very disappearance of politics itself? Waiting can also wait politically, but to give the image a political horizon as the only possible horizon is a way of substituting horizon for image, of falsely subordinating the image to its improbable primary politicity. The gleam in the night is the infrapolitical image, always a gleam without horizon.

In the story of Tobias, the wait is not redemptive—the angel does not return. The wait has to do with a deferred natality; it is a repetition of natality, the euphoric repetition of an awakening that nevertheless carries within it the pain of separation. What glimmers in the night is, in every life, what adapts to that temporal tension, that which appears, if it ever does, and then meets partially, through the very pain of separation, a desire that allows for much modulation (it can be a serene modulation, an abandonment to time, or it can be a desperate modulation, that of the addict, for example). The light is obscure light because it comes out of darkness, but it is an obscurity that glimmers. It is not mere absence of light; it is not nothing. The time that comes in every case is existential time. In a certain way, one could say that this waiting is thought—in the precise way in which thinking is a form of dwelling. One can inhabit politically or one can live for football or in the bar, but those are derivative options. Still, dwelling in them is a waiting for the return of an angel who does not redeem and does not arrive, but who may always do so. The night light arrives, or not, because the waiting prepares it; there is preparation, not redemption. Not for Tobias, who dies like all of us, prematurely, at age 117, after a sufficiently pious life. This confinement, caused by the pandemic, also feels like a preparation.

In one of his texts on the COVID-19 pandemic, Giorgio Agamben writes: "The threshold that separates humanity from barbarism has been breached... The first point, perhaps the most serious, concerns the bodies of the dead. How have we been able to accept, only in the name of a risk that it was not possible to specify, that people dear to us and human beings in general could not only die alone but also—something that has never before occurred in history, from Antigone up to the present—that their cadavers could be incinerated without a funeral?"[21] I will risk proposing that the necessary referent is not only Antigone but also Tobias, whose angelic help is prompted by parental piety. Tobit, whose first fortune and almost his life were sequestered by King Senacherib for burying his tribe's dead in such a way that the king was unable to find them, does it again when somebody appears, his throat slit, lying in the plaza. His neighbors laugh and say: "Is he still not afraid? He has already been hunted down to be put to death for doing this, and he ran away; yet here he is again burying the dead!"[22] Perhaps that is why the first instructions he gives his son, when he sends him to recover Gabael's money, are as follows: "My son, when I die, give me a proper burial.

Honor your mother and do not abandon her all the days of her life. Do whatever pleases her, and do not grieve her in anything. Remember her, my son, because she faced many dangers for you while you were in her womb. And when she dies, bury her beside me in the same grave."[23] We have always known that burying the dead is not a political act. For Agamben, to prohibit it is to enter into biopolitical barbarism. To submit to the prohibition, to abstain from burying the dead, is perhaps a renunciation of all that glimmers in the night, including the wait. One must clear a space for the wait.

APRIL 16, 2020

In "Building, Dwelling, Thinking," Heidegger speaks of a harassed unrest as a daily way of life in late capitalism.[24] I wonder if the opposite of it would be something like a calmness, or a state of rest, without the tension of harassment. An uncanny rest. The tortoise rests without harassment when its race with the damned hare comes to an end. That calm is a temporal condition, similar to the one we sometimes achieve while sleeping. But harassed unrest seems to refer to a spatial disruption, to some specific kind of dis-inhabitation, a dis-located location. It is not possible to achieve dwelling in dislocation. Deprived of space, deprived of air as well: you drown, you cannot breathe, you live without breathing. Dispositioned into a life without air, your unrest comes to you not as the opposite of unharassed rest but as a precondition that no rest will rectify. And perhaps today rest, for all of us, is only the attempt at putting harassed unrest to rest, a necessary distraction; hence rest is also dis-location, dis-position. And that is why unrest is not the negative condition of rest. On the contrary, unrest reaches an ominous positivity. It is rest that can no longer be experienced as anything other than a negation of unrest, as mere withdrawal, as escape.

If rest is a temporal point in our private negotiation with the absent space of our lives, the interruption of a spatial flow, the anxious search for oxygen in the night, it could be that time is no longer anything but the stasis of unrest. In dis-location, in dis-position, we deliver ourselves to a temporal avoidance of unrest; and that becomes the ultimate disposition of our lives. We are all, so to speak, tortoises impossibly dreaming of the end of our race with the hare, hoping for nightfall, for the final release. Tacitus would say that his compatriots in Germania had created a wasteland and they were calling it peace. We could say that we dream of resting and we call it a living. For example: when we head to the beach during the summer, or when we watch a series on Hulu, or when doctors instruct us to do physical exercise with pleasure and not disdain, and not for less than three days a week for seventy minutes each time. When we think of retirement. We interrupt harassed unrest by auto-disposing ourselves into a pre-paid box. Being inside the box marks our private time, and everything else is dis-location. But private time is also the time that is lacking, deprived time, hence the inevitable consequence of harassed unrest as the spatial disruption that defines our lives.

Heidegger tries to flip this structure around, saying that what is essential in undwelling is that the human does not think about his or her own plight, does not understand undwelling as a lack of inhabitation, but manipulates it and twists and turns it in such a way that undwelling comes to be understood as home itself. The plight of undwelling is forgotten. To understand undwelling properly would then be to think of an alternative dwelling. The radical plight is not then harassed unrest but rather misunderstanding it, not acknowledging it as such. We live in the box and forget things. But to think of the box as a box is already to prepare ourselves for another dwelling, to prepare ourselves to abandon that harassed unrest as the mindless rush of our lives. So thinking is but remembering that dwelling is the human task. We forget that, and forgetting it is our plight, our true dis-position, our real dis-location. Thinking thinks before all the end of harassed unrest. But thinking the end of harassed unrest presupposes an essential transformation of our lives.

Is that enough? There's another Heidegger text that seems to propose an additional meditation. In "The Question concerning Technology," he refers to a listening that the human forgets when he or she is given over for the moment only to the question, which is the question of domination, of how to dominate.[25] In harassed unrest, what harasses is the very subjectivity of the human, which interrogates and cannibalizes the being that is helpless not to ask about his or her own being. But to exist is precisely to think of an outside beyond any specular encounter. And so, between harassed unrest and the essential transformation regarding the thinking of harassed unrest, there is a point of absolute location that is also the maximum point of a-location, when the human, asking about the domination that is its own domination of existence, finds itself, and dis-poses itself, as an object to be dominated. Harassed unrest finds in that mirror of self-devouring subjectivity a principle of radical calculability, of total orderability, and we can think of it as the moment of accomplishment of biopolitical life, when life is only the risk of the evasion of risk; when the principle of domination not only makes its way to the objects of the world, but has already encompassed the human as object; when the subject has fallen under the shadow of the object and is no longer but the object of a calculation: extractable, orderable, radically available, as our institutional bosses would want for all of us to be. As social media companies make us be. Converted into a gene pool, into living labor, into a human resource, into mere data for extraction, or into acquisitive power, reduced to bare life, or dressed only in disguise, we will by then have already lost the minimum distance that allowed us to understand our undwelling as terminal plight. There is no longer an outside, only a general field of identity, but it is an identity that has managed to overcome the condition of harassed unrest toward the doubly sinister unharassed rest of biopolitical fixity, of biopolitical infinity. What is lost is the very capacity to understand that loss. And there is no longer any plight, or any experience of plight. But to think the dwelling, to listen to the demand of an outside, of an exteriority without which there can be no home, to find in it a free relationship with space against biopolitical rapture, against the abstract, unlimited, de-situated, and unbreathable space of biopolitics—there is no other option.

APRIL 18, 2020 One of the most pressing punctual problems in this phase of the pandemic is the dispute between what has been called biopolitics and what has been called the economy. If the economy is that which produces life's resources, then biopolitics addresses the administration of life by the state, or in any case by institutional bodies. There are big political differences—more apparent every day—between those who prefer to place greater emphasis on biopolitical care and those who prefer for there to be greater emphasis on economic concerns. There is a certain sector of the right that reclaims private liberty, limits on state-imposed confinement, or choice regarding the use of masks, without attending to the fact that their private options could result in sentencing others to contagion; and there is a certain sector of the left that, perhaps opportunistically, places favor on long-term total confinement, in plain awareness of possible catastrophic consequences to economic life that may serve their strategic plan, in this case a potentially idiotic one because it would be counterproductive. Or maybe, in the end, none of it is particularly measurable along the right/left spectrum, and it is instead something else we have not yet figured out. Let's reduce for a moment that "something else" to something other than the options of being either against biopolitics and for the economy, or against the economy and for biopolitics.

In any case, they are subjective options that are made in full reference to the perceived subject of the political. It is the subject who places itself at the center of that dilemma, measuring the world from its personal preference, or as a starting point for thinking about what might be best for its community. The subject, who sees the totality of the entities, wants to aspire to control such economic or biopolitical totality without attending to the fact that this totality is not controllable; and that elements of this totality—in this case, the virus—make it savage, ineluctable, and resistant to capture. From the point of view of that subject who seeks to remain in control of the totality of entities, or that wants its political agents and representatives to remain in control on its behalf, the pandemic is nothing more than a sinister interruption, a temporary desistence. At the heart of that subject who thought the economic regulation of its existence was threatened by biopolitical measures, or who thought, alternatively and complementarily, that the biopolitical order of its existence was threatened by economic pretense, something desists and escapes. In our world it is assumed that biopolitics is tendentially universal, or that the economy is, or that both are, and they generally coexist without major conflict. The medical and economic sciences handle the totality of entities from their perspectives, and within their ontic spheres there is nothing outside their reach. Nothing can threaten the claim of science to capture the totality of being. Nothing can threaten the absolute dominance of money in our lives. But the virus is like a little worm gnawing at such claims, at least until the invention of a successful vaccine confirms, temporarily at least, their absolute correction. The paradox then, for the time being, is that something pertaining to the totality of being—the virus—destabilizes claims to the capture of the totality of being. Against the insistence of the claims there is a desistence of the real.

What old Heidegger called "anxiety" is the type of experience in which nothing, or a particular placeholder or representative of nothing, or of the nothingness, displaces the subject's position against the totality of the entities. He also said that the experience of originary anxiety is rare, infrequent, while at the same time insisting that it is to be found everywhere unacknowledged or disguised: "In the clear night of the nothing of anxiety the original openness of beings as such arises: that they are beings, and not nothing. . . . The essence of the originally nihilating nothing lies in this, that it brings Da-sein for the first time before beings as such."[26] The "originally nihilating nothing" is the desistence in the real that brings forth an experience of anxiety. Heidegger gives various examples that, curiously, tend not to be taken into account and that represent diverse forms of desistence. He refers to the effects provoked in us by "unyielding antagonism and stinging rebuke," "galling failure and merciless prohibition," "bitter privation."[27] They would all be manifestations of an experience of desistence that originary anxiety unveils in full and that is not unrelated to "the cheerfulness and gentleness of creative longing," only its other side.[28] But in those experiences the human being, who experiences a lack or a withdrawal, who exists in the face of desistence, is brought up before "beings as such," Heidegger says. "Being held out into the nothing . . . on the ground of concealed anxiety makes the human being a lieutenant of the nothing" who can do something with it.[29] The nothing is not nothing, in that sense, but it is rather the giver of a transcendence away from the fullness of things. The human becomes able to use, to put to use, his or her relation with the nothing—that nothing that desists in the heart of the subject—in order to "liberate ourselves from those idols everyone has and to which they are wont to go cringing."[30] Are preferences for biopolitical care or for economic freedom not clear examples of those idols, manifest as such at the time of the pandemic, in whose latent aporia any aspiration to control the totality of beings is destroyed? Heidegger speaks of thought as a particular leap into the abandonment of the nothing that desists and, in desisting, opens up the possibility of a general critique of existence. But this abandonment is also an abandonment of the subject. It is the subject that desists in desistence. The subject is the first victim of the little worm that corrodes the aspirations to the domination of the totality of beings. Anxiety reveals this, and anxiety should not be disavowed.

The repeated voices that ask for a reform of the subject, for a transformation of the subject, for an entry into the interiority of the subject, and who express while doing so a new love for the wounded subject, are at the end voices who wish to evade desistence, since desistence is primarily the desistence of the subject, all the more profound the more originary the experience of anxiety is. To abandon the idols is also to abandon the central and totalizing idol of the subject, to whom we have assigned a role that it doesn't have and never has had. The particular leap of thought is a leap toward an outside beyond the subject—on which every possibility of another politics depends; of imagining another politics, beyond the tiresome and unproductive aporia of biopolitics and economy that I mentioned at the beginning of this note.

The pandemic is a warning and a symptom of the massively brutal instance of collective desistence in our time: climate change, the tendential destruction of the planet, of which we are now halfway conscious but to which we have devoted our blind efforts for several centuries, even immemorially. It now has sufficient force, perhaps, to take us to forms of life away from the subject's aspirations to the capture and domination of the totality of being, always deluded, and deluded also under that fallen form that has come to be called "hegemony." But we must listen to that force, a message of the nihilating nothing that desists both beyond the subject and the world reduced to an object—even if it contains them. Neither biopolitics nor the economy: what is needed is in some other place.

APRIL 24, 2020   Regarding Agamben and his positions on general governmental politics on the pandemic, it seems to me that there are many who imitate the Greek maiden who would laugh at Thales of Miletus for having fallen into a hole as a consequence of gazing at the sky. Yes, like Thales, we're all a bit idiotic when it comes down to it, but perhaps it is not in our interest to laugh so hard. During this last week of the academic semester we read and discussed the couple of chapters that José Luis Villacañas dedicates to the Spanish Inquisition in his book *Imperiofilia* (Empirephilia). Villacañas states that the "Party of Ferdinand," that is, the supporters of Ferdinand of Aragon, managed to stabilize a monarchist power whose most important negative political function was the destruction of the power of the Spanish cities and the dismantling and expropriation of their fiscal control; and that the Inquisition was an ideal instrument for these designs since the new forced converts were the political and, in many cases, economic elites. And then Villacañas says:

> The Holy Tribunal could only function by breaking previous community ties. The tighter they were, the more opportunities they afforded for the denunciation. Mistrust prevailed everywhere . . . At the end of the day everybody was *not yet a New Christian*. That is how fidelity to external rites that never fully protected was intensified to an extreme, in the face of the ancestral reality of blood, always debatable, since it depended on how far those [inquisitional] investigations were taken. We could call "negative community" this community forged by the Inquisition, since it only identifies the one who is forced to leave it. Everybody else remains inside but insecure . . . Even though everybody meets at the Church, or in the *auto de fé*, nobody feels secure in terms of being on this side of it. People will cling all the more forcefully to the public rite, the more they fear that the Tribunal will separate them from it. What united everybody was not reciprocal trust, simply the fact of not being looked at.[31]

We are not so far away from this. The *homo sacer* paradigm puts us all in a potentially marrano position, and therefore our community, to the extent that it still warrants that name, is a negative community, defined by its expulsions, defined by those who remain in the sense that they are not (yet) thrown out of it. The pandemic makes it explicit even in moments where basic human solidarity struggles to express itself against prevailing inertia. The negative community is marked by a belonging that is precarious and absolutely interruptible, therefore absolutely desirable; and at the same time constituted, paradoxically, by those who leave the community and enter the inquisitional outside, which immediately becomes the most intimate and terrifying inside. This contradictory community is like that figure of the unconscious Jacques Lacan liked to invoke: an aporetic figure, with no outside or inside, unlivable, but a condition of life. Henry Charles Lea, the old historian, would say that, under the Inquisition, nobody was able to exist except in the shadow of terror. The whole country was kept submerged in the shadow of terror, which was not less terror for being potential, since terror is always potential, it always ever anticipates, and never finds stasis. As for Agamben, we could think that his reduction of the position of the human in the present to *homo sacer* or bare life is excessive, inasmuch as we are not yet subject to bare life, in the same way that a Toledan convert was not yet in the hands of the Inquisition until he or she came to be taken by the Inquisition. But what Agamben principally proposes, as does Villacañas in terms of the community of the old Christians who have "not yet" lost their qualification, is that bare life is the tendential or potential meaning of life in our civilizational horizon, as might have been the case of a marrano life in sixteenth-century Spain.

From that point of view, it would not be farfetched to propose that our communities are also negative communities. If the reduction of life to bare life is the fundamental biopolitical horizon of our time, and if therefore, as Agamben proposes, there is always, in each and every one of us, a latent *homo sacer* ready to be executed without assassination or sacrifice, ready to be handed over to pertinent authority—political or medical or administrative—it should come as no surprise that the dominant political element in our world is negative and counter-communitarian. The Spanish Inquisition produced a negative and terrified social community, and the civilizational tendencies described by Agamben behave in the same way. This is what he points out. It is also perhaps what produces in his words, in these pandemic times, the most irritation. His worry—maybe monothematic and in that sense subject to the laughter of the Miletus maiden—is that general governmental attitudes are part of that logic and not an exception to it. It is not so easy to disagree with it. Finding an alternative solution that should have to go through civilizational change is not simple.

The inquisitional structure caused a collapse of all political possibility in Spain for centuries—there was a power within the state, an untouchable power, superior to the state itself; with regard to it there was no predictable emancipation or way out. In the same vein, the structure of *homo sacer* has the potential to produce political collapse and negative community: if we *are* only to the extent that we are not bare life, and we thus live in what remains between ourselves and our own abyss as bare life, into which we would never wish to fall, it is easy for our idea of community to become nothing more than a desirable imaginary impugnment of such an existential structure. It is not only the negative community that is organized after or according to the reductive potentiality of *homo sacer*; half-baked communitarian reactions and well-intentioned political proposals end up being just as counter-communitarian or give origin to perverse communities (nationalisms, sects, whimsical ideologies). This is, to my mind, important and valuable.

The question that worries me when I read Agamben is that his solution to all of that does not persuade me as a political solution. Agamben should be subjected to a small adjustment (Agamben greatly admires the "small adjustment" Benjamin mentions in relation to some story read in Gershom Scholem or Franz Kafka, or both). And here is that adjustment: if *we are* only to the extent that we are not bare life, that struggle for *being* should aim not toward the inversion of a negative community into an impossible positivity or glory, not toward the game of counter-communitarian inversion into the animality of the end of history, but more toward the achievement of a radical exteriority, neither biopolitical nor inquisitorial, with respect to the contemporary sociopolitical world. Aiming for that exteriority is an infrapolitical exercise that ends up constituting itself as a condition of all politics. The game cannot be the inversion of what exists, since there is no emancipation in that direction. What worries Agamben is neither sovereignty nor violence nor power, but the very opposite. He ought to be consistent with it. The time of the pandemic is exodic time.

APRIL 25, 2020
The tense nervousness of these past weeks has, in part, to do with the growing dependence on social media, with my waiting for reactions that only arrive sporadically, if at all. I wanted to compose these notes and immediately share them and expose the process of their composition: writing in confinement, but for all, by way of Facebook and the blog. But no, nothing works in digital communities that are, in their practical results—or at least as far as I am concerned—zombie communities. I should not postpone my flight from them, and I should look for a more radical retreat, without addictions. A retreat not toward interiority but toward another outside that might grant a quieter gaze, but that also is more resolute. In the current communication regime there is a lot of negative community in the precise sense of the note above. We are imprisoned in a community that only fears exclusion, which manifests itself as silence, as nonresponse. But one cannot fight against the civilizational drift except by separating oneself from it. To write only about

what interests, without critique, so as not to get caught up in the will to preach. What has no interest can be ignored. An act of sustained subtraction; one's notes, the more idiosyncratic, the better. To increase simplicity in everything. Not to look for anybody, not to ask for anything, not to wait. While waiting. This calls for a different writing.

APRIL 28, 2020   The absence of good news continues to weigh, and god knows that the last few years have prepared us well for it. It is difficult to establish productive routines; I'm still reacting to what keeps appearing, with few solid initiatives except what I did this past weekend when preparing some writing files. I have one last tedious batch of corrections to get through regarding the final papers my students have written. The writing of these notes is becoming imperative, all too imperative.

MAY 2, 2020   In that Empire, the art of Cartography attained such Perfection that the map of a single Province occupied the entirety of a City, and the map of the Empire, the entirety of a Province. In time, those Unconscionable Maps no longer satisfied, and the Cartographers Guilds struck a Map of the Empire whose size was that of the Empire, and which coincided point for point with it. The following Generations, who were not so fond of the Study of Cartography as their Forebears had been, saw that that vast Map was Useless, and not without some Pitilessness was it, that they delivered it up to the Inclemencies of Sun and Winters. In the Deserts of the West, still today, there are Tattered Ruins of that Map, inhabited by Animals and Beggars; in all the Land there is no other Relic of the Disciplines of Geography. —SUÁREZ MIRANDA, *Viajes de varones prudentes*, Libro IV, Cap. XLV, Lérida (1658)

Tiqqun's *The Cybernetic Hypothesis*, from 2001, but just published in an English translation, starts with an epigraph from Jean-François Lyotard in reference to Borges's text on maps and territories.[32] Perhaps the key to Tiqqun's work rests in its first sentence: "The great concentrator wants stable circuits, even cycles, predictable repetitions, untroubled accountability. It wants to eliminate every partial drive, it wants to immobilize the body."[33] To map a territory to the most exacting extent is to replace it, in perhaps the sense that Antonio Gramsci dreamed of when he said that the communist movement would not conquer the state but would perfect it by replacing it. This substitution, however, breeds a particular immobility: the map is, after all, territory brought to a standstill, to a fixity that only time can ruin. Time, or the plague: the Cartographers Guild could not have foreseen the invisible irruption of the virus that reintroduces a now irretrievable gap between map and territory. Any dream of reproduction and control, of reproduction by means of and in view of control, is shattered. The gap, the virus, destroys the speculative project through a multiplicity of zones of opacity. And then what? No speculative project will be possible from now on.

"Cybernetic [capitalism] asserts itself by a negation of everything that escapes regulation, of all the lines of escape that save existence in the interstices of the norm and its apparatuses, of all the behavioral fluctuations that ultimately would not follow from natural laws."[34] The "total modeling"[35] of the cybernetic hypothesis flounders. "Total transparency"[36] ends in a chaos of solitude. Surveillance and capture, after all, the twin apparatuses of cybernetic capitalism, are premised on the absolute equivalence of map and territory. The uncertainty introduced by the gap throws a wrench into the workings of their will to power, whose reconstruction is now, perhaps transitorily, in doubt. But it won't be forgotten. Another epigraph, this time from Giorgio Cesarano: "The fictitious constantly pays a higher price for its strength when beyond its screen the possible real becomes visible. It's only today, no doubt, that the domination of the fictitious has become totalitarian. But this is precisely its dialectical and 'natural' limit . . . in the bloody sinking of all the 'suns of the future,' there begins to dawn a possible future at last. Henceforth, in order to be, humans only need to separate themselves once and for all from every 'concrete utopia.'"[37] The separation is not simply willed: it occurs, dystopically and ineluctably. Its name is "panic,"[38] a "disintegration of the crowd *within* the crowd."[39] "It's the end of hope and of every concrete utopia that takes form as a bridge extended towards the fact of no longer expecting anything, of having nothing left to lose. And through a particular sensitivity to the possibilities of lived situations, to their possibilities of collapse, to the extreme fragility of their sequencing, it's a way of reintroducing a serene relationship with the headlong rush of cybernetic capitalism. At the twilight of nihilism, it's a matter of making fear just as *extravagant* as hope."[40]

The "invisible revolt,"[41] as invisible as the viral irruption, proliferates secretly, inconspicuously, through the constitution of zones of opacity "in which to circulate and experiment freely without conducting the Empire's information flows."[42] But this requires courage, a particular kind of it. There are anonymous singularities that have been and are breaking loose. They must now experiment. The thought experiment must go through what Jacques Derrida, in his Theory and Practice Seminar, called *l'incontournable* (the ineludible).[43] Thought returns to its calling as an attempt to open to what is both inevitable and obscure, ineluctable and necessary, but remote and forbidden. It cuts through Cesarano's *fictitious* because it has forcefully been exiled from it. The radical denarrativization the virus wreaks in the very fabric of the illusion of the speculative dream, cybernetic capitalism, leaves us open to a silence we have perhaps never heard before. That opaque silence is also the promise of a future. But it needs to be heard.

MAY 5, 2020

> If I myself can choose I would like as contemporaries Geronimo and Kakfa. The words in the story are beside the point, and the stupid meekness of Penelope. —MIGUEL MOREY, *Deseo de ser piel roja* (1999)

The head is now becoming a city only known to my feet—they lead me, and that's ok. They ignore the reasons for the straight path and the shortest distance—and instead they know well the virtue of all of the detours, all the good that comes from getting off track. Astray, here and there, things change: the city is another with every passing step and, above it, the skies are always open. I know. I know that I will soon be a free man—free even from threats like those of monsters in the night. I know, as the cowboy knew he would never return home after the death of the girl in white—that he had no other option but to heed the call of the prairie, and that it was among the redskins where he had his last hope of finding his land and people. Now I know—with that kind of certainty. —MIGUEL MOREY, *Deseo de ser piel roja* (1999)

Deseo de ser piel roja (Desire to be a redskin) is a text by Miguel Morey published in 1994; it ostensibly has little to do with the pandemic that surrounds us today.[44] But the narrator, undecidably the figure of the author or a creature of fiction (even though the text pushes to make the reader feel its autographic tone), does not stop insisting that his head is a city under siege, a city under threat: "Your head is always a city in a state of siege."[45] In addition, he says: "The times that began then were times to surveil oneself, to listen to oneself, to pay attention to oneself: when you feel as though you are learning something of the most elementary kind, that it is prudent for instance to not do more than one thing at a time, and to do it slowly . . . and that what is most important now is to be prudent."[46] I propose to dispense with the oedipal or post-oedipal structuring of the story in its central aspects ("the pages that follow are not, then, a psychoanalytic novel," Morey says, maybe in order to put in play the mechanism of disavowal and of lying with the truth)[47] and to look only at its *parergon*, at the framing, or at some aspects of the frame. It concerns "the wait," the "dead time of waiting,"[48] of which we shall all have learned something during these weeks.

The narrator seeks freedom, even if it is the threatened freedom of the Apache before extermination. If the Apache understands "that the life of liberty does not admit more than the present time,"[49] he or she can say to the good cowboy: "Get out of here—those of your race have been condemned to live forever in a land that does not exist, in something like that distance that separates lightning from thunder. You have chosen this path wherein it is always night."[50] The narrator, simultaneously hopeful and hopeless, searches for an "escape," of which he is suspicious: it could be "like living a reality where it is not possible to dream that the possible will one day create an opening."[51] That opening in the real is what awaits in the "city on whose outskirts only barbed wire flourishes" and where "the last red men should be hiding in the catacombs so as to dance the Dance of the Present."[52] With regard to it, "to know that one is somebody who flees [from the fixed gaze of all machine men[53]] is already a way of not being so lost."[54]

To avoid loss, what does one look for? Meditation, throughout all stories, is about the time of life, wherein one is always a survivor until one ceases to be one. That is why the narrator goes searching for another time, a present, understood as follows:

You know to the point of tedium that small sustained tear that it is to understand that the self-comfort of inhabiting a type of interminable instant will never be for you—the clean immediacy of he who is in the world as water should be inside water. That you are condemned not to be able to live your own life except in the revocation of what has already been lived, in the representation of a lived experience that is already an absence of itself once you come to identify it, when you interpret it and name it—which belongs to the instant, to the second, immediately anterior.[55]

But that small, sustained tear is precisely originary anxiety, the generator of all stories through the resolve of dispensing with story, of fleeing, not from time, but from time stolen into meaning, from hermeneutic time. The rift in the real follows the intent to destroy sense so as to find in its ruin, impossibly, its own redemption. Because of this, about the "latent imminence of sense in the interstitial opening," "something tells you that only this interstice can let you escape, fulfill your red man yearning for entering the present."[56]

The moment of the most perfect coincidence, the moment when the sound of thunder joins with the bolt of lightning, is the moment of annihilation, but the distance between lightning and thunder is the terrible time of an absence from which one creates meaning as compensation and consolation. That is, in each case, the dead time of waiting, time already charred in the nocturnal path of the machine-men. It is not Apache time, except in the sense that Apache time is the time destroyed. It is possible that the rift of dead and unproductive time in which we live, in the wait, rescues improbable memory from an existence not given over to "curricular transiting,"[57] which is today the common reason of singular solitude, what everybody does. That would be a plausible prudence, a political flight. The time of the pandemic opens the chance to escape curricular transiting. That would be both an exodus and a revolution.

MAY 6, 2020

Infrapolitics does not address the need for any one labor, or for any one central, oriented activity, or for a specific task; it is neither *energeia* nor *ergon*. Rather, it is a practice of the step back, an attempt to meditate, therefore, on the *dynamis* that enables and controls all *energeia*, all *ergon*, all *praxis*, all *poiesis*. We could call it a reflexive displacement toward the *parergon* that, as frame, is a condition of condition. If on the terrain of human action there are truths, or works, in art, in science, in technology in the sense of the manufacturing or invoicing of a product, in love or in politics, then infrapolitics is not that which meditates on the basis of those factual truths—that would be philosophy or also literature, since literature is not just a procedure of art but also something else—but a reflective exercise on the condition of condition: an exercise on the existential *parergon*, and therefore an antiphilosophy.

This confinement is, among other things, a time for retreat. I called it exodus before. The retreat can be understood as a retreat into inner consciousness, on the long-standing tradition adopted but not founded by Christianity. Why not imagine a retreat in an adverse sense, not toward inner consciousness, but toward the exteriority of the world? A step back toward the world as *parergon*, toward the outside, which is never just the outside, since it in-sists and re-sists in the dimension of the existential "ex-". Let us for a moment imagine man, or woman, as *argos*, *an-ergos*, that is, not turned toward production but removed or subtracted from it. This is one of the obvious possibilities or facts of confinement. Yes, in one of its faces, the *argos*, as Aristotle says and Giorgio Agamben repeats, addresses potency negatively, as not actualized, and so allows it to be seen in its privative character as im-potency. Potency or impotency, but there's something more, something else, that overflows and escapes those two conditions. That something else is the condition of condition, the infrapolitical condition, the original gift.

In confinement, landscape is the only thing we see, perhaps framed through a window—assuming there are still windows—like those of Andrew Wyeth. What follows are two quotes from recent reading, from Agamben's *Creation and Anarchy* and from Juan José Saer's *The Investigation*. First Saer:

> Being an adult signifies precisely having arrived at the understanding that one has not been born in one's native land, but in a larger, more neutral place, neither friend nor enemy, unknown, which no one could call his own and which does not give rise to affection but, rather, to

> strangeness, a home that is not spatial or geographical, or even verbal, but rather, and insofar as those words can continue to mean something, physical, chemical, biological, cosmic, and of which the invisible and the visible form a part; and that that whole which includes even the very limits of the inconceivable is not in reality his homeland but his prison, itself abandoned and locked from the outside—the boundless darkness that wanders, at once glacial and igneous, beyond the reach not only of the senses, but also of emotion, of nostalgia and of thought.[58]

And now Agamben:

> Insofar as it has in this sense gone beyond being, landscape is the outstanding form of use. In it, use-of-oneself and use of the world correspond without remainder. Justice, as a state of the world as inappropriable, is here the decisive experience. Landscape is a dwelling in the inappropriable as form-of-life, as justice. For this reason, if in the world the human being was necessarily thrown and disoriented, in landscape he is finally at home.... Landscape is the house of Being.[38]

The frame is the prison of landscape, its *parergon*. The *parergon* is not the house of being, but its condition. Confinement forces us to think about it, or, more commonly, to refuse to do it, to avoid thinking about it. Sheltered from all emotion, nostalgia, thought. If truths or works, which is to say, the appropriable, are conditions of philosophy—for Badiou, whom I'm following here, art, science, politics, and love are procedures of truth that frame the very possibility of philosophical thought, because philosophy does not produce truth but reflects on the truths of its own historical configuration—there is a thinking of the un-appropriable that surpasses, even if it includes, language and bodies. That thinking, itself overflowing, un-worked, is a condition of all works, for the most part a phantom and un-thematized condition. It is then a condition of all philosophical conditions, and therefore it is a form of antiphilosophy. Just as the inapparent is the condition of all appearance and impotency is the condition of all potency. Antiphilosophy, in its infrapolitical sense, tires itself out in the unproductive attempt to present the unpresentable. That is why it is an impoverished thinking, and a thinking of poverty, an im-potent thinking. That is its secret.

MAY 7, 2020

Bloomism is for Tiqqun the theory of the human without attributes at the same time produced and confronted by the authoritarian commodification of the society of the spectacle. If the Total Mobilization of 1914 was its qualitative leap toward historical presence, perhaps the Great Confinement of 2020 takes that presence toward its vanishing point, after which there will no longer be any confrontation—only a continuous and indifferent production.[60] But, Tiqqun adds, Bloomism "triumphs above all in those who run away from it,"[61] the champions of the global petite bourgeoisie whose ethos is defined by "bad substantiality."[62] It consists of this:

> Instead of considering their central vapidity, the majority of people recoil from the complete and dizzying absence of property, from radical indetermination, and therefore, deep down, from the abyss of their freedom. They still prefer to drown themselves in bad substantiality towards which everything is undoubtedly pushing them. But that won't result in surprise when they discover, through a detour headed toward a depression that is unevenly concealed, this or that incombustible quality. The French, the excluded minority, the woman, the artist, the homosexual, the doctor, the citizen, the firefighter, the Muslim, the Buddhist, or the unemployed, all that gives them voice is worthwhile, in some way or another, and their eyes blink toward infinity, before the miraculous I AM."[63]

Identity masks—it does not prevent—the lack of individuality; and in it, Bloom triumphs, if you can call it a triumph. Identity, in that form, like bad substantiality, as denial of the abyss of freedom, is the basis of the nonsubjects of today, and therefore also of their presumed political and emancipatory demands. The Western left has formalized all of this as a theory of hegemony, through the notion of chains of equivalence, but this is exactly the problem: through the theory of hegemony, people "quietly reenter the general system of merchandise, exchange, and equivalence, which reflects them and guides them."[64] Why do we still think of this as a leftist and emancipatory theory?

MAY 9, 2020

In trying to establish the historical genealogy of the concept of hegemony, I was prompted to read the entry on personal loyalty in Emile Benveniste's *Dictionary of Indo-European Concepts and Society*. Part of what I read was predictable (and consistent with Heidegger's analysis of Roman hegemonic domination in his *Parmenides*, from 1942):

> *Fides* develops into a subjective notion, no longer the concept which is inspired in somebody, but the trust which is placed in somebody . . . The one who holds the *fides* placed in him by a man has this man at his mercy. This is why *fides* becomes almost synonymous with *dicio* and *potestas*. In their primitive form these relations involve a certain reciprocity: placing one's *fides* in somebody secured in return his guarantee and his support. But this very fact underlines the inequality of the conditions. It is authority which is exercised at the same time as protection from somebody who submits to it, an exchange for, and to the extent of, submission.[65]

Calls for a hegemonic understanding of the political have that irreducible character of exchange—trust for submission, constraint, and obedience. This is clearly visible, by the way, in the early Gramsci, whom we are reading now in a working group. Persuasion, by the party that holds the secret of history, is obedience. Those who have faith in the party must first of all obey. As Benveniste notes, "*Fides* in Latin is the abstract noun corresponding to a different verb: *credo*. . . . In these terms we are back once again with notions in which there is no distinction between law and religion: the whole of ancient law is only a special domain regulated by practices and rules which are still pervaded by mysticism."[66] This is presumably why Gramsci may claim that "most people do not exist outside some organization, whether it calls itself the Church or the Party, and morality does not exist without some specific, spontaneous organ within which it is realized. The bourgeoisie is a moment of chaos not simply where production is concerned, but where the spirit is concerned."[67]

But there was something else in Benveniste's entry that intrigued me. It was the reference to Tacitus's description of the berserk, the Wotan army: "Those fierce men improve on their savage nature by enlisting the help of art and time: they blacken their shields, they dye their skin, and they choose the darkest nights for battle. The horror alone and the darkness which envelops that doleful army (*feralis exercitus*) spreads terror: there is no enemy who can withstand that strange and, so to speak, infernal aspect; because in each battle the eyes are the first to be vanquished."[68] Let us dwell for a second on that last phrase—"the eyes are the first to be vanquished." The attempt to think about the mere possibility of a posthegemonic politics, which means, first of all, a politics not bound by constraint and obedience, a politics that takes its point of departure from the assumption that persuasion means submission and domination, has been linked to the existential practice of freedom from domination that I call infrapolitics. Infrapolitics does not attempt persuasion to the extent that it does not attempt domination or calls for obedience. Indeed, it places itself at the limit of any political practice, in a dark area at the border of political logic. Benveniste starts his dictionary entry by talking about oaks, solid trees, an embodiment of firmness and reliability. In old Germanic, the oak was connected with the idea of trust, and trust was above all the virtue of a band of warriors. Friendship and community were originally and essentially the friendship and community of the warriors in a given band. The Greek word *laos* means both "army" and "the people." Politics is always first of all a politics of friendship, where friendship cannot avoid the hierarchies that pervade it, which are expressed in the obligations of submission and command. What happens when an obscure group of people, a group of friends, propose a form of thought that subtracts itself from submission and command, and that suspends war in that sense? What kind of strange politics of friendship is at stake in a group that denies the traditional understanding of politics as much as it denies the traditional understanding of friendship?

Infrapolitics (and its corollary, posthegemony) cannot constitute itself as a region of allegiances against a common enemy; it must subtract itself from it. It prefers not to engage in enmity as primary political deployment; it dwells otherwise. But this has two immediate effects. On the one hand, it preempts the deployment of any libidinal drive connected to group militancy (the unherdable cat is the referent here, not the *miles*), which means that it also preempts mimetic rivalry. These two—the mimetic drive and mimetic rivalry—are archaic characteristics or dimensions of the band of brothers, and they are probably un-renounceable as such. On the other hand, upon offering itself as an exception, it seems to undermine at every level the very constituting principle of community (trust, obedience, submission, mimetic drive, mimetic rivalry). It generates the impossible phantom of an ever more obscure, more abstract, radically opaque counter-community, which of course unleashes every instinct for danger and therefore every reason for rejection. That is to say, the infrapolitical form, as a theoretical option, must deal with two antinomic, hence, destructive problems (they are destructive to the extent that aporia, without exit, is destructive): it does not encourage any will for mimetic solidarity, and it cannot avoid being a target for the massive rejection of the rival (another warrior) who suspects an enemy to be all the more dangerous to the extent that it dissembles its enemy position; an enemy without a name, an obscure and unidentifiable enemy to the extent that it places itself outside the common light, the solar space. To that same extent it appears to be a berserk enemy, a feral and infernal soldier of the dead and nocturnal Wotan: it constitutes the *feralis exercitus* of the infrapolitical mofos, of those who have no *exercitus*. As far as infrapolitics and posthegemony go, the eyes are the first to be vanquished, and nobody wants to look farther out. Perhaps nobody can, or they prefer not to. This is, needless to say, unjust.

MAY 10, 2020

A letter from Nietzsche to Peter Gast about *The Wanderer and His Shadow*: "All of it—except for a few lines—was thought out on walks, and it was sketched in pencil in six small notebooks."[69] In *Vidas de Nietzsche* (Nietzsche's Lives), Miguel Morey, who mentions the letter, comments that, at that stage of his life, the option for the aphoristic style "is the effect of his critical disdain toward the lazy mendacity that all systematic will implies for thought; and toward its lack of courage as well."[70] But I wonder if the combination of certain physical factors wasn't far more decisive—Nietzsche's eyesight difficulties, the migraines that prostrated and incapacitated him for days, and the consequent hardship of sustaining the effort of reading and studying. For him, thinking brief and precise thoughts while on his walks, quickly drafting them in pencil, and later dictating them or transferring them over to his typewriter (which he used briefly at that time), with the necessary style and argumentation changes added in, were manageable tasks.

Nobody else is Nietzsche, but his way of intellectual production can perhaps be linked to contemporary conditions in one specific and perhaps unexpected way. Social media, at their best, are spurs for writing. One reacts to something one reads, to some brief comment, with pleasure or disdain, and that excitation generates a note that can then evolve, if not toward an aphorism, at least toward a punctual, concise text in which what is expressed is not only a verbal style, not only a style of thought, but also something on the terrain of affect or passion. For better or worse, the writing that results is opportunistic and unsystematic, heated or bland, but maybe out of it, as bleak as it may be (but it is not always bleak), a truth of our epoch comes to be expressed. At any rate, isn't that writing, when achieved with a certain sincerity and some modicum of intellectual integrity, infinitely more interesting and attractive than the deeply tedious academic paper, which terrorizes everyone and nobody can stand—even if the academic crowd still tenuously acts as if they revere it? It is, to such an extent that one begins to realize that the best opinion journalism today has incorporated that rhythmic quality of being a response to some excitation, whether noxious or pleasurable, in social media, derived from what one sees, almost always in casual, anecdotal, rarely systematic form. Surely that cannot be improvised and, when it does happen, in its good and not mediocre or disastrous form, it happens because the person behind the note is also a wanderer burdened with his or her own shadow, and not a pure spirit or beautiful soul like those who finally prevail on Facebook.

I think we would all be better off if academic meetings were, from now on, planned as a Nietzschean walk in some digital platform's Upper Engadin or Italian Riviera. Those forests of words, those sea cliffs, behind which we can in general assume there to be a body, would fulfill for us the function that for Nietzsche was the property of the sky and the sea and the light: the trees, the valleys or headlands, or the rocks of his favorite Swiss canton. Spontaneous thought and in that way free thought, not subject to passing through the hideous curricula of academic accumulation, where papers are so often no less pretentious than they are cowardly, inane in their measured formulations over the course of their twenty or thirty minutes of supposed rigor. We cannot and we would not want to repeat in ourselves Nietzsche's migraines or his eye infections, but we can try to learn what they made possible. Nietzsche liked to call them thoughts with dove's feet and the heart of a snake, the thoughts of the rare free spirits, from which he sought to take charge of, instead of avoiding, the conditions of his own existence.

Remark 4: Fools and Free Spirits

In his *Nietzsche's Journey to Sorrento,* Paolo D'Iorio notes a particular jotting in one of Nietzsche's 1877 notebooks: "Walking along the windless, twilight pathways, while above us the trees rustle, agitated by violent gales in a brighter light."[71] Nietzsche repeats the same thought in a March letter to Reinhart von Seydlitz,[72] but of course the reappearance of the thought in *Human, All Too Human* is more significant. It happens in #275, entitled *Cynic and Epicurean.* D'Iorio points out that the position of the Epicurean is the one occupied by Nietzsche.[73] He also says that the aphorism is a characterization of "one of the great antitheses of the philosophical tradition,"[74] that is, that of Cynics and Epicureans. But I think perhaps Nietzsche was after something more revealing for his own project than the rehearsal of a style difference in post-Platonic philosophy. Here is aphorism 275, which I transcribe in full:

> The Cynic perceives the connection between the multiplied and magnified pains of more highly cultivated people and the abundance of their needs; he therefore conceives that the host of opinions about what is beautiful, proper, seemly, delightful must give rise to copious sources not only of enjoyment, but also of displeasure. In accordance with this insight, he moves backward in his development by relinquishing many of these opinions and withdrawing from certain demands made by culture; he thereby obtains a feeling of freedom and empowerment; and gradually, once habit has made his way of life tolerable for him, he will in fact have fewer and fewer sensations of displeasure than cultivated people and will become very much like a domestic animal; in addition, everything that he does feel has the charm of contrast and—he can also curse to his heart's content, so that he thereby gets well beyond the animal's world of sensations.—The Epicurean adopts the same point of view as the Cynic; generally, only a difference of temperament sets them apart. And so the Epicurean uses his higher culture to make himself independent of prevailing opinions; he raises himself above them, whereas the Cynic merely continues to negate them. It is as if the for-

mer were strolling along in windless, well-protected, twilight avenues, while above him the treetops were being tossed in the wind and betrayed to him how violently the world outside was moving. The Cynic, on the other hand, acts as if he were going naked outside into the blowing wind and hardens himself to the point of insensibility.[75]

Let us imagine that both Epicureans and Cynics are potential examples of "free spirits" in the Nietzschean sense. The difference between them is a difference of "temperament," it is said. The Cynic "negates" prevailing opinion while the Epicurean "raises himself above" it. The Cynic's negation has two effects from which the Epicurean is shielded. On the one hand, he must "curse to his heart's content," as negation is necessarily militant and calls for a ceaseless fight. Consequently, on the other hand, because he goes "naked outside into the blowing wind," he must harden himself "to the point of insensibility." The Epicurean seems to have an advantage: he has simplified his life, has given up on a host of things that, while they may bring occasional enjoyment, are also sources of displeasure. He obtains thereby "a feeling of freedom and empowerment" that he may share with the Cynic, but his freedom does not make him curse endlessly, does not make him expose himself to the bitter winds. The difference may be a difference of style, but the impression is that the Epicurean is also smarter, less of a fool than the Cynic. Does that mean the Epicurean is no fool?

Are Epicureans or Cynics potential examples of free spirits in the Nietzschean sense? Both kinds of thinkers find their motivation in a desire for freedom. What follows seems to be the definition of a free spirit in *Human, All Too Human*. Again, I transcribe the full aphorism:

> *Cautiousness of free spirits.* —Free-minded people who live only for knowledge will quickly find they have reached their external goal in life, their final position in relation to society and the state, and will, for example, be content with a small official position or with only as much property as barely suffices for living; for they will arrange their lives in such a way that neither a great transformation in economic circumstances nor even the overthrow of the political order will overturn their life along with it. They expend as little energy as possible on all these things so that they can dive with all their collected forces and with a deep breath, as it were, into the element of knowledge. Thus, they can hope to dive deeply and even to see to the very bottom.—Such a spirit

prefers to take in only the fringes of an event; he does not love things in all the breadth and vastness of their folds: for he does not want to entangle himself in them.—He, too, knows the weekdays of unfreedom, of dependence, of servitude. But from time to time a Sunday of freedom must come to him, or else he will not be able to endure life.—It is likely that even his love for humanity will be cautious and somewhat shortwinded, for he wants to have only as much to do with the world of inclinations and blindness as is necessary for the purpose of knowledge. He must trust that the guiding spirit of justice will say something on behalf of its adherent and protegé if accusing voices describe him as poor in love.—There is in his way of living life and of thinking a *refined heroism* that disdains offering itself to the reverence of the masses, as his coarser brothers do, and that tends to pass quietly through and out of the world. Through whatever labyrinths he may wander, through whatever rocks his stream may make its torturous way—when he reaches the light, he goes his way clearly, lightly, and almost soundlessly and lets the sunlight play down into his depths.[76]

A Sunday of freedom, if I may have it: that would be my compensation as a cautious man of knowledge. Because, in the face of protracted unfreedom, dependence, servitude, I too have chosen to minimize my sources of potential displeasure, and I have consequently gone about that task in the only way I know how to do it: by minimizing everything else as well, so as not to risk too much, never to risk too much. I do not have a lot of property, I do not have much power, I do not get involved in much or if I do, I do so from the margins. I am a refined hero for the sake of diving into the element of knowledge. I may choose to walk my walks protectedly, never to venture beyond the treetops, stay in the lanes, or I may choose to bark my throat off like an enraged dog at the bitter gales of unfreedom. That is just a difference of temperament. But I am still a fool. Something else is needed if I am to stop being a fool. Did Nietzsche know it? But of course he did, or he came to know it.

The phrase in the late correspondence, already approaching the moment of disaster, when Nietzsche writes that he would prefer to be a professor at Basel rather than God, is not an arrogant sentence. It is not that Nietzsche thinks he is about to become God. Rather, he knows that his itinerary is inexorably leading him to a philosophical, or existential, or antiphilosophical act that, while it may or may not break into two the history of the world, it may break him into innumerable fragments. And that exceeds him. For probity's sake he must continue his path, but he would rather not have to do it and stay back. His Basel chair, the one he left so long ago, from which he could have thought dead thoughts, like so many academic sitters, now looks more inviting. But it is not on his path. His path goes through the now increasingly remote possibility of an act of affirmation, whose pathmarks were the free spirit, or the overman, or the eternal return, or the will to power. But those pathmarks are now behind, and what remains open is dangerous. The total affirmation of his conditions of existence, his final act of subjectivation, can have as a counterpart the most terrible de-subjectivation, madness, disaster. His wager, in the fateful fall of 1888, is not so much a wager for the difficulty of thought—his thinking, six thousand feet over everything academic, a thinking that isolates him and marginalizes him and takes him away from every community, a thinking whose main condition is hardening, personal firmness, on which survival depends. It is rather a wager for consistency. He looks for the great health he had mentioned in the preface to *Human, All Too Human*, and which he had briefly glimpsed in the halcyon days of his year in Sorrento. In *The Gay Science* he had also spoken about philosophy as a misunderstanding of the body, referring to priestly philosophy, to nihilist philosophy. His question had always been how to understand the body properly, how to turn the body into the site for thinking. But his own suffering and ailing body can only promise rather than reach great health through non-nihilist, counter-nihilist thought. It is not even a wager: he must simply accept his own demand; he must only subtract from the interdiction of doing it, which is what most people fail to do, including the thinkers. Not to give up on his own desire is Nietzsche's probity and the exorbitant modesty of his thinking: a thinking of non-submission.

Which is intolerable, for others, but also for himself. His non-submission to the forbidden, from which his own matheme derives, his insurrection against sense, his radical marranism, is his appropriating embrace of his own conditions of existence. But this move, this sustained gesture, makes the relation between necessity and freedom explode, leaving in its wake only the trace of an inhuman silence. Is that Nietzsche's final doctrine of being? Yes, the last, or the penultimate, it does not matter provided we understand it as a sort of Borromean knot. There is thinking, there is being, there is a body, and the production of truth consists of finding a consistency among the three. The condition of such a consistency is the knot whose slackening leads to dissolution and ruin. But is consistency not always already excessive? The Borromean knot is also a forbidden path if one must save one's existence from its malignancy. There is no return to the chair at Basel, only a demonic path, which is not quite so divine.

MAY 11, 2020

Jorge Alemán announces that for the discussion that is to take place in a couple of weeks his focus will be on the relationship between the Lacanian subject (the subject of the unconscious) and the Heideggerian Dasein. Insofar as I am not well prepared to speak about the subject of the unconscious, my observations will have to be limited to a partial glossing of what seems most decisive in Heidegger's existential analytics. Despite the fact that I do appreciate its pertinence in this time of the pandemic, it is possible that my proposals will seem untimely, because they will be linked to a theme that contemporary thought has not, in general terms, ceased to denigrate: the difference between authenticity and inauthenticity.

In its most basic sense, this difference could be formulated as a question having to do with the disjunctive syllogism: either me or them. But there is a lot to unfold there, and the essential thing to start with is not to vulgarize the difference—that is, the disjunction—as though it had to do with a disjunction between solipsism and community. The disjunction does not lie in the failure of the others—the "them"—to understand themselves as community, nor does it arise from the I's inability to understand itself as monadically constituted in itself. The disjunction is better understood if we explain it in reference to all decisions of existence: when that decision, which is logically and in each case necessarily my own, is made in favor of a social consensus that is always already imagined and interpreted, which is always in the region of the others, or when it is made in favor of an imperative of individuation, which can on the other hand certainly be a common or generic individuation (I choose to individualize myself as a philosopher, appealing to the community of philosophers, or as marrano, appealing to the community of those without community, and so forth). In the Baroque and post-Baroque moralists, and then in Nietzsche, or Kierkegaard, or Heidegger (maybe even in

Lacan too), that ontogenetic imperative of individuation is linked to the old Pindaric maxim *genoi oios essi*, "become what you are," "become who you are," don't let the anonymous and impersonal other dictate your life, your options, don't be a slave, and if you have to obey some voice let it only be the voice of a friend (but there are few friends).[77]

Alemán raised the possibility that the crisis precipitated by COVID-19 could promote or facilitate structural changes in capitalism that would make imagining another history, a new beginning, plausible. He then said that such a change in the global structure of rule and control would have to presuppose a "transformation of the subject." My question for Alemán at that point was about the kind of transformation he meant. How could we understand, in his terms, a "transformation of the subject"? Would it be a moral transformation or, more broadly, a transformation in the ethico-political relation between subject and community, or between subject and world? Does it have to do with an epistemic or cognitive transformation? With a spiritual transformation, or even a "religious" one, even if it only concerns a secular or generic religiosity and not a confessional one? With a psychic transformation, in the analytic sense? Or is what is required more of an existential transformation?

I know that the question is a difficult one. There will be no political (or economic) transformation unless there is a transformation of the subject, and the phrase could be reversed: there will be no transformation of the subject unless there is a structural sociopolitical transformation. From what I can tell, the conceptual limit of this proposition or dual proposition is the following: without an existential transformation, no ethico-political—or epistemic, or psychic, or religious—transformation can happen. But if the existential transformation posits itself as a consequence of effects that we could call pandemic, as, for example, a new desire for communitarian solidarity triggered by the confinement, or by massive unemployment, or by the vanishing in the medium term of social routines that had previously acted as support for everyday life (at the office, the club, the barber shop or the hairdresser's, the bar, the soccer game), that transformation will have been driven by the world of the others, by the demand for a new distribution of social consensus, by the need for construction of a new sociality. This could very well lead toward political change, and it remains to be seen whether for better or for worse. But, with regard to the so-called subject, it would have to do more with what Heidegger or Nietzsche or Kierkegaard—I'm not sure about Lacan—would have called an inauthentic transformation, which is to say, anything but a transformation. There may therefore be political transformation, unlikely as it may be, but the transformation of the subject is far more radically unlikely.

If a properly so-called transformation of the subject depends always in every case on a *principium individuationis* that is not assumable as such by any social consensus, and is in general far more linked to singular dissensus, which is to say, if we are not speaking about mere adjustments or changes of perspective in reference to social ideology, for better or worse, even if it has to do with an emergent social ideology and therefore one that is allegedly counter-hegemonic (but still aspires toward hegemony, still resides within the hegemonic game), is it really plausible to postulate it as the very effect of the pandemic? For Heidegger or Kierkegaard, the moment of authenticity, *Augenblick*, coincides with the moment of the decision of existence and does not have a duration; it is punctual and pertains to an instant, the instant. In no case does it bring about a transformation of the social subject, to the precise extent that it is, and only is and can be, an instance of singular subjectivation: with the decision of existence, the subject is born, and then immediately fades. No subject can therefore found a regime of life, or of thought. The subject does not last. There can be no transformation of the social subject that is not always already indoctrination, internalization, equivalential reification of a rule of obedience, and therefore social submission to the disjunction of the others, or of the Other.

What then is possible, properly or authentically speaking? Very little, almost nothing, even if in every case it be decisive. It boils down to a decision of existence, which can very well be propitiated by conditions of life in the face of a pandemic irruption, and that would orient itself toward a "learning to live" like the one Derrida proposed at the end of his life: to live otherwise, searching for the simple, or for the most simple.

MAY 12, 2020 A.M. We could ask Alemán if Lacanian analysis contemplates something similar to the Kierkegaardian notion of *instant, Augenblick*. For Kierkegaard the decision of existence takes place without duration, and therefore outside time. It constitutes the decisive step between the figure of the knight of resignation, who accepts structural and political conventions for existence such as they are, even if he or she tries to improve on them, and the figure of the knight of faith, who infinitely exposes him- or herself to finitude and death and abandons illusory compensations in the terrain of the public or of the "objective." Authentic temporality—what in yesterday's note I called "the simple"—opens in that extratemporal instant. It does not change the subject: it constitutes it. There is no transformation of the subject but rather unconcealment of a potency of subjective repetition whose character is formal, because it has no content. It is only a decision of existence, to make oneself into what one is, which is an unfinishable project, and demands therefore in each case ceaseless repetition. It is a repetition of the simple, of the very *factum* of an existence, my own, which is neither consumed nor consummates itself in any interiority. It is in that sense a simple opening, against the existential concealment of the knight of resignation, who remains perpetually enclosed and buried in the universe of the determinant and the public, no matter how much misery it brings him or her. (One of our favorite readings for these times should be, in this sense, *Walden*, by Henry Thoreau.) That simple opening to the simple, to the most simple, is to be understood as a rupture, a *Durchbruch* or *breakthrough*, a crossing. Toward the simple but from where? We could translate the Heideggerian concept of *Befindlichkeit*, often poorly rendered as state of mind, by the word "dis/position." The dis/positioned is the badly exposed and, therefore, submitted. Alemán can no doubt tell us if this notion of submitted dis/position finds a counterpart in Lacanian analysis; for example, if the Lacanian notion of "traversing the phantasy" may refer to it, and reverse it.[78]

Meanwhile, I could risk proposing that the search for the simple in the decision of existence, unfinishable and repeated, always extratemporal in the sense that it opens time (it is the instant of a present that is something other than the undifferentiated and undetectable *now* between the past and the future), is potentially available to every one of us in the strange and unprecedented experience of pandemic confinement. Does it not trace the adventure of a project of emancipation that is not simply a political emancipation, but also, first and foremost, an emancipation from politics, understood as that which governs and controls our dis/position in every case? That is how, under a different vocabulary, I understand what I have imagined Alemán calls "transformation of the subject," ultimately capable of supporting another politics, another beginning of politics, no matter how much the latter remains doubtful and improbable.

MAY 12, 2020 P.M.　　The problem that arises in the previous notes, as far as I can tell, is related to the difficult issue of incessant repetition as actualization of a potency of being, that is, as a reactivation in every case of a state of relative plenitude, which would be the asymptotic endgame of "become who you are," to the extent that we are not yet speaking of your cadaver (or that you are thinking of mine). We know that the historical origin of that imperative is to be found in Pindar; traditionally understood as an imperative of subjective formation, it reaches its peak but also stalls in suspense and crisis in Nietzsche's *Ecce Homo*. It is not so obvious that the imperative is also at the heart of the Aristotelian disquisition in *Metaphysics*, book Z, on *dynamis* and *energeia*. Both notions are linked to the movement of bodies, to *kinesis*. *Dynamis*, as potentiality, becomes concretized in each *energeia* as actualization, but actualization is not in itself static (not even in your cadaver or in mine, as we know). In this sense, *dynamis* does not stop in *energeia*, potency does not cease in its actualization: the chair, for example, continues to move as a chair, as it perseveres in its being-chair, just as the sea does as it perseveres in its being. But this means that for the animal, and more precisely for the human animal, "to become what one is" in endless perseverance is also infinitely or indefinitely an always and ceaseless becoming other, since *dynamis* does not end and is incessantly *arche metaboles (o kineseos) en allo e he allo*—the principle of change or movement of something to something.

Yes, there is a *kalos pathein*, a beautiful suffering, which has to do with the fact that each entity finds, against all resistance, its perfection and exercises itself in it. The decision of existence can then be understood in every case as the injunction not only to "become what you are" but also "to become *all* that you are." Like the sea or the chair. But there's an intuitively visible conflict between the "be all that you are" injunction and its subsidiary "and do it one thousand and one times, over and over again." If the decision of existence demands an incessant repetition, it is because it finds no end point, it finds no stasis. And it is so because it brushes up against a lack, a difficulty or impossibility of being fully, a hole in its totality, determined by time as change and by change as time. In this way, the decision of existence, repeated a thousand times, does not achieve rest, does not obtain satisfaction, and gets entangled in a proliferation of becomings, in difference and in the trace of difference. Another way to put it is to say that the existence of every person is essentially unworked, and the more so, the more the illusion prevails in it of consummated work, of selfsame identity, of a stable and final presence to itself. (It is not necessary to go very far to find this active illusion: it is enough to look at whatever collection of university administrators you happen to work under.)

An unworked existence—that of the rest of the mortals—is, however, not a negative quality but precisely the very possibility of freedom, above and below every production of the subject. The nonsubject enables Dasein to become something other than achieved fixity. It is inapparent because, in each case, it is what does not enter into appearance, what does not enter into presence: the constitutive lack, in retreat; that which remains concealed in all possible unconcealment, as its enabler and very possibility. Is it also not therefore the condition of possibility itself of Lacanian analysis and of its interminable character? It is the condition of possibility and the region of elective dwelling of the infrapolitical exercise as such, that is, as a form of being human, outside its political determination.

MAY 13, 2020 A.M. This writing is also rehearsing repetition and retrieval. Firstly, a repetition of things that I have been thinking about for some time. In the writing it tends to constitute itself as a piece of work, even if it is full of holes. The decision of existence is in this case tied to the production of a writing facilitated or prompted by the situation of confinement, by what in confinement is a call to recollection, to the reduction of distraction. It tends toward a book form, as it seeks consistency, as it accepts the burden of what precedes it and looks for a solution to it. To convert these notes into a book that is sufficiently unworked and opened so as to not be inconsistent with what the book itself is saying is the task ahead. That is what I thought of last night. I have been reading some secondary bibliography on Aristotle, Heidegger, Kierkegaard, and Nietzsche, and I just reread an old article by Thomas

Sheehan, "Heidegger's Interpretation of Aristotle: *Dynamis* and *Ereignis*," which I found in my computer's files scanned from a typewritten manuscript, though I don't remember how I came to obtain it. I must say something about it, and I must also comment on some chapters from the Agamben book that I read a few days ago in its English translation, *Creation and Anarchy*, because of the resonance it carries with all of this. To repeat, then: the themes will be expanded echoes of what has already been said, and the writing will trace itself in circles, whether centripetal or centrifugal. And the overall idea is for everything to end up as a personal revision of Nietzsche and his antiphilosophy, which I can no longer postpone—I've been postponing it since I was more or less twenty years old. It is only therefore another repetition, and I cannot help thinking that this repetition comes along with its "eternal return," *circulus vitiosus deus*. But I must prepare it. And for it.

This will turn out to be a writing disengaged from academic conventions and not tipping over toward the supposed impact that should be sought, in administrative terms, on the community, which condemns all academic writing to exercise itself, vapidly, on the disjunction of the others. We should write, we are told, for the Other, and that means, in the doubly fallen form of writing in the academic humanities, whose impact can only be singular, whose improductivity is real and necessary, that it should be written for the consumption of an anonymous machine, for a spectral and spectrally hostile body only interested in the principle of equivalence and indifferentiation that the writing may deploy. It is bad enough that the institution only counts numbers, dismissing the form and content of what is done. But our colleagues? More and more these are their questions: Is this fellow who writes a feminist like I am? Is this fellow a leftist like me? Is the Latin Americanism here of the kind I approve of? Does he write so that I can feel safe through his writing? If not, and I am the one who decides, on the basis of what there is in me of an anonymous and undifferentiated brain, of ideological precipitate, then let this fellow take a walk and go jump in the lake, piss up a rope. We will ignore the writing and send the author off to limbo, or else I will sharpen my knives to deal with him or her as soon as the opportunity presents itself.

It has been some time since I first found the idea of writing for that sort of pious reception to be unbearable. I detest its filters and its more or less well-meaning violence. It no longer matters to me, or if it does, I will have to assume the risk of being silenced, or of conflict. I have never done anything but this, truth be told. I have no interest in proving myself a good Derridean here, or a bit of a Marxist, or nice for a world image that is not mine and to which I am in the best of cases indifferent. Out of cowardice we do not reflect enough on the question of up to what point writing for the Other, that is, for the Public, for the academic community, is always already a writing for traitors, structurally so. I don't know if I have in me the ability to write singularly, for singular reception, but that is the only thing that interests me in terms of writing. And yet I will insist on putting all of this up on the blog, and secondarily up on Facebook. It's a meager gesture, poor, and certainly there is nothing heroic about it. It recognizes, as plainly as possible, that there can only be compensation in writing through interlocution; it recognizes that singular writing is always a searching for improbable reception, and I don't want to dissemble on that, because it would be a falsity. On the other hand, the gesture will likely be interpreted with rancor and hostility. At this point, I can afford it because I don't have anything to lose. Nor do I have great expectations.

MAY 13, 2020 P.M.
Energeia ateles, a work without an end, without a final determination, without fixity—that is what Sheehan announces in his interpretation of Heidegger's interpretation of Aristotle concerning the question of being. Heidegger first developed his "phenomenological" interpretation of Aristotle between 1919 and 1931. Gramsci's first writings are fairly close in time to Heidegger's first seminars on Aristotle. The *energeia ateles* comes like a blow to Gramsci's idealistic view of Hegel, for whom there is clearly a teleology of history. In my notes for the working group discussion I wrote:

> The Hegelian ethical state, accomplished through the bourgeois revolution, is not enough, Gramsci says; we must move towards the construction of an organic state, which only the Party, as the shadow government of the proletariat, can prepare. It is just a matter of culture over economics: culture enables the proletariat to know itself, that is, to accomplish self-consciousness through the "disciplining of one's inner self," through the "mastery of one's own personality," through the "attainment of higher awareness," that will lead to understanding the place

of the proletariat as universal class in history. That will naturally determine "our function, rights and duties."⁷⁹

History is therefore "the supreme reason."⁸⁰ And history teaches us that the unleashing of productive forces will bring about communism, resulting from a "greater productive efficiency" that will eliminate all the "artificial factors that limit productivity."⁸¹ It is therefore a matter of "exploiting capital more profitably and using it more effectively."⁸² Yes, toward equality and solidarity, love and compassion, of course.⁸³ This is the truth of history, and "to tell the truth, to reach the truth together is a revolutionary, communist act."⁸⁴ This will be "the final act, the final event, which subsumes them all, with no trace of privilege and exploitation remaining."⁸⁵ Thinking is being, and being is history. There is an "identification of philosophy and history."⁸⁶ That is why Marxism is "the advent of intelligence into human history,"⁸⁷ which is equal to "identifying [historical] necessity with [man's] own ends."⁸⁸ This is the task of the Party. "Voluntarism" is the task of the Party, and it is "about the class becoming distinct and individuated, with a political life independent, disciplined, without deviations or hesitations."⁸⁹ Until it can replace the state rather than conquer it, The Party is all, but it is only the vanguard of the all. "Most people do not exist outside some organization, whether it calls itself the Church or the Party, and morality does not exist without some specific, spontaneous organ within which it is realized. The bourgeoisie is a moment of chaos not simply where production is concerned, but where the spirit is concerned."⁹¹ When Gramsci discusses the Italian liberal constitution existing in 1919, he notes that Italians have been living under a state of exception for several years during the war. The exception reveals the rule, he says, and the rule is the rule of domination by bourgeois interests as expressed by liberalism. The situation post–state of exception, in the wake of the Russian Revolution, might enable the unleashing of true history. "The proletariat is born out of protest on the part of the historical process against anything which attempts to bog down or to strait-jacket the dynamism of social development."⁹² By submitting to history and its unleashing, the Party will lead the people in order to create, through "ceaseless work of propaganda and persuasion," an "all-encompassing and highly organized system."⁹³ Freedom, after all, is party discipline.⁹⁴

But *energeia ateles* leads to another place, and to another understanding of freedom. The incompatibility is noteworthy. At the time

Gramsci was writing, one hundred years ago, two possible ways of thinking emerged, two structures of thinking, and my option for the first of them is unconditional at this point. My job is to make it explicit, nothing more, not to look for some other thing but to make it explicit, to take it up to wherever it will go, or to where I am able to take it. The term *telos* does not mean above all goal or purpose, but achievement, completion, end in the sense of termination. It is the same with *peras*, translated as "limit" or "border," which does not signal primarily a special restriction, but a space that allows abiding by oneself, a constancy or stability in being. Both words, in their Greek meaning, refer to a confinement understood as a place of containment. If confinement is telic containment, what could result from it is the production of a substance, *sub-stantia*, a "work" as persistence within the limit. Assuming that the world itself were the place of confinement, then Gramsci is clear in what he says: the end of history is "the final act, the final event," without residue, a historical entelechy, an *ergon*, a finished work. This would be consistent with the long-held interpretation of Aristotelean ontology as centered on *ousía* as the unified name for the being of the entities. Western ontotheology—that is, metaphysics—finds its principal, and principial, manifestation, from that structuring of being as unification in the telic *ousía*, which carries directly into Hegel and Marx, and therefore into Gramsci, wherein the replacement of God as the name of the primary substance in favor of telic history makes itself explicit: history is "supreme reason." But *energeia ateles* opens another history that is not understandable as supreme reason, not primarily linked to a production of finished work or to the union with maximum perfection, whether it is called God or Party or whatever other instance of hegemonic domination, but to what Aristotle kept somehow concealed or subordinate as a condition of the unconcealment of substance: *dynamis* as time and movement, *dynamis* as an alternative name for being. *Energeia* does not find perfection because it encloses and conceals that which sustains it: potency as the name for time in movement, or for movement in time.

In *Physics*, Aristotle delimits a group of entities, called natural entities, whose peculiarity is that they have within themselves the principle of their own movement. In order for a rock to move, it needs something or somebody to move it. That is not the case for a mouse, which moves by itself. To move by itself, and to do it time and again, appealing to its own principle of movement, is to repeat. Movement, as ontological conscription of the natural being, that is, the state of moving oneself, implies and entails repetition as a basic existential characteristic. Just like the rose bush, which dies when its repetition ceases. But this means that the natural being moves and appears under a double manifestation as presence and absence. It moves, and its appearance as mover conceals its destiny. *Dynamis*, potency, is concealed in its own manifestation in each case. *Dynamis* is potency of repetition, based on its secret, on its non-manifestation, on its factual im-potency, which is its *energeia ateles*, its lack of completion, which is its condition of existence (since completion is death). But it is, precisely, a lack of dynamic completion, in the sense that it ceaselessly depends on its own movement as movement of appropriation. Repetition appropriates, and the process of appropriation repeats itself. The mouse perseveres in its being as mouse; it wants to be a mouse, and it seeks to be mouselike until the end. I do the same, when at my best: I want to be, not a mouse, but myself, and that is my condition of existence. This is not solipsism, but the irreducible destiny of all natural beings in the state of moving oneself in time. Heidegger calls this *Eignung*, appropriation, which defines movement for all natural beings as perseverance in repetition, as open possibility.

But this leads to the revolutionary position of *Being and Time*: the Dasein is appropriative possibility, and what it seeks to appropriate is its own principle of movement, its *dynamis* as *kinesis*, and its *kinesis* as time, which is, in all cases, my time and not the time of the others. The appropriation of time itself as auto-appropriation is kairological, not chronological—it occurs in an instant outside of time, because it founds or opens time as appropriative repetition. In it we risk the possibility—the mere possibility—of "becoming what we are," attending to the old Pindaric call that accompanied Nietzsche to his tragic moment. The decision of existence does not preserve but exposes. But to expose and to be exposed—is that not a more attractive calling than the security of self-protection proposed by confinement? Confinement both conceals and manifests its most proper possibility, which is its destructive appropriation in resolute repetition. Against, in ultimate terms, whatever canny or uncanny rest.

MAY 14, 2020

If antiphilosophy is a mode of thought, as well as a concealed dimension of all philosophical work, it is so because it does not attend to its specification as a work. Its specific drive is to plot or prepare the decision of existence. Insofar as this plot ends up being formulated through language and constituting one discourse among others, antiphilosophy is always aporetic: it is the discourse of those who do not wish to constitute themselves in or through discourse, or the antidiscourse of those who, in all discourse, seek their resolution of drive, their unworking at the same time concealed and enabling. Antiphilosophy is necessarily *energeia ateles*. Maybe this is, at its best, the secret of critique: whoever decides to give practical priority not to the production of work, that is, not to the production of art, but to its examination, can be following an antiphilosophical imperative, can be seeking, in that examination of what is produced by others, their own decision of existence, and therefore manifesting their unproductive impotency. The problem is how easy it is to fall on the other side, through an automatism that is merely a reproduction of social discourse, one that receives and installs art, also, as the very production of the Other.

Antiphilosophy as critique runs the lethal risk of understanding itself as ideological production, which is what it mostly is: empty talk, and at the same time, violent; it is a policing and a disciplining. The critic (I have been this) who strives to avoid that determination, which chases him in each of his activities and generally ends up devouring him, becomes stranded on some anonymous beach, as residue and wreckage of multiple ships or as some gigantic end product of anonymous digestion. Critics deserve it when they have not been able to see, when it was still possible, that their fundamental option, in the margins of their primary intention, in a determining *parergon*, structurally condemned them to be mercenaries in a market of interpretation, to objectify themselves as ornaments or dejections of the production of work, functional parasites or maybe police officers, preservers or condemners, pedagogues or inquisitors. Or all of it at once. And that is no longer a learning how to live but a self-constituting into judges and administrators of other people's lives, from an archaeological militancy in which appropriation is now only archival appropriation, appropriation of the time of others, precarious as it might be.

It is difficult for a militant to escape the compromised situation of the *miles gloriosus*, the braggart of classical comedy. I prefer belligerence. The belligerent is the one who does not stop defending his or her positions, from some savage moralism linked to a decision of existence. Militants accept a discipline through which their positions are immediately and indifferently the positions of the Other. Hence the need for confession that Gramsci sponsored: "The Club has among its objectives a full acceptance of reciprocal control by the members of each person's daily activity—family life, work, and social interaction. We want each member to have the courage and moral energy to make a public confession and to accept the advice and guidance of his friends. We want to create a reciprocal bond of trust: an intellectual and moral communion, uniting us all."[95] As we know all too well, this sinister structure, *mutatis mutandis*, has dominated academic life, which is the place of the contemporary critic par excellence, even in times of an ideological eclipse of the left, as occurred in the 1980s and 1990s. And it is returning now, in more and more desperate forms, as police thought. That is why some, presumably on the left, are not offended by the Chinese option of a surveillance state. Surveillance has always been internalized within a certain mental structure that corresponds to fallen criticism, after it abandons the substance of its antiphilosophical drive. Belligerence, not militancy, can only help here.

In "The Archaeology of the Work of Art," Agamben recognizes the aporia that I have called constitutive of antiphilosophy, and shows it in the intrinsic conflict of artistic production between the finished work, *ergon*, and *energeia* on the side of the maker—that is, between *poiesis* and *performance*.[96] The transposition of art's locus in the twentieth century toward *performance* would have had to do with something in art that escapes art itself, something in the work that exceeds or sub-cedes the work, which "demands to be realized not in a work but in life."[97] The aporia governs the risk of both the unworking of the work and the objectification or reification of life—when the body of the artist is made to be no more than another tool of use or a form of use as advertisement. Here is the limit of what Agamben seems to be proposing when he says: "Art is only the way in which the anonymous ones we call artists, by maintaining themselves constantly in relation with a practice, seek to constitute their life as a form of life: the life of the painter, of the carpenter, of the architect, of the contrabassist, in which, as in every form-of-life, what is in question is nothing less than their happiness."[98] But the happiness of the one who ends up being celebrated as influential or famous, although still a form of life, pertains to the fallen daily routines of the public and is not an antiphilosophical decision of existence. There is also, in the form of life, something that escapes the very form of life itself. More interesting in this sense is the reflection with which Agamben concludes another one of his essays, "What Is the Act of Creation?": "Everything desires and strives to persevere in its being; but at the same time, it resists this desire; at least for an instant it renders it inoperative and contemplates it. . . . This is a resistance internal to desire, an inoperativity internal to the operation. But it alone confers on *conatus* its justice and its truth."[99] There is no happiness in that unheard-of resistance to the supposed happiness of becoming what one is. There is, perhaps, enjoyment, linked as such to a dark death drive, to an alternative drive that contradicts the telos of appropriation. It is a disappropriating drive, atelic, that forms a part of antiphilosophical *energeia*. How should we understand this?

The Chinese sage says that the only thing necessary in life is a square meter of earth to plant your feet on and not fall. But if somebody were to come and eliminate all other ground surrounding that square meter, we would not be able to take a step without falling into the abyss. So the unnecessary is also necessary. The sum of both things constitutes, in each case, our facticity, the panorama of our life, the always inalienable—we are ineluctably condemned to being away from ourselves, fallen or thrown into what is the particular case of our existence. And only from there, and not from any other place, can we proceed to a decision of existence that opens a clearing in our lives. That decision of existence is in every case a transition, a path in which it is a question not just of following the Pindaric imperative, but also of accepting its resistances. Becoming what you are is not moving to a cloud or to a small swath of land. What is essential to understand and accept is the transition, and the moment of the transition as specific movement. We know that the notion of existence is tied to movement since existence is *energeia ateles*. In movement, the entity achieves, finishes, or tends toward completion, at least when it deploys its own potency. That potency is potency of appropriation, which can be understood as the entity's force of appropriation toward the entity's own telos. For the human being, the notion of *Ereignis* supplements the notion of *Eignung*, appropriation. Human appropriation is appropriation, not of an interiority, but rather of the "there" of the *Da-sein*, of its circumstance, of its very facticity. And it is an unfinishable appropriation. Sheehan retrieves for it a word that Heidegger borrows from Heraclitus and uses in a slightly different context. The word is *ankhibasie*, which means "ever approaching."[100] In referring to it as the "asymptotic condition of ex-istence" Sheehan gets it right. That which is ever approaching never arrives, the infinite final stretch never intersects with the bend to which it leans. Existence is never achieved, but it can aspire to get closer and closer to that which would determine it as achievement through the very resistances that are placed in opposition to it. *Ankhibasie* designates that existential practice of radical transition that is never consummated. This is a drive that pertains to *Dasein*—not to the subject, which tends only toward reified perseverance—and that goes beyond the animal drives of the human as *animal rationale*. It is worth understanding this, to some extent against Agamben and against all philosophy of life. The *animal rationale* can find a closeness to life, an intensification of vital processes, better health, better power, more strength, more money, more sex so as to recover life and rescue it and redeem it. The counterpart that tradition has called "spiritual," which is already invoked in the word *rationale* as an inversion of, or a complement to, animality, remains within its circle. What is asked for is neither a spiritual transformation nor a vital redemption, but something other that *ankhibasie* names, which refers only to the tension in the asymptotic movement of existence invoked and conjured by the Pindaric imperative.

Dasein accepts the need for a transitional thinking toward the asymptotic condition of existence, which necessarily includes the acceptance and transfiguration of all resistance to it, in the sense marked by Agamben's reference to the Spinozan *conatus*. In *Contributions to Philosophy*, Heidegger gives a name to that transition as the transition from *Wegsein*, or being away, to *Dasein*, or being there. The decision of existence, for *ankhibasie*, responds to an intimation or to a presentiment. Who has it? Those who can listen to the Pindaric imperative and avoid the machination controlling our lives under the figure of the public, the disjunction of the Other and of the others: those who resist the call of the principle of general equivalence as the primary engine of our world. In this resistance, one can glimpse a form of the death drive that is also the appropriation of death: the *conatus* becomes what it is also through the absent presence of death in every instance of our lives. Antiphilosophical belligerence can, then, constitute something like the death drive of Dasein, alien to the biological or religious drives of the *animal rationale* and situated beyond the pleasure principle and beyond the posited simple happiness of the Agambenian form-of-life. It is *ankhibasie*, which, in the decision of existence, repeats for the human the curious heliotropic principle of the moth and the butterfly, and also of the firefly.

MAY 15, 2020

I reread my notes. Damn it, they are becoming more like short academic papers, less like what I was aiming to do. I cannot help myself. I read, and the reading forces the writing. And then, of course, my warhorses—infrapolitics, the wait, the decision of existence, posthegemony—keep popping up. Also, at the same time an exigency to move away from any writing to or from the "them," the machine, the apparatus. I suppose I have my own apparatus, and I talk to it. I can only write from my own references, and yet it is not my references I write about. I write about, and from, the uncanny and disquieting experience of the time of confinement, which is suspended time, its possibility, its chance for a step back. Spring is in full splendor, there is life everywhere, the turtles have laid their eggs and calmly wait for what happens (but there are too many armadillos around here), and yet there is silence, an almost overwhelming one, and there is an ominous waiting, not the turtles', from which the thought of death cannot be subtracted. I read and write, and I post what I've written, and nobody responds. And reading and writing and posting are distractions.

MAY 16, 2020 A.M.

DEAR ALBERTO,

How are you?

I'm writing because I have just read the last text you posted on the blog, about antiphilosophical belligerence as decision of existence.

To cut directly to the chase: I find the way in which you distance yourself from militant and vitalist positions tremendously convincing. I have, without prejudice of the above, three questions, regarding not so much the way you demarcate your position but rather the position that demarcates itself from your text.

1. Firstly, I wonder if perhaps the way in which you pose the decision of existence does not end by reintroducing the teleological schema (despite your declared attempt to limit your position in terms of *energeia ateles*), when the transition that encrypts the *ankhibasie* is defined as asymptotic tendency. The first trend of that kind that occurs to me is, of course, the one consigned to the schema of the infinite task. If this occurrence can be conceded to me, it is worth asking why and how the decision of existence would not be coupled to such a schema; and if it is the contrary, how could it be exempt from it, if it is to be teleological, a finalism of ego, a

teleo-egology? Is the difference you propose in your text between enjoyment and happiness a way of beginning to answer this question? Let me insist on the question of the infinite task: when I say happiness I am not thinking so much about Agamben but of Kant's notion of happiness, when toward the end of the first Critique he speaks on what I can expect when I act as I should. I am emphasizing that Kantian possibility in order to elicit your reference to "savage moralism."

2. Secondly, very briefly, in relation to *energeia ateles*: I understand that for you, in relation to this "concept," it is a matter of signaling a way of doing subtracted from the "militant" position, from all moralisms (commitments that would be rather renunciations, subjugations), and from all crystallized historical-political closings, as well as from the metaphysical (teleological?) capturing of the activity, since said capture would end, if I understand your argument, in the cancelation of what you call freedom. To defend such freedom, an antiphilosophical belligerence would be required wherein the decision of existence would already be implicated. My question is this: The Aristotelian definition of the immobile mover, the eternal principle of movement, as pure *energeia* without *dynamis* (a definition based on the priority of *energeia* above *dynamis* with respect to *ousia*, since "nothing that is potentiality is eternal," which makes *energeia* without *dynamis* the fundamental ontological principle of Aristotelian finalism, insofar as it is necessarily incorruptible and, in this sense, atelic because it already coincides completely with itself, it is subtracted from *telos* as an expression of its fulfillment as a life in which being and Good coincide), this definition of the immobile mover, *ousia energeia* (*ateles*?), does this not threaten to rehabilitate the vitalism that the decision of existence had to transgress toward freedom? From, let's say, a Plotinian perspective (as it may have been possible to guess, I'm thinking of Gwenaëlle Aubry's work, although I'm keeping myself from following her through to all of her conclusions), could it not be said that Aristotle neutralizes the chance of transgressing vitalism by thinking the Good (*agatón*) as *ousia energeia* exempted from a *dynamis* that, in Plato, surpasses the Good beyond the *eidos* and the *ousia*, opening an outside to metaphysics in its origin, and because of this, as Derrida shows in

"Plato's Pharmacy," the figure without the figure of death? Doesn't the Aristotelian *ousia energeia* cancel the Platonic transgression of the *ousia* toward an indeterminacy that, according to Heidegger, we would too quickly determine? How can the *energeia ateles* be subtracted from the structure of the *ousia energeia*, Aristotle's life without death?

3. I am using the word transgression strategically, in order to retake the difference I mentioned above between enjoyment and happiness in reference to your blog post. I'll say this very quickly, since the opposition I'm going to raise can (and should) be a complicated one: the Platonic transcendence of the good would be, I think, an image of enjoyment; the Aristotelian *ousia energeia*, of happiness (nevertheless, in Rogues, Derrida translates as jouissance, in a perhaps somewhat idiosyncratic way, the *hedoné* that characterizes the *energeia* of the immobile mover). But unmeasured *jouissance*, as we all well know, is exceedingly dangerous. Your opting to call it a "death drive" seems to me, therefore, fitting. That being said, I wonder if there is some existence that can completely rest in that drive, because what existence (I don't wish to say life, sticking to your register) could open itself up in unmeasured *jouissance* without disappearing immediately (the Id does not give a damn about the Ego; the Bataillean moment of expenditure without calculation strikes down any life, no matter how contaminated it is, and so on)? In other words, what existence is there that embraces infinite difference without a remainder? Would it not instead be the case that existence, assuming we can speak in this way, is the differential economy between the same and the other; that is, neither the one nor the other? In this way, if antiphilosophical belligerence is the death drive of Dasein, would we not be speaking instead of a decision of inexistence? And if this is the case—I move quickly—could the phantom of the worst politics not reappear there, in the praise of the death drive, just the same as when the life drive is being glorified? I'll end this outburst in three questions here.

Big Hugs,

Matías
May 16, 2020

DEAR MATÍAS,

It was a long day today, but I kept my promise as you see. I'll answer briefly and with as much simplicity as possible, though I encourage you to keep the conversation going if you want.

1. My interest is not to say that there is no teleology, that is, no orientation to goals in human existence, but rather that those goals, insofar as what matters most, are never given, they are never accomplished. Still, undoubtedly, they are also present at the same time and at all times but in a derived kind of way: if the end of your existence is to become famous, and you do become famous, you will have achieved your goal. But if your goal is to follow the Pindaric, or Eckhartian, or Nietzschean imperative, then no—you should start by understanding that your end is atelic, it does not have an end (there is no end in the experience of the eternal return, for example, which is an experience of radical dislocation, of radical displacement, where what is appropriated is the dislocation, the displacement itself). In Aristotle, the primary meaning of *telos* is that it refers to a perfection or state of plenitude, a *completeness*—the *energeia ateles* remits to the impossibility of finding an end to the decision of existence, which is exercised only in an interminable asymptotic operation. Notice that my interest is to follow the thematics of kinetic appropriation in *Physics*, through which every natural being seeks to be what they are, and that is what is called appropriation, something that Heidegger translates as *Eignung*. Hence the demystification of *Ereignis*, which is now understood as the tendency toward an appropriation of existence which is in every case my own, since my existence holds the drift of its own movement. We could even say, if you want—although going down this path holds no particular interest to me, because my interest is precisely its opposite—that it could be accepted that there is an egological subjectivity that is telic, and which is exercised daily. The ego wants to rest at night, it wants to have a sexually active life, it wants to dress with elegance, it wants to receive smiles, and it generally seeks compensation through the public. Kant is certainly there with his notion of happiness, as is the average citizen, etc. But the savage moralist—say Pascal, or Kierkegaard, or the detective Philip Marlowe—is not there. And, incidentally, the militant is there too, the militant who finds in his or her doc-

trine—feminism, socialism, environmentalism, vegetarianism—a *promesse de bonheur*. Which, unfortunately, almost always stays as a mere promise anyway. But in them there is a frustrated goal, which is not the case with the deployment of *energeia ateles*, where the path is everything, including the path of errancy whenever it is a misguided errancy, that is, whenever the errancy is an error (yes, since the errancy of the one who wishes to wander, to lose themselves in the world, is not atelic).

2. Of course, in breaking away from Spinoza, and after him from the German idealism that accepts his notion, including Marx and Gramsci in the latter, freedom is therefore not a conformity with the "real" necessity of things. Neither is freedom to be understood as submission to the moral law, like in Kant. It is not even the resigned acceptance of the material conditions of existence. I want to think about it from the vantage point of the decision of existence. One example that is too simplistic but when well thought out opens some doors: If my institution tells me that it is necessary for me—a friend of the humanities—to do whatever I can to find money elsewhere, even though to do so would mean that I sacrifice certain ideas and replace them with, say, some more socially useful ideas, more promising, more in accordance with dominant ideology, to say yes to it is anything but freedom, even if saying yes can be justified through the deluded thought that such is the real logic of the institution, that what they request is what is necessary for present academic life, that being good according to their standards will bring me compensation in the long run, rather than stubbornly continuing to write more of the whimsical nonsense that *nobody* can understand. The more or less legitimately constituted institutional authority may ask things of me according to a certain necessity, but freedom, perhaps crossed by the death drive, by anarchic desire, is certainly somewhere else. Which is where I would rather be.

3. Lastly, it is not that existence rests in the death drive; rather the death drive is a non-renounceable aspect of the will to be who one is. I would call it a condition of possibility for the decision of existence. But in my text that death drive is intended as resistance—resistance to the negation or the disavowal of death and at the same time resistance to the negation of inexistence. So the decision of inexistence, as you call it, in a certain way is a part of the decision of

existence. A resistance to the negation of inexistence is also, from the other side, which occurs simultaneously, in the same instant, a resistance to inexistence. Whoever exists, by necessity, does not cease to inexist. It is like that Lewis Carroll bit that Gilles Deleuze liked: the moment when Alice gets bigger and bigger is the same moment when Alice gets smaller and smaller.[101] That is what I am referring to: the inversion or reversal of temporality in the decision of existence. Which is not a unique and rare decision but rather one that occurs every day, which is born in and out of the everyday, and that endlessly repeats itself. That is life, which can be happy or not. I do not oppose happiness, but it is a life that pursues *jouissance* rather than or before happiness. Tragically or not, that is contingent and, in a sense, beside the point.

I think those are the three answers I can offer you. There are other things in your questions that perhaps I am not able to understand, like the theme of transgression or the Plotinian issue, and other things that are not exactly my questions, or at least I don't see them as being in direct relation with my own text, and which I therefore would rather let be in your text, without trying to respond to them.

Thank you so much again, Matías. As I said, I wrote this on the fly, with no intention of doing anything other than following my own drive; I am not looking for justifications or new arrangements here, and I wrote this and would like to keep it without revisions—I'm only using what I already had, the stuff I carry with me. But those pages you read are justified, or I hope they are, in the previous sixty or seventy pages, most of which (although not all) are up on the blog.

Big hug, and hope all is well.

Alberto

MAY 16, 2020 P.M.   I was thinking of the phrases that Jean-Luc Nancy uses to conclude his short book *The Banality of Heidegger*: "We must learn to exist without being and without destination, to claim to begin or rebegin nothing—and also not to conclude."[102] And just yesterday, during a Zoom call to discuss Gramsci's early work, Gerardo quoted the epigraph Villacañas put at the beginning of his new book *Neoliberalismo como teología política* (*Neoliberalism as Political Theology*). They are Carl Schmitt's words: "It would be more exact to say that politics continues to remain the destiny, but what has occurred is that economics has become political and thereby the destiny." Now, saying that politics is destiny is—or is very close to being—either an incontestable truism: yes, yes, political circumstances radically affect my life and they condition it; or else it constitutes a supreme theologico-political affirmation, which must be the meaning José Luis assigns to it. In this context, how should Nancy's affirmation on learning to live "without being and without destiny" be read? Would such a thing mean a subtraction from politics and a renunciation of all political responsibility? Is what I previously called antiphilosophical belligerence in the decision of existence also a subtraction and renunciation of political responsibility? Confinement seems to encourage this insofar as, in confinement, political life understood as the administration of collective life continues to flow outside any practical possibility for us. Why then get involved in the management or modification of an impossible destiny? To the extent that one can, it might be better to withdraw from destiny and look some other way.

The theologico-political articulation of thought, secularized, certainly, is very visible in those early writings by Gramsci, but Schmitt himself taught that secularization does not change the structure. Gramsci offers a political theology of history in the time of God's death, which pretty much amounts to using the backdoor to reintroduce God—and this is why in his text, the Party ends up looking a lot like the Church. The old Christian morality is transcended in favor of a discipline of work along the lines of the Hegelian articulation of the master/slave dialectic, in which the slave finds redemption and emancipation in and through work, and conformity, understood as an unending task. And this leads Gramsci to wager that the shadow state that constitutes the Party and waits for its opportunity to morph into the dictatorship of the proletariat does not mean primarily destroying capitalism, but perfecting it, and taking it to its plenitude: the proletariat, through labor discipline, will effectuate and accomplish the liberation of all productive energies and forces, and will remove the obstacles and fetters imposed on the chain of production by the bourgeois administration of capitalism. But this amounts to supporting, even to dictating as the course of history, the destructive power of the technical configuration of late metaphysics, asking for it to be taken all the way to its ultimate consequence, linked to the "final act, the final event, which subsumes them all, with no trace of privilege and exploitation remaining."[103] This will be the time when the absolute Spirit can enjoy what Hegel, at the end of *Phenomenology*, calls "the foam of infinity."[104] If Gramscian communism is "the foam of infinity," and if it is based on a productionism that is perfectly unleashed and free from all chains and restrictions, today we know that such foam is formed through and by the tendential destruction of the planet as the structure of all life. And it is therefore inoperable as a political principle. The erasure of all traces of privilege and exploitation will not be accomplished that way, or only catastrophically, through total destruction.

Outside of its tautological form, the constitution of politics as an ineluctable destiny is the postulation of a principle to be understood as the principle of all principles: whatever the very principle of politics is, nothing is outside politics, politics itself is your principle. And your end. Nancy objects to this, surely. And he does so, presumably, from the refusal of all principles and archic notions. In the era of the end of political theology, there are no principles—that is, there is no obtainable legitimacy in reference to any principle that, as such, may found and sustain political praxis. If an emancipatory political practice is still possible today, it is so as a consequence of that archic cancelation that constitutes the end of any privilege not nakedly sustained on the sheer force of expropriation. If there is only expropriatory power, and if the expropriatory power is not a principial power but merely a practice of force, then no domination is legitimate, including any hegemonic domination, whatever its content. The de-archization of the principle implies that only real rascals without principles are the ones today invoking principles. For me, posthegemony names the fact that there is no—and cannot be—(legitimate) principle of politics; that nobody is in a position to invoke any privilege guaranteeing their right to power. The absence of legitimacy undermines any and all hegemony, including counterhegemonic bids for the construction of social majorities on post-foundational grounds tied to the production of chains of equivalence. In this sense, posthegemony is an-archic, and takes pride in it.

Gareth Williams, in yesterday's Zoom session, proposed that "when we say 'posthegemony' we are trying to move in the direction of what emerges on the outside, on the exterior, of politicization itself, of self-governance (biopolitics), of political sovereignty (decisionism), or whatever other master signifier one may want to invoke (patriotism, nationalism, the list is endless). Posthegemony would therefore be what lives at a distance from the principles of organization of political power, pointing, certainly, in the direction of the political, but exceeding without sharing the postulates of mediated subordination." Gareth accepted the notion that posthegemony, which for the same reason cannot move toward any anarchism, is the an-archic dimension of the political. As an-archic dimension it may perhaps constitute a tragedy or bring grace, but it does not constitute a destiny. I prefer to reserve the term *destiny* for what can be linked to the decision of existence, or to its lack thereof, which is in all cases another form of decision. Derrida offers a reflection at the heart of *Of Spirit* that has always seemed to me strangely provocative. From the point of view of the critique of subjectivity carried out in *Being and Time*, which is not a simple critique of subjectivity but rather the central demand of the work against modernity, Derrida says that it is hardly possible to found a (proper) politics, insofar as all political proposals emanate from the inauthentic and fallen subjectivity that Heidegger following Kierkegaard defines. Whatever it is, Dasein is not a *political animal* in the modern sense; Dasein may be a political animal in no sense. Derrida's conclusion is the following: "The only choice is the choice between the terrifying contaminations it assigns . . . Even if all forms of complicity are not equivalent, they are *irreducible*. The question of knowing which is the least grave of these forms of complicity is always there."[105] Derrida asks for a politics of the lesser evil and repeats something he previously said in his 1963 essay on Emmanuel Levinas: that seeking the lesser evil—that is, the less violent path—is the primary obligation of politics. What then hurts is that, whatever the wager placed on the lesser evil, it is still a wager for evil, and therefore politically cursed. It is not about dispensing with violence, which would be an impossible and misleading task. There are only shades of difference that, while they may be important, do not establish a qualitative difference between, let us say, the democrat, the populist, the anti-democrat, or the anarchist. A politics of the lesser evil is still a calculative politics, unable to overcome its condition of impropriety, its fallen condition, its average and mediocre facticity.

That facticity always comes back, it returns eternally, it is precisely what returns, and whichever decision of existence seeks to subtract itself from it does not subtract itself toward politics but necessarily toward its outside. Does this subtraction at the limit, which I called above posthegemonic or an-archic subtraction, still have political weight? Another way to ask this would be: Is a political responsibility still exercised in or from it? In 1988, Derrida, along with Philippe Lacoue-Labarthe, was invited to have a conversation with Hans-Georg Gadamer at the University of Heidelberg regarding the scandal caused by the publication of Victor Farías's book *Heidegger and Nazism*. Obviously, none of the participants had any interest in exonerating Heidegger from his political commitments to Nazism or hyper-Nazism over a certain ultimately indeterminable period of time in his life. But the conversation's point of departure stemmed from the basis that in Heidegger, in addition to Nazism, or to logocentrism, or to provincial reactionary-ism, or to false piety, there was also to be found, in Derrida's words, an "*aussi autre chose, beaucoup plus complexe*" (an entirely other thing, much more complex).[106] That other thing, with which Lacoue-Labarthe concurred, demands to leave behind fascist determinations, and even offers a means of getting out of them, of moving toward a necessary thinking, which is also a thinking necessarily incapable of reverting to Heidegger's political mistake. In his "2014 Note," which serves as a preface to the French publication of the Heidelberg conversation, Nancy elaborates on this question, attending to what today should be preserved and what should be abandoned in Heidegger's text. Nancy addresses a comment Gadamer made: "What [Heidegger] was prepared to think finds itself condensed here in . . . Gadamer's phrase when he says that '*l'être*' (being), with the definite article, 'is already a falsification.'"[107] The substantivation of being brings back the worst of ontotheology, and it is more than possible that Heidegger, beyond his Nazi or hyper-Nazi incursions, fell into logocentrism, into phallogocentrism, into national-aestheticism, all of them things that Derrida and Lacoue-Labarthe did not stop accusing him of doing. But, Nancy says, if we leave all that behind—and Gadamer says that Heidegger did achieve this—then a new notion of "responsibility" emerges that Nancy acknowledges as expressed in the conversation. In light of the devastating effects that confinement is having on many countries' economies, and in view of the imminent and obvious risk of the abduction of these same effects in favor of expropriating capitalism in this very crisis, this other notion of "responsibility" seems particularly significant today—and more than ever before.

Derrida's critiques do not revolve around easily impugnable neoliberalism, a tenuous battlefield for the left. His critical interest extends to social democracy as an alternative, about which he says that its referential values are "those of the rights of man, of democracy, of the liberty of the subject. But that discourse is becoming conscious that it remains philosophically very fragile, that the strength of its consensus in official political discourses, or elsewhere, rests on very traditional philosophical axioms that often appear . . . in any case incapable of resisting what they are meant to oppose."[108] The legacy of the Enlightenment has been failing us for much of the last two hundred years. It is true that Heidegger's positions threaten the pious who continue to believe, or simulate their belief, in the liberal or social-democratic discourse, understood from the theologico-political tradition. But it is time to propose to the diehard Kantians and Gramscians and Hegelians out there that there is no future in their desired repetition. As Derrida says, "To trust in traditional categories of responsibility seems to me today to be, precisely, irresponsible."[109] Of these traditional categories, none are as fundamental to the secularized political theology of modernity as Kant's notion of voluntarist and intentional responsibility based on humankind's response to itself, on the moral law installed in the heart of the human, which for Kant founds and constitutes human freedom. But let us go back, as Derrida says, to the question of the question. For many years, Heidegger thought that questioning was thinking at its highest point of dignity; but he changed his mind in the 1950s when he understood something that had always been latent in his thinking, namely, that questioning was always already an answer to something. "Questioning is already a listening—a listening to but also of or from the other. I do not have the initiative, even in this piety of thought that is the question," Derrida glosses.[110] The sovereign subject of modernity, as subject of responsibility, is also displaced in this. "The moment of the *Zusage* (acceptance and commitment, promise of correspondence)" goes beyond the moment and subsequent years of *Being and Time*, when already, of course, Dasein was imputable and in need of responding. But *Zusage* introduced something else: "to determine what and who I respond to."[111] It was no longer taken for granted that the human responds to the human in accordance with the law at the heart of Dasein. It is here where, for Derrida and Nancy, another politics begins, another political possibility, which is, however, left undetermined in its concrete possibilities. All we know, all we are told, is that it has to do with a response (to some other, to another, to all others or to all that is other) that is a consequence of a listening in the decision of existence, that it cor-responds in it, and that it belongs within its framework of belligerent repetition. Its conventional name is being, but that word, so openly contaminated by the metaphysical tradition, still holds possibilities of translation that go beyond productionism, beyond equivalence, and beyond hegemonic exploitation. In being the place of an undecidable (to what or whom do I respond through listening?), it is also the place of a political decision: of the political decision of our present, say Derrida and Lacoue-Labarthe in 1988. Nothing is given in advance, and that is why the decision is also a "terrifying test."[112] But in this affair contemporary politics risks it all, as it risks our very planet.

MAY 17, 2020

How should we connect minor violence to the decision of existence? In his *Discourse on Voluntary Servitude*, the young Etienne de La Boétie linked the decision of existence to the abandonment of all voluntary servitude, thus making it accessible to all from the postulate of the radical equality of humans. If the tyrant—understood as the one who imposes servitude—has nothing but the power given to him by his servant, which he then turns against the latter, then everyone can abstain from giving it, everyone can retain their consent and their will to serve. That, for La Boétie, is minor violence against the greater violence of all despotic imposition. And it is a condition of freedom. "Resolve not to serve and you are immediately free." But it isn't always so simple. For the Apache chief Geronimo, it becomes clear that his own resolve not to submit may imply the extermination of his people. Geronimo was not partial to light or measured violence. At war with the Mexicans ever since Mexican troops killed his mother, his wife, and their children in 1859, he would later tell his biographer S. M. Barrett: "I have killed many Mexicans; I do not know how many, for frequently I did not count them. Some of them were not worth counting. It has been a long time since then, I still have no love for the Mexicans. With me they were always treacherous and malicious. I am old now and shall never go on the warpath again, but if I were young, and followed the warpath, it would lead into Old Mexico."[113] But Geronimo understood that it was a battle to the death, and that he could only sustain it in order to last as long as he or the last of his warriors could remain alive: a matter of time.

In 1883, Geronimo, who is fleeing the combined pressures of the Mexican and American troops, finds himself in a ditch, from which he hears the Mexican general tell his men: "Officers, yonder in those ditches is the red devil Geronimo and his hated band. This must be his last day. Ride on him from both sides of the ditches; kill men, women, and children; take no prisoners; dead Indians are what we want. Do not spare your own men; exterminate this band at any cost; I will post the wounded to shoot all deserters; go back to your companies and advance."[114] For Geronimo, revenge is a decision of existence, because, as a mechanism of war, only relentless attack could delay, although not stop, the extermination of his people. But he could have chosen to renounce revenge and accept submission, which he did do, albeit late—when there was no alternative. This was no voluntary submission; it was not chosen. In that sense, the terrible violence of Geronimo and his band of Apaches should be understood as such: as a minor violence, as a decision of existence, and as what I have called savage moralism.

This evening, as I was finishing Geronimo's autobiography, an email came into my mailbox from a former student, Yoandy Cabrera, now a professor at a university in Illinois. He was asking for my consent to publish in the journal he edits an old review I had written of Javier Marías's novel *Thus Bad Begins*, which I had posted—and later forgotten about—on www.infrapolitica.com. I copy it partially with minimal formal adjustments: Marías maintains the cultic—the call or cultivation of a certain mimetic addiction that has to do with style always present in his novels in subterranean fashion, with the exception of his first two novels. Like it or not, Marías's novels construct and prolong style as form, while also interrogating the world, and being in the world. His novels not only show but also summon forth a form of inhabitation out of the notion of what I would call "savage moralism," or rather, a form of savage moralism, a savage moralism already turned into a style, which leaves its mark in the writing. This is the mark that captivates or alienates the reader. The agent of style is, in *Thus Bad Begins*, a young philologist, or rather, a Bachelor of Arts in philology, who reflects in the present on events that occurred around 1980, in the midst of the post-

Franco transition. In that year, Juan de Vere acts as a secretary or assistant to Eduardo Muriel, a capable, intelligent, and educated film director, who is nevertheless trapped in the precarious structures of the cinematic industry of the times and therefore constantly frustrated in his attempts at glory. Juan spends a lot of time in Muriel's home and cannot help but get involved in Muriel's family history and become familiar with the family's friends. At some point he receives a strange and compromising directive from Muriel, an errand that sets him off to discreetly investigate something that, if confirmed, would be seriously disturbing for the friendship between Muriel and Dr. Van Vechten—the latter a doctor of a certain age who had a recognized prestige in Madrid during the long reign of Franco. Juan has been noticing Muriel's mistreatment of his wife, Beatriz Noguera—whom he seems to love but insults, undermines, and ignores on a regular and consistent basis. The apparent contradiction between Muriel's preoccupation with an alleged issue having to do with the abuse of women in Dr. Van Vechten's dark past and his own daily conduct—to any observer, he is daily abusing his wife—triggers the narrative's central conflict.

It is a conflict between the public and the private, or better yet, between the political and the intimate. Whatever the doctor did, serious as it might be, belongs to the sphere of his life as a successful doctor in the postwar years, to his medical and political, hence civil and public, activity insofar as the doctor cared outside of institutional channels for the children (the doctor is a pediatrician) of those who were targeted by Francoism. While Muriel is described numerous times as a righteous and just man, he seems in his relationship with his wife to stage a dull and punishing resentment whose origin is secretive and strictly private, and may have to do with something unforgivable. Muriel's behavior tears down and destroys Beatriz, whose relationship with Muriel is both of absolute fidelity and of absolute abjection.

Loyalty and betrayal are the themes that unify both histories. Is betrayal what is unforgivable? If being a just and righteous man means never to betray, what should we make of a just and righteous man who, on feeling betrayed, no longer forgives, and in his will for revenge resorts to the cruelty of a betrayal that is perpetual, of a sordid and daily nature? Or, inversely, if loyalty is kept out of love, what happens when it is love itself that resorts to betrayal in order to consolidate itself, to be able to guarantee perpetual loyalty, to establish lasting conditions of real and non-phantasmatic fidelity? Is loyalty unforgivable? Or maybe there is never loyalty or betrayal, but a radical indifferentiation between the two that does not absolve either. These are questions that philosophy might be able to address by cutting the knot, appealing to normative ethics with respect to which conditions of consistent or inconsistent behavior could be determined, and therefore also possibilities for judgment, appreciation, or condemnation regarding any personal or even collective attitude. If the judgmental attitude is collective, then philosophy enters its political dimension. Through his reflections on memory and forgetting, on truth and lies, Marías's novel takes on the weight of the problem in the context of the post-Franco transition.

But Marías is not interested in solving these problems, which remain forever complicated, speculated on in contrary resolutions, deconstructed, dispersed in dramatic tension, abandoned to their singular temporality every time. This might be a condition of the literary function, which is then exercised from an infrapolitical *ethos* that moralizes without a norm. Marías's novels can rarely be considered political works; they are moral or antimoral novels, depending on how you look at them, except that the derangement they operate in any possible prescription should not be understood as a renunciation of morality. It is rather a matter of a moral intensification, of an extreme moralism without rules that becomes antiphilosophical. All of Marías's novels, after a certain early moment in his career, seek an extreme infrapolitical intensification and play with the denarrativization of stories in favor of individual temporality, of personal life, which can be more or less tragic, more or less catastrophic, more or less interesting, more or less ripped apart, more or less given over to pleasure (although "pleasure" in Marías does not allow for pedestrian definitions). Marías's savage moralism places itself beyond judgment, beyond any possibility of ethical control from stable philosophico-political positions. "It is up to them," Marías says every time, and the decisions that are therefore allowed are not to be tampered with, bracketed, sanctioned, condemned, praised: they are only what is most properly singular, hence sacred, in a life, in every life. And also in every death, hence in what is sacred in them as well. Regarding those decisions, there is no justice, only practices of forgiveness or resentment that are in themselves infinitely complex, since each of them carries along grave implications. It is in view of them that Marías titles his novel using a Shakespearian leitmotif: "Thus bad begins, and worse remains behind." Marías's extreme moralism is centered on a categorical imperative with strictly savage characteristics: "Do what will cause you the least pain, what you'll find easiest to live with." The price of doing so belongs to the tragic, to the residue of the tragic in every one of our lives. What will cause you the least pain, that is your politics in your decision of existence. Because nobody is more or better than any other person, and so there should be no voluntary servitude. And not even you would want to impose it. But looking for what you will find easiest to live with is also a task of loyalty, a task of respect, a task of care, and a savage practice of freedom beyond domination. This is a politics that infrapolitics can live with.

MAY 18, 2020
In a couple of days, two months will have passed since I started writing these notes. The confinement, perhaps only the first confinement, which here in Texas has never been very extreme—even though we have taken it very seriously at home—will confusingly come to an end, and therefore I will finish this book, just as institutional media are announcing vague ominous measures that are to be enacted in the foreseeable future—announcements that are preceded by or immersed in obvious perplexity. No one really knows how things will go except that they are bound to get worse, and there is little hope of a positive political transformation. Yesterday, Naomi Klein published an article in *The Intercept* on agreements made between the State of New York and Eric Schmidt, representing Google, and the Bill and Melinda Gates Foundation, which is Microsoft. These agreements announce the beginning of a heinous dystopia that is digital and securitarian, something awful for this country, though they are touted as being on the salvific cutting edge of technological innovation. It becomes ever more urgent to pay attention to our own conditions of existence in order to face what is coming with some equanimity, some degree of alertness.

MAY 19, 2020
Neither the next few months nor the next few years will bring any kind of political salvation. We can break our necks insisting that this will happen without so much as thinking of its

improbable conditions, or we can choose something else: the practical compromise in every case with a decision of existence that may rescue singular time and help us prepare, for the long haul, a new administration of common time that would be deserving of the name of a new politics, of an alternative proposal for political life.

Remark 5: The Fourth Position

La Boétie warns of the endemic lack of enthusiasm in a regime of voluntary servitude. I've seen this in the university for years, in my colleagues, in the students: how nothing seems to disturb the banal dream of the righteous, how everybody prefers sleepwalking servitude without even thinking about it, without any consciousness of it. There is hardly any thought; that is the necessary conclusion to draw. It is enough to quickly scroll through Facebook or Twitter to know this—and to see what all that noise masks over and shuts up. In Walter Hill's film from 1993, *Geronimo: An American Legend,* Geronimo tells Lieutenant Gatewood, while he is on the San Carlos Reservation preparing for his own long confinement, that an Apache shaman had announced that many more Apaches would die fighting against the white-eyes. "In the end we will win because we would die free of them," says Geronimo, quoting the shaman. To die free of the despot who is imposing servitude is, for Geronimo and his last Apaches, not a goal but a condition. As a condition, it derives from an imperative: the refusal of submission. The confinement of the Apaches—in Turkey Creek, at Fort Marion, in the forest of Alabama, or at Fort Sills—was real. Assuming that we are fortunate enough not to be left on the sidelines of the system of exploitation after summarily losing our jobs, our confinement will, from now on, largely be digital and cybernetic. But this won't keep it from having real effects. My conclusion cannot be anything other than an insistence on the need for a decision of existence somewhere between the kind recommended by the *Discourse on Voluntary Servitude* and the one embodied in Geronimo's life, even if our material situation is not as desperate as his was. Our courage won't be either. "Apache refusal," John Kraniauskas calls it.[115] Well, Apache refusal is another name for antiphilosophical infrapolitics.

Badiou may be right when he says that philosophy "is never an interpretation of existence."[116] And in that sense, philosophy is not as urgent as antiphilosophy, which stems from a specific existential position, from a concrete, personal, and autographic situation, which is the one that we cannot avoid and for which we must take responsibility. But this runs counter to contemporary trends, which are much more geared toward mere ideological production or toward political praxis blindly understood as the only possibility for thought. Badiou and Ernesto Laclau insist on the constraints for left political thought that so-called global capitalism imposes. Badiou says that only a communist, or neocommunist, idea, which can unleash a faithful militancy, will have sufficient force to allow for an opposition to capitalism that would be capable of turning the latter into history, that is, into the past; for Laclau the theory of hegemony is equated with political possibility itself, and so for him there is no other option but to seek necessarily contingent and temporally finite equivalential alliances between social segments that can build anti-capitalist formations of power. All of that is well and good: if Badiou's "communism" seeks movement toward a postcapitalist social configuration, based on equalitarian symbolization, and if Laclau's theory serves to configure political operations of alliance against despotism and servitude, I don't have any issue with accepting either notion, or both. But I am more interested in determining what the role of an existential infraphilosophy is in all of it—communism will neither come to pass nor will we have any interest in new hegemonic formations unless both communism and hegemony bring along new modes for understanding our relationship with existence, which also includes the political relation. One of the obvious problems in the recent history of the global left is that, to the real lack of a program, whether political or economic, one has to add a largely miserable charisma, with few exceptions—Bernie Sanders, in the United States, is one example. This is a defect that politics itself is incapable of resolving. If philosophy, in its metaphysical incarnation, or in its latest avatar as political philosophy, has had for centuries in the West a certain powerful hegemony, it is radically incumbent on us to examine what the status of such hegemony is now. Concretely, the question is whether such a hegemony is already dead, just as metaphors also die, and whether today it is meant only for zombies, still capable of dragging all politics along toward death. Antiphilosophy is born, and lives, in our present, in the context of the passage to death of hegemonic politics, of the politics of hegemony. And as infrapolitical resistance to the politics of hegemony.

Appropriating a phrase from one of Fernando Pessoa's heteronyms, Alberto Caeiro, a poet from the "age of the poets" and himself an antiphilosopher, Badiou in *The Immanence of Truths* proposes a "metaphysics without metaphysics."[117] And yes, a "metaphysics without metaphysics" infinitely complicates the apparent opposition between philosophy and the end of philosophy, which is also the opposition between metaphysics and thought, and which is also called, in another of its forms, the opposition between antiphilosophy and philosophy. Philosophy—far from having been brought by Marx, Nietzsche, and Husserl to its "final stage," where, in Heidegger's words, only an "epigonal renaissance and variations of that renaissance" would be possible[118]—could still offer new and multiple figures of the thinkable for Badiou, not supplementary but alternative to those offered by the tradition of modernity—which can be encoded, beyond the establishment of its subjectivist ground by Descartes, in the sequence that goes from Leibniz to Nietzsche: "The ground has the character of grounding as the ontic causation of the real, as the transcendental making possible of the objectivity of objects, as the dialectical mediation of the movement of the Absolute Spirit, of the historical process of production, or as the will to power positing values."[119] In the meantime, however, and until there is an occasion to decide for one or the other, we can accept the undeniable fascination offered by the theme of antiphilosophy that Badiou has been developing since the 1980s, but that finds its first apparent culmination in the first half of the '90s with the seminars that were dedicated to Nietzsche, Wittgenstein, Lacan, and Paul of Tarsus, respectively.

However, it can be argued that the seminar Badiou offered to his students on Heidegger in 1986–87, a period that coincides with the final writing of *Being and Event*, is at the origin of Badiou's antiphilosophical inquiry.[120] His interest in antiphilosophy has something or everything to do with the Heideggerian demand concerning the end of metaphysics and the beginning of an alternative way of thinking that, were it to occur, would be no more and no less than a transformation of thought—that is, into something other than what has been called metaphysics by the history of the West, a history that coincides with that of philosophy. "Philosophy is metaphysics," Heidegger says, which seems to imply that the "end" of metaphysics would also be the end of philosophy.[121] The question is what would come next in the field of thought, to the dubious extent that, at this point, there will be thought as something other than—to use the

Lacanian expression—a service of the goods, which is what fundamentally occupies the contemporary sciences under the aegis of cybernetics, that is, under calculative-representational domination. In the conversation with Jean-Claude Milner that concludes his 1994–95 seminar on Lacan, Badiou recognizes that the issue of whether or not there is thought is controversial. This is what he tells Milner: "You are taking a stand by asserting that there is thought, at any rate in Lacan's work—a view that runs counter to the dominant view that there isn't any."[122] But is there thought today? Is there politics, is there love, is there art? Is there scientific truth beyond the logico-mathematized technologization of the productionism that is the dominant aspect of capitalist discourse, which seems destined not to disappear but to continue on even more ominously than before in the wake of the seeming economic catastrophe brought about by the coronavirus? In the eighth session of the seminar on Lacan, Badiou says: "Lacan's final thesis is that, as regards the real, there is no politics . . . there's no politics other than the politics whose hole is plugged by philosophy. I'd even say—this isn't something Lacan said—that what he fundamentally thought is that there's no politics at all; there's only political philosophy."[123]

Badiou is partially aligning Lacan with the Heideggerian position, from the quote he previously commented on in the seminar, which comes from the introduction to the German edition of Lacan's *Écrits*, where Lacan says: "For my 'friend' Heidegger . . . consider the idea that metaphysics has never been anything and can only continue by plugging the hole of politics."[124] There is neither metaphysics nor politics for Lacan, insofar as the latter becomes only present as a hole, as it does for a certain Heidegger, whose Nazi commitment would have already been antipolitical (and also inconsistent with *Being and Time*); what remains is antiphilosophy. But the antiphilosophical position is not merely the position that says that there is no politics, that there is only political philosophy, and that political philosophy is also sufficiently useless to the extent that it only serves to plug the hole of politics. We can give an example regarding the antiphilosophical radicalization of politics that is not just any example. These are among the last words of Ernesto Laclau's book *Emancipation(s)*, where, from a perspective that Laclau himself recognizes as Heideggerian—although ultimately that is more than controversial—we read:

The metaphysical discourse of the West is coming to an end, and philosophy in its dusk has performed, through the great names of the century, a last service for us: the deconstruction of its own terrain and the creation of the conditions for its own impossibility. Let us think, for instance, of Derrida's undecidables. Once undecidability has reached the ground itself, once the organization of a certain camp is governed by a hegemonic decision—hegemonic because it is not objectively determined, because different decisions were also possible—the realm of philosophy comes to an end and the realm of politics begins.[125]

There is no politics, according to Lacan, there is only a useless and outdated political philosophy that simply plugs holes; or there is no philosophy, according to Laclau, and there is only a heroic hegemonic politics that will bring to our time "its most radical and exhilarating possibilities."[126] Both positions are examples of antiphilosophy, even if they are partially contrary—their only agreement, which is exactly what Badiou does not agree with, is that there is no longer philosophy, there is no longer metaphysics. But, for Badiou, Laclau's words couldn't be understood as something other than a dark disaster—I must return to this.

Badiou doesn't believe in the end of philosophy, and he therefore doesn't believe in the end of metaphysics; he takes a stance that is perhaps not so much anti-Heideggerian as simply an alternative to Heidegger's. Heidegger is Badiou's great antagonist. Badiou nevertheless seeks to inquire about the problem that Heidegger's position opens up regarding contemporary historicity, and that inquiry is his extraordinary analytical effort to establish a history of antiphilosophy in which Heidegger would be subsumed. We understand, and Badiou doesn't stop repeating this, that Nietzsche and Wittgenstein, Lacan and Paul, do not exhaustively constitute the antiphilosophical pantheon, but rather Heraclitus would already be an antiphilosopher to Parmenides, just as Pascal would be an antiphilosopher to Descartes, Rousseau the antiphilosopher to rationalism, and Kierkegaard the antiphilosopher to Hegel. There are many antiphilosophers, Badiou says, which from the outset effectively counters the Heideggerian claim that the philosophical tradition is unitary, all of it subsumed in the medley assortment of historical metaphysics: philosophy is itself divided, it is more than one, but one of its divisions touches on extreme liminality, and even without withdrawing entirely from philosophy, it positions itself as antiphilosophy.

The position that we can take as central in Badiou's reflection on the necessity of philosophy is under the aegis of what is forcefully stated in *Manifesto for Philosophy*, to wit: philosophy is never an interpretation of existence. For Badiou, thinking of or interpreting existence would therefore fall resolutely on the side of antiphilosophy. Should we take this delimitation on board? Wouldn't that lead us to accept that we would not be speaking philosophically when we speak of existence? Will we have to choose and guide our own discourse based on the division between philosophy—given over as such to knowledge of truths only produced by art and science, politics and love—and antiphilosophy, which would directly be thought in existence, of existence, about existence, untethered from the condition of truth? In other words, from thinking truth as its condition? Or would there be a third position, even a fourth position that we could more modestly call thought, so as not to end up in a Badiouan mimesis adopting the tempting formula of "metaphysics without metaphysics"? How, in any case, are these pages, my pages, inscribed in this?

Badiou has spoken of a "fourth position" that was precisely not developed in his article "The Philosophical Status of the Poem according to Heidegger."[127] Badiou begins by referring to the necessarily desacralizing interruption proper to the philosophical dimension in the context of Parmenides's poem (see also his seminar on Parmenides). Parmenides's poem is a philosophical poem insofar as there is an argumentative secularism in it that desacralizes and interrupts the path of the goddess. For Badiou, Parmenides's poem emblematizes the first of the "three possible regimes for the link between poem and philosophy."[128] The second regime would be assigned to Plato, and it is the regime of distance. For Plato, "philosophy cannot establish itself except in the contrast between poem and matheme, which are its primordial conditions."[129] And Plato insists on an argumentative distance that is no longer the contrasting rivalry that appears in the Parmenidean poem. Badiou assigns the third regime to Aristotle, whose *Poetics* includes the knowledge of the poem within philosophy in the technical sense of aesthetics: "The poem is no longer thought according to the drama of its distance or its intimate proximity, it is caught in the category of the object."[130] According to Badiou, Heidegger—based on his interest since the mid-1930s in Hölderlin's work—sanctions the idea that the poem holds truths that are concealed in the hijacking of philosophy by science or politics, and both reject the reduction of the poem to an object of a regional ontology in the Aristotelian sense, since that would amount to the poem's expulsion from philosophical reflection. But Heidegger is unable to find a fourth possible relation. He therefore does not found a fourth regime of the relation between poem and philosophy but instead reverts to the Parmenidean regime: "In the place of the invention of a *fourth relation* between philosophy and poetry, which would be neither fusional nor distanced nor aesthetic, Heidegger prophesies in the void a reactivation of the sacred within the undecipherable coupling of the saying of the poets and the thinking of the thinkers."[131] There is no denying Badiou's reason for claiming an end to "the age of poets," which would require, in his terms, de-suturing the thought from its poetic condition. The great Heideggerian era, which according to Badiou, was defined precisely by that poetico-philosophical suture against the scientific-political kidnapping of philosophy by analytical and Marxist traditions, would have come to an end not only when Paul Celan "encounters the silence of the master, which is precisely the sutured abdication of philosophy,"[132] but also when poetological tropology excessively saturates the field of expression and turns literary-theoretical reflection into mere culturalism that produces those "experiences" that are the dark face of technical machination. From my perspective, the age of the poets has long since expired in its radical inauthenticity at the hands of university discourse in the humanities such as it is today.

But does the establishment of this fourth position regarding the thought-poem relation not remain a possibility? Badiou indeed seems to concede as much when he refers already in *The Age of the Poets* to Alberto Caeiro's "metaphysics without metaphysics." In a recent book of interviews, Badiou responds to Giovanbattista Tusa about a question regarding the closure of the "age of poets": "In poetry . . . the real potential of the poem lies in its piecing together a certain saying that is manifestly the saying of that which cannot be said . . . we come back naturally to the immanent exception, and the immanent exception is also this dialectic of subtraction—that is to say, the fact that the proper essence of a thing is not so much the intensity of its presence as the figure of that which is fugitive yet which it nonetheless manages to retain, to hold on to somehow."[133] But with this, and insofar as the "immanent exception" is a figure of the totality of Badiou's philosophical production,[134] Badiou approaches a formulation of the task of thought that is dangerously close (for Badiou's ostensible will) to the Heideggerian formulation of the ontico-ontological difference, and therefore in the precise genealogy of that which is the absolute condition of every "other beginning" of thought. What I have been calling the decision of existence is, after all, nothing more than the attempt, repeated and ceaseless and belligerent, to listen to and take responsibility for the ontological difference in my life and in every life: to appropriate my time and to live that difference between becoming who I am or becoming only its mirage and slavish parody.

Is the age of poets, however, replaceable with an age of politics, in the Laclauian sense? Let us remember Laclau's opinion, quoted above, according to which we would be facing a historical moment—the moment of globalized capitalism—when it is possible to affirm the end of philosophy and the beginning of politics ("the realm of philosophy comes to an end and the realm of politics begins"). Toward the end of *On Populist Reason*, Laclau insists on that perspective: "Perhaps what is dawning as a possibility in our political experience is something radically different from what postmodern prophets of the 'end of politics' are announcing: the arrival at a fully political era, because the dissolution of the marks of certainty does not give the political game any aprioristic necessary terrain but, rather, the possibility of constantly redefining the terrain itself."[135] The age of politics would then succeed the age of the poets. For Laclau, there is the age of politics in the precise way that there is no longer a necessary and *a priori* terrain—that is, a metaphysically constituted one—for political practice. Given that there are no truths, as Laclau says, hegemonic practice is what remains. But, upon presenting itself as a substitute for a notion of truth—not as truth but as the empty signifier occupying the absent fullness of a truth—Laclauian politics, in Badiou's terms, opens itself up to disaster. For Badiou, philosophy moves toward disaster precisely when it tries to present itself as a "situation of truth," which occurs when it tries to fill the void: the void of absent fullness, the void of the empty signifier in Laclau's vocabulary. In other words, precisely when thought, or political action, which for Laclau amounts to the same thing, indulges in what in his theory would be a hegemonic procedure: hegemonically to fill a void, which is the social void in Laclau and the void of truth in Badiou. When that happens, for Badiou, thought ecstatically presents itself as the *topos noetos* of truth, it incorporates and incarnates the sacredness of the Name, and is formulated as the presence of Presence, which necessarily operates through terror, looking for the separation or the annihilation of what has been left out. Badiou does not expressly mention Laclau when he makes these comments, but in my opinion there is no other critique that is as clear on the consequences of enthroning the theory of hegemony as political procedure par excellence, which, consequently, condemns us all to be a parody of the more or less heroic or submissive but insubstantial public subject of modernity, the citizen, whose greatest virtue would be his or her questionable, because improbable, emancipatory political enthusiasm.

Laclau's antiphilosophy is offered up as a hegemonic re-substantialization that cannot but give itself over to disaster. Laclau says: "No social fullness is achievable except through hegemony; and hegemony is nothing more than the investment, in a partial object, of a fullness which will always evade us because it is purely mythical."[136] We can look at this in two ways. In the first of the two, we make an affective investment; we know that it is consolatory and substitutive, we know that through it we are not going to get to any stable place, we know that it will come loaded with problems and disappointments, that the leader will fail us because leaders always do, that the historical myth that we have invoked will take water everywhere as soon as some time comes to pass and the seams get weathered, but in any case, the gnashing and grinding of teeth will always be less than those derived from the absence of all affective cathexis in politics, from an absence and a void uncompensated, and therefore nakedly accepted, without ornaments. In the second way, if the history of philosophy ends up being the history of a desubstantialization of truth, and if the history of politics cannot be formulated as anything but the history of the successive dis-incarnations that trace the ruin of successive hegemonic formations, antiphilosophy should open itself up to a critical suspension of politics that renounces certain affective investments and that understands that what is politically relevant can no longer be tied to the bandwagon of any false mythical fullness, of any hegemonic fullness. It should do the opposite: in each case, it must demystify representational life, undo the chain of equivalences, denounce the epochal hypocrisy that confuses politics with the hegemonic maintenance or establishment of power, and prefer an antihegemonic structuration, always concretely antihegemonic, which is to say, always grounded in the rejection of the mythical pretenses of dominant formations, wherever they come from.

MAY 20, 2020 A.M.   Antiphilosophy happens when a thinker, having come to the end of her or his particular ontological itinerary, refers to an altogether alternative kind of experience of thought, normally posited as yet to come or barely glimpsed, hence futural but immanent, and it is an experience of a nearness where things will have come to be accomplished in terms of that thinker's itinerary of thought: Nietzsche and his notion that he was just about to have an insight that would break the history of the world in two in the weeks prior to his mental collapse; or Wittgenstein and his notion that thought opened up in the silence of which one could no longer talk, having exhausted the talkable, at the end of the *Tractatus*; or the later Lacan and his notion of the analytic matheme. Heidegger reaches a particular antiphilosophical formulation in the 1950s, and his path to it is narrated in the lectures titled "The Danger" and "The Turn." The experience of "the turn" is an antiphilosophical experience.[137]

    Antiphilosophy could not be further away from antithinking, if "thinking is the authentic action (*Handeln*), where action means to give a hand (*an die Hand geben*) to the essence of being in order to prepare for it that site in which it brings itself and its essence to speech."[138] At the limit of thought, when a certain occlusion in the presuppositions makes itself impassable, further thought is possible, provided a displacement takes place. But this only ever happens when a thinker comes to the end of his or her own ontological itinerary. There is no antiphilosophy without philosophy pushed to the limit. To that extent, antiphilosophy requires a history in every case, requires a thickness of ontology that somehow becomes void and needs to be displaced. Antiphilosophy is not an overcoming, it is not a transcending. It is a displacement. History moves, and the thinker at the limit of ontology may prepare for a "traversal of the errancy," a "traversal of the zone of dangerousness of the danger"—these are Heideggerian expressions—in the way that an analysand prepares for a "traversal of the phantasy" or a monk for satori. Coming to the other side of the traversing is the antiphilosophical step—it comes at a theoretical end, but it is no longer a theoretical step. It enacts the relation of (mortal, pained, poor) existence to world. It is a transfiguration of thought.

Remark 6: An Invitation to Social Death

That transfiguration is not merely private, it does not simply reference what happens to you as you attempt to become all who you are, all that you are. It has political implications, political overtones, but they call for a change in presuppositions. In an essay I just read, Samuele Mazzolini claims that Laclau's theory of the political is reductive, particularly as it concerns hegemony theory. And that it therefore needs to be "re-Gramscianized." Mazzolini rejects Laclau's claim about the identification of populism with hegemony and politics: all politics are hegemonic politics, and all hegemonic politics are always already populist politics. He calls for a restitutive de-identification of the three terms. Fundamentally, for Mazzolini, Laclau's notion of hegemony is too simple, or excessively simplified, as it points toward an ever-punctual, ever-contingent bid for power without the necessary social depth. This is the reason why Laclauian hegemony is doomed to pass every time—that is, politically to fail—always to end up in its own desubstantialization, as it has happened both to Podemos in Spain and to the different Latin American pink-tide governments, which were unable to capitalize on any properly constructed socially hegemonic depth. For Mazzolini the only half-successful hegemonic articulation from the left in relatively recent times was the one almost accomplished by the Italian Communist Party in the years after World War II and until the 1970s. Yes, the PCI ultimately failed, for other reasons, and did not reach its primary political objective. In the process, however, it was able to sustain a long and almost successful hegemonic struggle.

Hegemony, then, for Mazzolini, who is following Gramsci, is and can only be the long pedagogical march toward communist society, always led by a minority elite, an intellectual class, whether it is communist party cadres or the duly committed members of the academic intelligentsia and its pedagogy of the politically correct. Only through a long and successful internalization of the awareness of good politics could we ever accomplish proper hegemonic change, and such an internalization can only be a function of sustained pedagogic interventions cutting through time, institutions, and social classes. The rest is perhaps populism, as a fleeting and unrooted or ungrounded move toward a quick political change that will leave, alas, the underlying structures unchanged, thus dooming itself. Mazzolini's diagnosis is good, but the prognosis (that is, "without an endless Gramscianism nothing real will be accomplished") is not just rather boring but also misguided. Witness the state of play in the North American university, where there has been an obvious ideological dominance of the left since the 1980s, only to get Donald Trump and full corporatization forty years later, and counting . . . with the added injury that what is going on today in the North American right, for instance, is something the left could not predict. So pedagogy be damned—it cannot be the way to go. And yet the more I read in and about current Gramscians, the more convinced I am that is the only thing they can come up with in their quest for political power.

What is summed up in or by the notion of infrapolitics is at the same time the analysis and the subversion of the myriad micropractices of everyday life in every region of life, at the existential and the social level, which are levels that are obviously not independent from one another. Politically, what is summed up by its companion concept, posthegemony, is an operationalization of political practice in every case, whose primary object is not persuasion, not the establishment of consent, not pedagogy of any kind, not the move toward any accomplishment of genuine or deluded agreement. Instead, posthegemony proposes a practice of general dissensus, that is, a refusal of hegemonic intrusion in singular life (whether personal or collective), wherever it comes from. This results, or should result, in political practice understood as the permanent negotiation of conflict on ever-pragmatic, that is, tactical grounds, and in view of whatever is possible at every given conjuncture, and at every step in the conjuncture. Posthegemony gives up on hegemonic pedagogy, which it denounces as only ever committed to domination, whether it is the sedimented pedagogy of the status quo or the politically correct pedagogy of the converted. It postulates an emancipation from the state apparatus, which includes an emancipation from any counterhegemonic inversion of the state apparatus. To that extent it affirms or presupposes a "communism of intelligence" in Jacques Rancière's terms.[139] For posthegemony, pedagogy is for the birds. Posthegemony is an operational indicator for political practice, not a political doctrine. Its strategy is the accomplishment of democratic equality both now and for the future, but tactically it prescribes nothing beyond the permanent use of thought at the service of a (pragmatic) refusal of domination, formally defined as hegemonic intrusion in singular life.

Posthegemony is therefore perfectly capable of unleashing a new political sequence based on the equalitarian symbolization of the social. But only as a result of the abandonment of the policies of hegemonic intrusion that seem to be all the left is capable of providing us with nowadays (paradoxically prompting, not consensus, but a radical if not terminal dissensus, as the recent results for Podemos in Galicia and the Basque Country in Spain show—not to mention the Trumpists' reaction to well-meaning political correctness at the moral level in the United States). If an example of posthegemonic thought and practice were needed, the example I can adduce is Afropessimist practice. Afropessimism is a radical position marked against "the death of Black desire," which is a function of the three fundamental aspects of political terror in contemporary societies. From the position that Black life is the radical *constitutive outside* of humanity, the radical other of the Human, Frank Wilderson presents the three terrors succinctly in his recent *Afropessimism*. They are, first, the terror of political society as embodied by the police apparatus, the military apparatus, and the incarceration regime; the terror of hegemonic force as embodied institutionally by the mainstream media, the university, and the churches; and, finally and most polemically, the terror of "counter-hegemonic and revolutionary thought: the logic of White feminism, the logic of working-class struggle, the logic of multicultural coalitions, and the logic of immigrant rights. The unrelenting terror elaborated whenever Black people's so-called allies think out loud."[140] It is clear that Wilderson is not out to make many friends, yet his words should nevertheless be heard. Not just hegemony but the counter-hegemonic positions of the social left enjoy powerful narratives, which they constantly build on at the expense of subaltern life as embodied by Black desire. If political narrative is organically anti-Black, as Wilderson claims, this has two difficult implications. Political narratives would always be about contingent violence, not about the gratuitous violence that assails Black life. For Blacks, violence is always already totalizing, which "makes narrative inaccessible." If the Human is "a construct that requires its Other in order to be legible,"[141] all narrative coherence evaporates: so-called Human narrative is inconsistent as it avoids and preempts, or falsifies, a thematization of the abjected Black other; this absence spectralizes and destroys narrative form even if narrative form remains unaware of its fundamental and constitutive exclusion or precisely because of it. And Black narrative is also impossible because there can be no narrative of epistemological catastrophe. There can be stories, but they will not be conceptually coherent. They will be broken stories. Narrative subjects, particularly those in a political narrative, are always parasitic on Black suffering. A liberation from all social fictions, but particularly from the one that constitutes the fulcrum of Human life, namely, Black social death, implies a radical denarrativization. Narratives may be deemed to be always already (insufficiently) political, but this can only refer to Human narratives. *Saying* the structure of Black suffering, that is, cannot be political, cannot be conceptualized as primarily political. "It actually takes the problem outside of politics."[142] It is infrapolitical.

No wonder understanding this prompts a nervous breakdown. There is "sadism" as "a generalized condition [of political life] . . . in that pleasure, as a constituent element of communal life, cannot be disentangled from anti-Black violence."[143] The exit from sadistic narrative is a difficult one, as it does require an epistemological catastrophe, that is, the end of the world as we know it. If so, then Afropessimism is an attempt to think, to use a phrase borrowed from Badiou, *"le réel impensé de l'epoque"* (the real unthought of the epoch). Its condition is to undo shackles: "The Black people were shackled to the cognitive maps of their well-meaning masters."[144] But undoing the shackles brings no redress, no redemption, as there is nothing (thinkable) to be put in place; there are no alternative cognitive maps. The "absolute dereliction" of Black life "cannot be made legible through counter-hegemonic interventions."[145] "Without the Black, one would not be able to know what a world devoid of redemption looks like—and if one could not conceive of the absence of redemption, then redemption would be inconceivable as well."[146]

This is what Afropessimism proposes to us non-Blacks: Given hegemonic *and* counter-hegemonic terror, the latter no less "essential," "if a social movement is to be neither social democratic nor Marxist, in terms of its structure of political desire, then it should grasp the invitation of social death embodied in Black beings."[147] Even non-Blacks, on occasion if not structurally, have had to contend or must contend with hostile and violent events that cannot be turned into any kind of conceptual coherence. There are times when consignment to social death, if not the physical one, is administered to you or to me because of some transgression, real or imaginary. But there are times when consignment to death, to the radical precaritization of your life, traumatically, does not happen under the principle of sufficient reason. It exceeds it. Through a sadistic cathexis. The claim is that a sadistic cathexis rules every moment of Black life and organizes ceaseless social death. Saying it, through which act the Blacks become "worthy of [their] suffering,"[148] is something. Once said, the issue of how it should orient our lives, politically and infrapolitically, is a matter of thought. Accepting the invitation of social death, as Wilderson prompts us to do by way of a precarious alliance with Black life, does not of course mean accepting your own consignment to death. Rather, it means making it the existential basis of your thinking in order to resist it and fight it, to survive it, to move outside of it. There are, to my mind, two fundamental ways of proceeding. I will call the first one "archipolitical" and the second one "infrapolitical." Both of them are, for me, forms of posthegemonic practice.

What is the difference between saying "there is no Humanity, Humanity is not one," as it excludes Black life, and saying "there is a Humanity, it is called Whiteness"? I think both statements come to the same, that is, to a humanism that posits itself always and ever in counterdistinction to its constitutive outside. The space of humanism has defined the space of modern politics, and it still does. And it is because there is a political, if not ontological, conflation of humanity with whiteness that the archipolitical statement about the necessary end of humanity becomes possible on the side of Black life. I call it archipolitical because it seems to me that Blackness, as a name, becomes in Afropessimist terms both the name of an extraordinary political power and the name for a dissolution of politics altogether. One historical example for this definition is, of course, the Nietzschean conception of "grand politics," but this time it is enacted from a subaltern perspective. This is actually historically unprecedented in my opinion, at least in the languages of the West. And it also offers a double path to follow in the wake of pandemic confinement.

Blackness, in Afropessimist usage, is no longer a common name, but it takes on the character of a proper name. It is premised on an abyssal ground: it is at the same time a name of slavery and a name of freedom. There is something in Blackness as a proper name that exceeds slavery, and it is freedom: an excess that dissolves. That is the archipolitical gesture of Afropessimism: an extreme identification of political conditions that ruins politics and opens (itself up for) another sequence. It is an archipolitical gesture because it is a redoubling of the political stakes. When

Afropessimism seeks primarily and for the most part the production of political effects through the very destruction of politics, Afropessimism is archipolitical. Stéphane Mallarmé used to talk about Igitur's throw of the dice as the production of *l'unique nombre qui ne peut pas être un autre* (the unique number that cannot be another). This is the Afropessimist throw of the dice. It is a declaration after which politics is not possible any more except as erasure and mystification. Politics is, in fact, from the perspective of Blackness (proper name), nihilism. Something else, a non-political insurgency, opens up in it. This is one of the possibilities of posthegemonic practice: archipolitical posthegemony. But there is another one.

I find no better way of introducing it than by quoting a long paragraph in a recent book by Saidiya Hartman associated with Afropessimism, in order to follow up with a comment on it:

> Wayward, related to the family of words: errant, fugitive, recalcitrant, anarchic, willful, reckless, troublesome, riotous, tumultuous, rebellious and wild. To inhabit the world in ways inimical to those deemed proper and respectable, to be deeply aware of the gulf between where you stayed and how you might live. Waywardness: the avid longing for a world not ruled by master, man or the police. The errant path taken by the leaderless swarm in search of a place better than here. The social poesis that sustains the dispossessed. Wayward: the unregulated movement of drifting and wandering; sojourns without a fixed destination, ambulatory possibility, interminable migrations, rush and flight, black locomotion; the everyday struggle to live free. The attempt to elude capture by never settling. Not the master's tools, but the ex-slave's fugitive gestures, her traveling shoes. Waywardness articulates the paradox of cramped creation, the entanglement of escape and confinement, flight and captivity. Wayward: to wander, to be unmoored, adrift, rambling, roving, cruising, strolling, and seeking. To claim the right to opacity. To strike, to riot, to refuse. To love what is not loved. To be lost to the world. It is the practice of the social otherwise, the insurgent ground that enables new possibilities and new vocabularies; it is the lived experience of enclosure and segregation, assembling and huddling together. It is the directionless search for a free territory; it is a practice of making and relation that enfolds within the policed boundaries of the dark ghetto; it is the mutual aid offered in the open-air prison. It is a queer resource of black survival. It is a beautiful experiment in how-to-live.[149]

Can we then speak of the "wayward subject" as the subject of posthegemony? We may want to cross out the word "subject," put it under erasure, since there is inevitably a dual distortion linked to the word: on the one hand, certainly in modernity, the equivalence of subject with citizen; on the other hand, the pretense that the subject rules absolutely over the object. The wayward subject (under erasure, crossed out) would reject both determinations—there is no claim to mastery, and there is no vindication of citizenship, which is always premised on subordination to the sovereign. In a recent conversation Fred Moten, another important thinker of Black studies, says that Frank Wilderson could be taken to be the "last great theorist of the subject." Wilderson's position would be that Blackness is the site of the nonsubject that makes subjectivity possible: all subjectivity is parasitic on the Black (non)subject. It would then seem that Wilderson's theory of the subject is rather more like a countertheory, a theoretical destruction whose momentum might well come from waywardness as existential projection. This goes, it would seem to me, beyond the Lacanian theorization of the split subject—the wayward (non)subject does not accumulate in the last instance, does not recoup or redress, finds no passage to itself. So, my question: does the wayward (non)subject, whose historical possibility is social death, constitute not just an instance of posthegemonic practice but also itself as a "philosophical act"? Or is it, radically, an act of antiphilosophy?

In his 1992–93 seminar on Nietzsche, Badiou, who calls Nietzsche the *prince pauvre et définitif de l'antiphilosophie* (the poor and decisive prince of antiphilosophy),[150] links Nietzsche's final antiphilosophical act—he is talking about the last year of Nietzsche's writerly life, before his plunge into silence—to the terrible accomplishment of an absolute reduction of the gap between "the one who says and what is said."[151] This accomplishment is premised on a thorough de-subjectification whereby the very name of Nietzsche becomes "a name without a name, an anonymous name, without the mark of nominal recognition."[152] The name is only what the name says, and if there is an excess it is only the excess of desire, and it cannot be converted into nominative capital, into subjective accumulation, into identity. But is that not, then, the name of every wayward life? Of every wayward (non)subject. I would not think we need to posit any kind of identification, no matter how remote, between Nietzsche's waywardness, although it clearly existed, and Blackness as subaltern form-of-life. Both of them could be forms of what I am calling antiphilosophical existence. Both of them insurgent. Both of them appropriate to post-confinement life.

But then antiphilosophical existence, as posthegemonic practice, takes exception to archipolitical posthegemony. Its interest is no longer the political intensification of desire through the destruction of politics, but rather an infrapolitical enactment. To finish with Hartman's words:

> Waywardness is a practice of possibility at a time when all roads, except the ones created by smashing out, are foreclosed. It obeys no rules and abides no authorities. It is unrepentant. It traffics in occult visions of other worlds and dreams of a different kind of life. Waywardness is an ongoing exploration of what might be; it is an improvisation with the terms of social existence, when the terms have already been dictated, where there is little room to breathe, when you have been sentenced to a life of servitude, when the house of bondage looms in whatever direction you move. It is the untiring practice of trying to live when you were never meant to survive.[153]

And is that not the practice of a freedom that leaves behind both slavery and its concurrent historical effects in hegemony, wherever it may come from?

MAY 20, 2020 P.M.

There is something that I was trying to think through when the viral outbreak changed the coordinates of everyday life. At the end of this book, of the first two months of pandemic confinement, I might as well return to it, also because essentially I never left it. *Commodious vicus of recirculation*.[154] We had a conference in Michigan in February, only a couple of weeks before the pandemic was declared as such, on Derrida's 1975–76 seminar *Life Death*.[155] In those February days, we didn't yet imagine we would be entering a kind of suspension of time, in which, among other things, the conditions for writing would also be altered for all of us. Or at least for me. After a lifetime occupied in producing more or less academic texts, which is to say, texts fundamentally oriented toward interpretation, which is another way of saying paraphrasis or exegesis, with all its accompanying tics (the necessity of saying something new or relatively new, the necessity of more or less covering the critical tradition for any given issue, the necessity of speaking, in specialized form, to those already specialized, and to do all of that through invitations one receives, with their consequent deadlines and time limitations—always the time of the other, where it was necessary to adapt to their time frame, at the price, when refusing to do any of those things, of becoming something of a pariah, marginalized and forgotten, an outlaw handed over to his or her desert solitude), after so many years I can no longer conceive of returning to such structures—and that is a gift of the viral irruption and of its temporal interruption, which I have lived, or am living, as an interruption in temporality. All those forthcoming conferences needed to be canceled, that is to say, the four or five that I had already planned on attending for the months ahead, whose sequence would have organized my time. In those cancelations another time emerged, which I can no longer understand but as the late time of a return.

What I called above the asymptotic condition of existence, the fact that existence is always already a form of arriving at what cannot be reached, *ankhibasie*—and it is worth recalling here the Nietzschean word: *the smallest of abysses is also the most difficult to cross*—forces, then, a movement that can no longer be exercised in the time of the others, in academic time. If what matters in writing is in every case its autographic drive, that is, its contribution to the decision of existence, does it not become necessary to insist on it, and therefore, to flee from all other modes? Yes, *ankhibasie* is a practice of transfiguration, a practice of transition toward what is important in life more than life itself, however much it remains and should remain in every case unnameable. Perhaps the Nietzsche of *Ecce Homo*, a work definable as a radical anchibasic practice, is the model here. Nietzsche thought that his writing was going to split the history of the world in two; he was going to formulate the possibility of another beginning of thought; he was going to transfigure history. To think *Ecce Homo* was, curiously, my academic task in the days leading up to the viral irruption.

The Derridean interpretation of Nietzsche in *Life Death* revolves around *Ecce Homo*. It is laborious and unfinished and takes the apparent form of a critique of Heidegger's determination of the so-called fundamental position in Nietzsche's work. Derrida focuses those sessions of his seminar on Heidegger's *Nietzsche*, published in 1961, but compiled from materials mostly put together in the 1940s. Derrida begins by referring to an "impossible protocol," the aporetic *pas au-delà*, by asking how that step *out of* life, in life and beyond it, is an impractical and at the same time necessary step. He quotes a fragment from *The Will to Power*: "Life is only a means to something: it is the expression of the forms of growth in power."[156] And he glosses: "Life would not be the last resort, or the origin or the end, only a means toward something else here called 'growth in power,' a growth in power thus referred to a will to power that is no longer in its last or essential form *life*, force of life."[157] If the will to power is no longer a force of life, it must be because it somehow incorporates death unto itself, understanding that death is not opposed to life and that the logic linking life and death is far from being one of opposition: "It is death, I say at the end, a death that is not opposable, that is not different, in the sense of opposite, from the pleasure principle, from the reality principle, or from the difference between them [*la différance détournante*], but is inscribed in the functioning of this structure."[158] The will to power is a form of death that creates a duplicity, an at least partial contradiction, an impossible protocol when invoking its step beyond which is also a not-beyond (*pas au-delà*).

At the beginning of the eighth session of the seminar, Derrida focuses on "how the interpretation of Western metaphysics in its totality, or as totality, implies a decision about unity or the unity of a thought, which in and of itself implies a decision about the biographical, the proper name, the autobiographical, and the signature."[159] For Heidegger "Nietzsche's name . . . is not the name of an individual or a signatory, but the name of a thought, of a unified thought."[160] For Derrida this is a problem, since "at the moment when a certain otherwise-than metaphysics insinuates itself and when Nietzsche is placed at the limit, at the apex of achievement," Heidegger would be reintroducing "a classic gesture that ultimately consists in dissociating the thing from life or from the proper name of the thing of thought."[161] Derrida thinks that Heidegger is moving too fast toward a what-is-Nietzsche, against the very question Heidegger ostensibly thematized: that is, who-is-Nietzsche. But this is not all together fair, in my opinion. Let us look at Heidegger's 1954 essay "Who Is Nietzsche's Zarathustra?," an essay that up to a certain point repeats and summarizes the most essential part of the larger text published in 1961. In my opinion, the interpretive impulse starts from a radically personalized instance, that is, autographic, in the sense that it is the autographic in Nietzsche that is read with the greatest passion, and precisely at the moment in which Heidegger presents his most controversial criticism—the one that bothers Derrida the most—which is the claim that Nietzsche is still a metaphysical thinker, a thinker of metaphysics.

But Heidegger says and claims a bit more than that. These are the final words of the 1954 essay: "That Nietzsche experienced and expounded his most abysmal thought from the Dionysian standpoint, only suggests that he was still compelled to think it metaphysically, and only metaphysically. But it does not preclude that this most abysmal thought conceals something unthought, which also is impenetrable to metaphysical thinking."[162] The most abysmal thought, which is to say, the eternal recurrence of the same,[163] is experienced metaphysically by him because he experiences it as a Dionysian inversion of the Platonic-Christian experience of time. As a direct inversion of metaphysics, it cannot yet abandon (it could not have abandoned) metaphysics: the logic between the Apollonian and the Dionysian is oppositional, much like the oppositional one between the Christian and the Dionysian, and Nietzsche—this is Heidegger's thesis—has not explicitly moved toward a possibility not marked by this opposition. He remains within a contradiction that is, like all contradictions, also a phantasmatic identification. And yet it is a contradiction signed by Nietzsche, inscribed over his very name, and not only in that famous last line of *Ecce Homo*, which reads: "Have I been understood?—*Dionysus against the Crucified*. . . ."[164] I will copy here a paragraph from Heidegger and another from Nietzsche quoted by Heidegger. These two paragraphs mark to my mind the decisive moment of the Heideggerian position regarding Nietzsche as a thinker of the decision of existence. Heidegger says: "'to *impress* the character of Being upon Becoming—that is *the highest will to power*'. . . . This thinking takes becoming under its care and protection—becoming of which constant collision, suffering, is a part. Is reflection-to-date, is the spirit of revenge overcome by this thinking? Or is it that in this 'impressing,' which takes all becoming under the protection of the eternal recurrence of the same, there is nonetheless concealed an aversion to mere transience and, therefore, a supremely spiritualized spirit of revenge?"[165] And this is a quote from one of the drafts of the preface to Nietzsche's *The Gay Science*: "The spirit strengthened by wars and victories, to whom conquest, adventure, danger, even pain have become a necessity; the habituation to sharp mountain air, to wintery walks, to ice and mountains in every sense; a sort of sublime malice and extreme exuberance of revenge—for there is *revenge* in it, revenge against life itself, when one who suffers greatly *takes life under his protection*."[166]

Nietzsche signs his suffering, but that is not enough for him: he also signs the suffering that his suffering causes in him. His decision of existence is doubled, and it traverses the interruption of all decisions of existence. This is the radical moment of autographic inscription on which the Heideggerian interpretation is based. Despite Nietzsche's establishing in *Thus Spoke Zarathustra* that to free oneself from revenge and the spirit of revenge was the ultimate goal of his thinking ("For *that man be delivered from revenge*, that is the bridge to the highest hope for me and a rainbow after long storms"[167]), he himself recognizes that revenge still governs his thinking: if the eternal recurrence of the same is protection against the suffering of revenge, it is still revenge from revenge, and therefore reactive thinking. Precisely here, in this moment of radical autography, wherein Nietzsche recognizes himself within the will to punishment that he had ostensibly tried to avoid, in a sinister doubling, Heidegger situates the "something" that "comes to the fore in Nietzsche's thought which that thinking itself can no longer think."[168] That unthought is what for him also remains "impenetrable to metaphysical thinking," and therefore exceeds it.[169] It is unthought, in *ankhibasie*, but it is an unthought signed as such, registered as such, which exceeds metaphysical parameters to the extent that it moves beyond the mere inversion of temporality (from the aversion to the transcurrent and to the fixation on eternity as a form of a continuous present to the affirmation of becoming or of becoming-who-one-is) to an astonished realization of the trickery and the trap of inversion: there, in the very inversion, a punishment was wanted, a punishment was sought. The decision of existence could rather be revealed, then, as a simple rebellion against its sequestering by a will to revenge. But that wasn't, isn't, enough.[170]

And that is the aporetic point of the impossible protocol of the *pas au-delà*. Is there more, in the decision of existence? Can that decision lead farther than its own intrinsic disappropriation? The subtitle to *Ecce Homo* is *How One Becomes What One Is*. Can that be teachable, or do we end up encountering a limit similar to the limit Derrida perceived in political terms as the impossibility of transcending minor violence? Politics, as a praxis of the subject seeking emancipation, Derrida tells us, is condemned to infinitely repeat its own violence. Emancipation can therefore only be contingent and partial; the difference between one form of politics and another is a difference of degrees, for better or for worse, more or less, and it is therefore ultimately discardable, inessential, forgettable. In the same way, the decision of existence, far from leading to any telic authenticity, finds in its *energeia ateles* the doubling of its possibility into impossibility. And there is therefore no decision of existence, only its illusion: at the moment of greatest appropriation, of greatest authenticity, we see in the mirror the fallen monster of ourselves that we had been trying to disavow. Is that it?

Perhaps beyond the nameable and the teachable, beyond the word, beyond philosophy, there is a gesture, at the limit, that dissolves the aporia. And that gesture, if it appears, if it can *be*, is the gesture that we will never be able to learn from the other, the gesture of the singular secret in all of existence and in every existence. Beyond writing and toward the late temporality of return that dictates the other imperative, this time Derridean: become what you are and learn then how to live.

Remark 7: Infracendence — Unpublished Fragments from Fernando Pessoa's (Posthumous?) Milieu

I found four typewritten sheets among old family papers I had never bothered to examine.[171] Two photographs were glued to them. They are undated, and they seem to be consistent with the delirious style of my uncle Timoteo Moreiras, who was a wolfram smuggler for the British across the Spanish-Portuguese border post of Bande, in Galicia, during the big war. He was arrested by a Civil Guard commander who was new to the post and very severe, and who happened to be a relative of ours, but that is another story. In any case, the commander brought my uncle's career to an abrupt end. Timoteo had many friends in the anti-Salazar resistance. The sheets tell an enigmatic story. Timoteo, who was half a poet himself and an affiliate of the nationalist group Nós, seems to have taken down notes subsequent to a visitation by either a ghost of Pessoa (Pessoa had died a few years earlier, in 1935, if my approximate dating of the sheets is correct — I figure 1941 or 1942) or else by someone from the Pessoa circle. It happened in Vigo, also in Galicia, where several of the Pessoa heteronyms had lived for a time.[172] Ostensibly they deal with the poems of Alberto Caeiro, one of the heteronyms. My uncle seems to have used his own heteronym, a game of brothers, since he signs his name as Alberto Moreira—my grandfather, his brother, was Alberto, but Moreiras, not Moreira. I will transcribe those sheets here, although imperfectly, since I will suppress the typos and flaws of the typescript. I want to do it in particular because there is something infrapolitical in them, above all in the reference to what *transcende para baixo* (transcends from below or toward the below), a nice find. Those sheets, never published, are themselves proof of a certain *survie* of the poetic word in obscure circumstances (those of 1941–42 Galicia) and even beyond death, since the typescript could not have been written without ghosts.

If it was truly my uncle who penned these pages, and not some, for the moment, unidentifiable collaborator of his, he mixes Spanish, Galician, and Portuguese with some English sentences, and he frequently forgets some of the Portuguese circumflexes and accents. A rather mysterious reference to the "ontological difference" links this text more or less directly to the group of cryptofalangists led by Eugenio Montes, another relative of ours, in post–Civil War Galicia. The reader should not be particularly taken aback by the references to ghosts, or the *fantasme*, perhaps just a product of Timoteo's style, a phantasy in itself. In fact, in Galician it is perfectly possible to talk about someone living as a *fantasma* or *fantasme*, even when he is made of flesh and bones: "*Oi, fantasme,* how are you doing today?" Nobody takes offense, although the form of address has undertones of an accusation of tendential dissembling and lying and de-realizing, beyond the reference to a certain de-realization.

What follows is the imperfect transcription of what I found, among other papers, the dissemination of which I will be thinking about, in a cardboard shoe box damaged by time and humidity, with an only semilegible rubric (covered by old mildew) that says: "Calzados Antonio SL, Para su buen pie, Palma de Mallorca":

Notebook of Alberto Moreira, Heteronym

1. I detest pedagogy: "*A única coisa boa que há en qualquer pessoa é o que não sabe.*" (The only good thing about any person is what he or she doesn't know.)

   I encountered Caeiro's ghost in Vigo, at the terrace of La Aldeana, some time ago. He told me: "*O que existe transcende para baixo o que julgamos que existe.*" (What exists transcends from below what we judge to exist.) Transcends from below? Infracendence. To pass a judgment of existence is already to lose the thing.

   "*Uma aprendizagem de desaprender*" (a learning how to unlearn), [he said].[173]

   "*Uma gargalhada de rapariga soa do ar da estrada.*" (Laughter from a girl resounds in the road's air.)

   Dark three piece suit, white cotton shirt, ascot bow tie, English shoes. A cigarette (possibly a Players Navy Cut or a Craven A) dangles from the left corner of his mouth. The radical materialist walks in the city's streets; I suppose he is going to the café or the post office.

   "*Passa un momento uma figura de homem . . . E os passos vão com o sistema antigo que faz pernas andar.*" (A man's figure passes by for a moment . . . And the steps are like the old system that makes legs walk.)

   Is he or is he not the best poet in the world? He said, "*Que a Natureza existe . . . Nunca ninguém tinha pensado nisto.*" (That Nature exists . . . Nobody had ever thought that.) It is "*a maior descoberta que vale a pena fazer e ao pé da qual todas as outras descobertas são entretenimentos de crianças estúpidas*" (the greatest discovery worth making and in comparison to which all the other discoveries are stupid children's amusements).

   Countercartesian. Not I [whatever the I refers to], *that* exists, but it only exists if I do not think it exists. If I think it exists, I've already lost it. It only exists in infracendence. I [exist] not even so, since I am trapped in time.

   Metaphysics without metaphysics. In La Aldeana, as I was eating a crab, he said: "*As coisas não tem nome nem personalidade,*" (Things have neither a name nor a personality.) And: "*Há metafísica bastante en não pensar em nada."* (There is enough metaphysics in not thinking of anything.)

Excessively nothing—there is no other path to things.

2. We had lunch at the restaurant of the Hotel Universal. We had the splendor of the estuary right in front of us, and some sailboats in the docks. The poet *"fala sempre com frases dogmáticas, excesivamente sintéticas . . . com absolutismo, despoticamente"* (always speaks through dogmatic, excessively synthetic sentences . . . with absolutism, despotically). A pain. I asked him: *"O senhor poeta, ama-se?"* (Mr. Poet, do you love yourself?)

Caeiro *"de tal curioso modo acentua o eu, o mim, que se ve a funda emocão com que fala"* (accentuates the I, the me, in such a curious way, that one can see the deep emotion with which he speaks).

"Amo-me." (I love myself.) Because I seek existence not signification. To be a thing is not to signify anything. *"Eu vejo ausência de significaçao em todas as coisas."* (I see an absence of signification in everything.) And *"amo-me."* (I love myself). With the only possible love of the one who does not see transitions [that is, hermeneutic displacements, always false, since nothing refers to anything] in things. I love myself coldly. I am only eyes to see. *"Se não estou doente."* (If I am not ill.)

Only whoever does not think of it exists clearly. It is difficult to have eyes and see only what is visible [note from Alberto Moreiras, the author, not his grandfather: this is Timoteo's reference to his profession as a smuggler, where he trusted only those eyes that could not see. But it is also a reference to the thought that humans tend to fantasize beyond vision and can hardly attain what is merely visible as such.] *"O único sentido das coisas é elas não terem sentido íntimo nenhum."* (The only sense of things is that they have no intimate sense whatsoever.)

The best metaphysics, that of the trees: they neither know for what they are alive nor know that they do not know.

To think is to be sick from the eyes. *"Não sei o que é conhecerme. Não vejo para dentro. Não acredito que eu exista por detrás de mim."* (I do not know what to know myself is. I do not see inward. I do not believe I exist behind myself.)

Cuaderno de Alberto Moreira, heterónimo.

1.

Detesto la pedagogía. "A única coisa boa que há em qualquer pessoa é o que ela não sabe."

Me encontré en Vigo, hace algún tiempo, en la terraza de La Aldeana, con el fantasma de Caeiro. Me dijo: "O que existe transcende para baixo o que julgamos que existe."

¿Trascender para abajo? Infratendencia. Pasar juicio de existencia es ya perder la cosa.

"Uma aprendizagem de desaprender."

"Uma gargalhada de rapariga soa do ar da estrada."

Traje oscuro de tres piezas, camisa blanca de algodón, pajarita y sombrero. Zapatos ingleses. Cigarrillo cuelga de la comisura derecha. El materialista radical camina por la calle de la ciudad, supongo que va al café o a correos.

"Passa um momento uma figura de homem. ... E os passos vão com o sistema antigo que faz pernas andar."

¿Es o no es o maior poeta do mundo? Dijo "que a Natureza existe ... Nunca ninguém tinha pensado nisto." Es "a maior descoberta que vale a pena fazer e ao pé da qual todas as outras descobertas são entretenimentos de crianças estúpidas."

Contracartesiano. No yo, eso existe, pero solo existe si yo no pienso que existe. Si pienso que existe ya lo perdí, ya lo maté. Solo existe en infratendencia. Yo ni eso, por estar atrapado en el tiempo.

Metafísica sin metafísica. En La aldeana, mientras comía una nécora, decía: "As coisas não tem nome nem personalidade." Y "Há metafísica bastante em não pensar em nada."

Excesivamente nada--no hay otro camino a las cosas.

We went up to the Castro in the afternoon. He was saying that there were no trees, only *"muitas vezes uma árvore"* (many times a tree). And not even. Concrete abstraction [taken to a limit of impossibility, beyond anything reasonable], infracendent exercise. Neither *sobreiro* (corn-oak) nor *carvalho* (oak) nor *pinheiro* (pine tree). Only this and that and that.

Ah, mystical soul, absolute materialism. He loves himself so much because he does not have a conscience of his conscience [in Portuguese in the text, but this is not Pessoa's Portuguese]. Ill, he is aware of his conscience. And he hates himself.

To explicitate his facticity is to lose it. To de-realize, to ghost himself. To die. To exist is to exist *"sem nome nenhum"* (without any name).

3. "And what the hell are you doing in Vigo, ghost?" Two things: I am looking for another ghost I met here [to be understood: before the war, when the ghost was flesh and bones], a friend. And I wanted to try the tripe with chickpeas in Adolfo's inn [that tavern, near the Falperra fountain, continued to serve that delicious dish until well into the 1980s every Wednesday. They also served Ponche Cuesta and vanilla biscuits for dessert, or as a snack if one wanted it.]

What there is is all there is. The ghost you do not see and there is none. To look for it is hermeneutics. "Where did you hide, Beloved?" [John of the Cross verse continues: "and left me groaning." But this groan is a proof of illness unacceptable for Caeiro. In the cold love of the real there is only stunned joy.] You cannot follow tracks if you are not ill. "The only occult meaning of things are things themselves" [in English in the original].

Exercitium: I dis-enclose, I de-contain. The *fantasme* (ghost) no longer bothers with time, hence it does not look for presence. I do not want the presence of the friend, I do not seek his temporal trace. "*Não quero pensar nas coisas como presentes; quero pensar nelas como coisas. Não quero separa-las de elas própias, tratando-as por presentes.*" (I do not want to think of things as present; I want to think of them as things. I do not want to separate them from themselves, dealing with them as present.) The *fantasme* is no longer trapped in time. Things are no longer present or absent, not even real. *O exercicio é pensar a coisa sem o tempo que lhes damos, que o fantasme não da mais.* (The

2.

Comimos en el restaurante del Hotel Universal. Teníamos delante el esplendor de la ría, y algunos veleros en la dársena. El poeta "fala sempre com frases dogmáticas, excesivamente sintéticas ... com absolutismo, despoticamente." Una leria. Le pregunté: "O senhor poeta, ¿ama-se?"

Caeiro "de tal curioso modo acentua o eu, o mim, que se vê a funda emoção com que fala."

"Amo-me." Porque busco encontrar existencia y no significación. Ser una cosa es no significar nada. "Eu vejo ausência de significação em todas as coisas." Y "amo-me." Con el único amor posible del que no ve transiciones en la cosa. Me amo fríamente. Solo soy ojos para ver. "Se não estou doente."

Solo existe claramente quien no piensa en ello. Es difícil tener ojos y ver solo lo visible. "O único sentido das coisas é elas não terem sentido íntimo nenhum."

La mejor metafísica, la de los árboles: ni saben para qué viven ni saben que no lo saben.

Pensar es estar enfermo de los ojos. "Nao sei o que é conhecer-me. Nao vejo para dentro. Nao acredito que eu exista por detrás de mim."

Subimos al Castro por la tarde. Decía que no había árboles, solo "muitas vezes uma árvore." Y ni siquiera. Abstracción concreta, ejercicio infrascendente. Ni sobreiro ni carvalho ni pinheiro. Solo esto y eso y aquello.

Ah, alma mística, materialismo absoluto. Amasse tanto porque nao tem consciência da sua consciência. Enfermo, tiene conciencia de su inconsciencia. E detesta-se.

Explicitar su facticidad es perderla. Desrealizarse, afantasmarse. Morir. Existir es existir "sem nome nenhum."

exercise is to think things without the time we give them, which the ghost no longer gives them.) [This last sentence appears in the text without quotation marks, so it may or may not be quoting Caeiro; it is more likely Timoteo trying out his Portuguese, which was good enough but not perfect.]

Entón, ver as coisas sem tempo nem lugar, sem tudo menos o que se vé. Ciencia poética, que não é nemhuma. (Therefore, to see things without time or place, without anything but what can be seen. Poetic science, which is none.) [Same as before: is this a *verbatim* quotation or is it Timoteo mimicking Caeiro's language in symbolic identification with it? I cannot tell.] And so we go.

A new simplicity [in English in the original], said I in the 1914 text. [This, however, can no longer be Timoteo speaking, in spite of the absence of quotation marks, since it is unlikely that Timoteo, who was in 1914 hardly sixteen or seventeen years old, could already be a connoisseur of Caeiro's texts. Caeiro was virtually unknown at the time. In fact, Pessoa developed him into existence that very same year, but Pessoa himself was largely unknown in 1914. Nobody outside of Lisbon knew of him as a promising poet.] *Qué pensas da pedra cando não pensas nela?* (What do you think of the stone when you are not thinking of it?) That is impoetic. What you see is always what you do not see [because you are not thinking of it], but you only see what you do not see [since you do not think of it]. "*O pensamento é uma doença.*" (Thought is an illness.)

You are the greatest world poet because you are an impossible poet, without a word, without a language. In you poetry is its dissolution into a blind gaze, which you turn into a full gaze through blindness itself [this is the way in which Caeiro, a maximum protagonist of what Badiou calls the Age of the Poets, would also at the same time bring the Age of the Poets to closure, well before Paul Celan]. The exercise of poetic unveiling [transpoetic] is a murderous ascesis. And only through that destruction something appears. That something, a remainder, a pain, what is it? [The word "*es*" (is) is erased in the typescript, covered over by two dashes.] (It is not, it only is.) [That second "*es*" is also under erasure, and my impression is that it is not a simple erasure, but something else is intended that cannot be represented in the language, neither in spoken nor in written form.]

This was my friend. Did you see him? [The question seems to refer to the second picture glued to the typescript.][174]

3.

"¿E que carallo andas ti a fazer en Vigo, fantasme?" Dos cosas: busco a otro fantasme que conocí aquí, un amigo. Y quería probar los callos na tasca do Adolfo.

Lo que hay es todo lo que hay. Al fantasme no lo ves y no lo hay. Buscarlo es hermenéutica: "¿Adonde te escondiste, Amado?" No puedes seguir rastros sin doencia. "The only occult meaning of things are things themselves."

Exercitium. Des-encierro, des-contengo. El fantasme ya no ha de ocuparse del tiempo y así no busca presencia. No quiero la presencia del amigo, no busco su rastro temporal. "Não quero pensar nas coisas como presentes; quero pensar nelas como coisas. Nao quero separá-las de elas própias, tratando-as por presentes." El fantasme ya no está atrapado en el tiempo. Las cosas no son ya presentes o ausentes, ni reales siquiera. O exercicio é pensar a coisa sem o tempo que lhes damos, que o fantasme nao da mais.

Entón, ver as coisas sem tempo nem lugar, sem tudo menos o que se vé. Ciencia poética, que nao é nenhuma. Y así andamos.

A new simplicity, decía yo en el texto de 1914. ¿Qué pensas da pedra cando não pensas em ela? Eso es impoético. Lo que ves es siempre lo que no ves, pero solo ves lo que no ves. "O pensamento é uma doença."

Eres o maior poeta do mundo porque eres un poeta imposible, sin palabra, sin lengua. En ti la poesía es su disolución en mirada ciega, que conviertes en mirada plena en la ceguera misma. El ejercicio de desocultamiento es áscesis asesina. Y solo en esa destrucción algo aparece. Ese algo, un resto, una leria, ¿qué es? (No es, solo es.)

Este fue mi amigo. ¿Lo viste?

4. And who were you? [The question is in Galician, so it should be attributed to Timoteo.]

> This one. [Probably a deictic reference to the picture in the last sheet, which the tradition has conveniently agreed is a picture of Pessoa himself.]
>
> Transitive eyes = thought. [But here "thought" is under erasure, which is not the same thing as erased. I suspect it is no mere erasure, not a mere replacement of that white liquid that was used to erase typos when typewriters were in use. But I doubt it existed in Galicia in the early 1940s.]
>
> *Não existo por detrás de mim.* (I do not exist behind myself.)
>
> *Sou partes sem um todo.* (I am parts without a whole.)
>
> "*A Natureza é partes sem un todo.*" (Nature is parts without a whole.)
>
> Multiple of multiples.
>
> *Só penso.* (I only think ["think" showing erasure].) "*Que todos andam a achar e que não acham, e que só eu, porque não fui achar, achei.*" (That everybody is trying to find, and that they do not find, and that only I, because I did not try to find, found.)
>
> *Penso* [under erasure] *o rio.* "*O rio da minha aldeia não faz pensar em nada. Quem está ao pé está só alí.*" (The river in my village does not make you think of anything. Whoever is by it is only there.)
>
> *Saír do tempo e do lugar, saír da presença. Infracendencia.* (To subtract from time and place, from presence. Infracendence.)
>
> We were going to the Roxo [another old restaurant, it still exists]. The interview—with a ghost the view is always interdicted—was coming to an end. I realized the greatness of the poet could not be measured except in the apathetic [but total] repetition of his text. He thought of an ontological difference [in the typescript, "ontological difference" shows erasure] without sacredness. Beyond words. Beyond names and nomination. Impoetic poetry. The rest are traps. "Nothing can give an adequate idea of the work except total quotation of it" [in English in the typescript]. There is no nonpresent language; there is no

4.
¿E ti quem fuches?

Iste.

Olhos transitivos = ~~pensamente~~

Nao existo por detrás de mim.

Sou partes sem um todo.

"A Natureza é partes sem um todo"

Múltiple de múltiples.

Só ~~pense~~. "Que todos andam a achar
e que nao acham,
E que só eu, porque não fui achar,
achei."

~~Pense~~ o río. "O rio da minha aldeia nao faz pensar em nada.
Quem está ao pé está só alí."

Saír do tempo e do lugar, saír da presença. Infradendencia.

Ibamos al Roxo. Anochecía. La entrevista—con un fantasme solo hay
entre-vista—llegaba a su fin. Me di cuenta de que a grandeza do
poeta no podía medirse excepto en la repetición apática de su texto.
Pensó una ~~diferencia ontológica~~ sin sagrado. Más allá delas palabras.
Más allá del nombre, de la nominación. Poesía impoética. Lo demás son
trampas. "Nothing can give an adequate idea of the work except total
quotation of it." No hay lengua impresente, no hay lengua trasespacio-
temporal. ~~Espacio-temporal~~. Solo el ruido o la imagen—"gargalhada de
rapariga"—que son porque no son.

"Vivo a meio dum outeiro/ Numa casa calada e sozinha/ E essa é a
minha definição."

COURTESY OF KRISTI SWEET

trans-spatiotemporal language. Spatio-temporal [under erasure]. Only the noise or the image—"a girl's laughter"—and they are because they are not.

"*Vivo a meio dum outeiro / Numa casa calada e sozinha / E essa é a minha definição.*" (I live on top of a hill, / in a solitary and silent house, / and that is my definition.) [But "*calada*" may also mean "whitewashed," which is Richard Zenith's preferred translation.[175] And yet it seems to me important to underscore the silence in Caeiro's home.]

APPENDIX 1   MORE QUESTIONS FOR JORGE ALEMÁN

A Presentation for 17 Instituto de Estudios Críticos, Ciudad de México, May 25, 2020

No emancipation without thought: thought is a condition of emancipation. But this thought must not be understood as the infinite task of interpretation and deciphering of signs, but rather as an operation, even as an operationalization of existence: a setting into act, a setting into praxis. Thought is an emancipatory operationalization of existence—this would be the initial thesis, although I would rather state it as a question, and a question voluntarily exposed to a confrontation with psychoanalysis and with Lacanian thought. Under what conditions is it possible to understand thought, and one's own thought, as an emancipatory operationalization of existence? Even: as care or *cura*, in the widest sense of the notion, which includes its Latin sense.

The emancipatory operationalization of existence I call thought is primarily reflection on one's own facticity. It goes through a making explicit, in the most radical form possible, of facticity, which is to say, it goes through the understanding and explicitation of one's position in the world, in the structure of signification that surrounds us and that we call world. The old Greek world that can be read in Pindar's Second Pythian Ode is my referent here. Pindar says what has been understood as an imperative: learning or having learned who you are, become that being. The relevant word here is *mathon*, a present participle, on *learning* who you are, become it. Be that one who you know, or will have known, that you are. Or, in the Nietzschean version, become who you are. This is my second question for Alemán: is the Pindaric imperative effective, still acting, on the horizon of Lacanian analysis? Is the Pindaric imperative to be read though psychoanalysis still a call to the emancipatory operationalization of existence from one's own fallen facticity?

To become conscious of it—to make oneself conscious of the task of thought as the task of an explicitation of facticity that has, as such, an emancipatory character—is what I call the decision of existence. All existential decisions must take on what has been learned by acting on the Pindaric. The operationalization of the Pindaric imperative is also the discovery and acknowledgment of one's own finitude, one's mortality. And such a discovery emancipates to the very extent that it leaves behind habits, dispositions, occlusions, and concealments—but it is a leaving behind that is also at the same time a bringing along. This is a strange structure that is nevertheless intuitively graspable: upon getting to know your own facticity, you do not primarily leave it behind, you rather bring it up and along. Emancipation is never simply an emancipation from facticity—that would be pure metaphysics or ontotheology or political theology, depending on the case. You drag your facticity along, bringing it with you, and it is making it sustain your decision of existence that becomes emancipatory. And this is my third question: is a decision of existence conceived along those lines comparable to the Lacanian notion of traversing the phantasy?[1]

Is thought to be understood as an operationalization, a putting into praxis, as a move toward an emancipatory decision of existence? If so, could it be linked to the Pindaric imperative that calls for an unconditional appropriation of one's facticity? And could those two questions amount to the question about the Lacanian notion of traversing the phantasy? The three are antiphilosophical questions, even the very questions of antiphilosophy. For Jacques Lacan the antiphilosopher would have saved the honor of philosophy after having come to express what the analyst understands as the missing page. In the missing page of the analyst, we can cipher the whole problem of emancipation, and also the entire problem of the Pindaric imperative. It is also the problem, not of being, but of nonbeing, of what there is not, the lack at the heart of the existent, or at the heart of the subject. But the operationalization of thought is an attempt at liberating that lack, by making it explicit and bringing it along.

Which brings us to the COVID-19 pandemic. The text that Alemán circulated, titled "Emancipation," says: "The serial extension of death, the automatism in the distribution of corpses, steals from finitude the singular experience of one's own death. The effects of this situation are incalculable." From a certain point of view, then, it can be stated that the pandemic, or at any rate, the biopolitical or economico-biopolitical treatment it receives, cooperates with the serial production of death and with the calculability of corpse distribution. Which means that the economico-biopolitical treatment of death reduces mortals to their condition as bodies, to naked life in the Benjamin-Agamben formulation. In other words, it steals mortality and cooperates with the infinite capitalist production of world as standing reserve. But would it be possible to turn all of that around and to think that the forms of economico-biopolitical treatment of existence in confined pandemic times could bring mortality back to human facticity? Would it be possible to think that *there will be mortals* again, after the pandemic? An emancipatory operationalization of thought, the discovery of the radical facticity of existence, is facilitated by the pandemic experience and hands over at the limit a new experience, a new knowledge of mortality, a new self-understanding that has traversed the phantasy. My fourth question: Is becoming mortal again not a potency of the sinister experience of the pandemic?

APPENDIX 2   FROM A CONVERSATION WITH JAIME

A recent conversation with Jaime Rodríguez Matos led me to reread Jean Birnbaum's interview with Jacques Derrida, which appeared in *Le Monde* a few weeks before Derrida's death.[1] It was Derrida's last interview, done in full awareness of the gravity of the disease that would end up winning the battle and taking his life. The interview, crossed by the difficult pain of "learning how to live" at the end of one's life, in any case an always inconclusive and never finishable task, ends with words that refer to the structural and never-wanted, unenforceable *interruption* of the experience of the appropriation of time. We may call this interruption the structural *interdictum* regarding the possibility of a full appropriation of time (and it may have something to do with the interdiction of thought mentioned at the beginning of this book). It is not an objection against understanding the human being as radically mortal; it is rather the opposite: the interruption makes us mortals, hence it prepares—only it prepares—the possibility of learning how to live. These are Derrida's words: "To feel joy and to weep over the death that awaits are for me the same thing. When I recall my life, I tend to think that I have had the good fortune to love even the unhappy moments of my life, and to bless them. Almost all of them, with just one exception."[2] That singular exception (but you, dear reader, how many exceptions would you propose? It would be better for you not to claim too many) is at the same time an obstacle and a confirmation of the affirmative relation with one's own death. It could not be otherwise. "When I recall the happy moments, I bless them too, of course, at the same time as they propel me toward the thought of death, toward death, because all that has passed comes to an end."[3]

I want to comment on two other moments of the interview, certainly related to the already mentioned one but more narrowly limited to the experience of the intellectual in a direct labor relationship with the university. In the first of them, Derrida, after remembering the extraordinary generation of thinkers that surrounded his life, "from Lacan to Althusser, and including Levinas, Foucault, Barthes, Deleuze, Blanchot, Lyotard, Sarah Kofman, and so on,"[4] speaks about "an intransigent or indeed incorruptible *ethos* . . . without any concession even to philosophy, an *ethos* that does not let itself be scared off by what public opinion, the media, or the phantasm of an intimidating readership might pressure one to simplify or repress. . . . It is thus necessary to save that or to bring it up at any cost. And the responsibility for it is today so urgent: it calls for an unrelenting war against any *doxa*, against those who are today called 'media intellectuals,' against a general discourse that has been preformatted by media powers that are themselves in the hands of certain politico-economic, editorial, and academic lobbies."[5] This was said in 2004, and since then a lot of water has gone under the bridge, almost all of it forgetful of the responsibility Derrida invoked, which is today rather the object of a presumptuous and inane ridicule.

The second of those moments refers to the university understood as an "unconditional" space for the production of truth. Derrida says that Kant posited it particularly "for philosophy, whose superiority derives from the fact that it must be free to say everything it considers to be true, on the condition that it says it within the university and not outside it—and that was my objection to Kant. In the originary concept of the university there is this absolute claim to an unconditional freedom to think, speak, and critique."[6] I believe the last fifteen years or so have radically modified the context out of which Derrida spoke, and that today it is no longer possible to continue to maintain the pretension of that "originary concept of the university," a concept to which the institution no longer responds but that it has instead been avidly burying for years—in a way that I hold to be irreversible, although I would like to be wrong.

Both issues are related: Facebook and Twitter may absolutely mark the possibility of expression, the (political?) battle for the reception of thought may be a battle that can only be fought in the media (we may add Academia.edu), and both things are probably lamentable. But who today believes anybody reads anything that has not been previously posted on Facebook, etc.? When did you last devote yourself, from your comfortable lazy chair, to review the articles published in the volume edited by Professor K. from Bucharest that you had checked out of the library on a whim? The radical decline of the university as a site for the production of truths not directly linked to economic exploitation, and therefore subject to market demands, is systemic with the mode of intellectual production sanctioned by the blessed Facebook public. Derrida could have suspected such developments in 2004, or he could not even have begun to imagine them—we will never know. To my mind, those late Derrida reflections are indicative of the place of a loss, and they convey, from our perspective, a certain naiveté—which is indefensible as naiveté, I regret to say. Derrida remarks: "In principle, the university remains the only place where critical debate must remain unconditionally open."[7] Is that the case? Go plan an open critical debate in the university today and you will see how quickly you will be catalogued as an unconditional fool, and then a poor pariah.

I do not think being thought of as a pariah at the university was Derrida's "sole exception" to the affirmative experience of the eternal return of his past. One can have enough energy to *love* that experience of rejection and to turn it into joy. The problem, in general terms, is that to be perceived in such a way, at the university or on Facebook (but is there today a real difference between the two institutions?), does not help the task of the unconditional production of truths, and it does not help the task of the maintenance of that intransigent or incorruptible *ethos*—a task that has become so openly anachronistic that it is now little more than an archival curiosity. What is there to do, then? What must we give up in order to find, in intellectual life and in its professional praxis, the possibility of "learning how to live"?

APPENDIX 3

FROM A CONVERSATION WITH GERARDO

Gerardo Muñoz published a blog note titled "¿Democracia o anarquía?" (Democracy or Anarchy?). In that text a number of tendencies in contemporary thought come together, among others those associated with Emmanuel Levinas, Derrida, Reiner Schürmann, Giorgio Agamben, and Jacques Rancière. Agamben is the main theoretical reference in Muñoz's text. In *Creation and Anarchy* Agamben says:

> A good description of the so-called democratic societies in which we live consists in defining them as societies in which the ontology of the command has taken the place of the ontology of assertion, yet not in the clear form of an imperative but in the more underhanded form of advice, of invitation, of the warning given in the name of security, in such a way that obedience to a command takes the form of a cooperation and, often, of a command given to oneself.... The free citizens of democratic-technological societies are beings who incessantly obey in the very gesture with which they impart a command.[1]

Think of your iPhone or your laptop computer: to make them work you must follow commands that are inscribed in the gadget. "These apparatuses are defined by the fact that the subjects who use them believe themselves to command them (and in fact push buttons defined as 'commands'), but in truth do nothing but obey a command inscribed in the very structure of the apparatus."[2] Agamben is well aware of the Nietzschean doctrine of the will to power as well as of Heidegger's position regarding technology as the goal and final consummation of metaphysics. Also, of positions such as Jacques Lacan's when he refers to capitalist discourse.[3] Or of Tiqqun in *The Cybernetic Hypothesis*. Agamben gives an example that one would have to use metonymically, as he is referring to the entire structuration of our societies as archic, based on embedded commands. Agamben does not shy away from saying that "anarchy has always seemed more interesting to me than democracy, but it goes without saying that everyone here is free to think as they believe best."[4] He marks a difference between Reiner Schürmann's option—in the book originally titled *Le principe de l'anarchie* (The principle of anarchy), Schürmann proposes a liquidation of the notion of *arché* toward a simple "coming into presence"—and that of Derrida, who attempts to neutralize every *arché* in order to reach a "pure imperative, without any content but the injunction: interpret!"[5] Agamben's anarchic option refers, with some objections, to Schürmann's rather than to Derrida's, in the search for a dismantling of the archic principle of liberal democracy that we might do well to call "hegemony" (but Agamben does not make that explicit).

In the chapter headed "Principle and Anarchy" in *Otherwise Than Being*, Levinas argues that consciousness does not exhaust the horizon of being. The being of beings cannot be considered, as they have been in modernity, under the name of transcendental subjectivity. Or perhaps, perversely, modern subjectivity can be considered to name the being of beings but only in order to immediately claim that there is a me-ontological region that would be placed beyond being and beyond consciousness. Such a me-ontological structure would be, for Levinas, an-archic, as every notion of principle (*arché*) would be on the side of consciousness. Subjectivity is then what is invoked in the phrase "principle and anarchy," as the following words lay out: "Being a theme, being intelligible or open, possessing oneself, the moment of *having* in *being*—all that is articulated in the movement of essence, losing itself and finding itself out of an ideal principle, an *arché*, in its thematic exposition, being thus carries on its affair of being. The detour of ideality [Levinas has just said that "even an empirical, individual being is broached across the ideality of logos"] leads to coinciding with oneself, that is, to certainty, which remains the guide and guarantee of the whole spiritual adventure of being. But this is why this adventure is no adventure. It is never dangerous; it is self-possession, sovereignty, *arché*."[6] It is archic, not an-archic, and it responds to a principle of command and control. Contemporary subjectivity is not only an accomplice; it is the very configuration and the product of will to power, of an ontology of command, of a will to rule at the outset. The subject, consciousness, is will to power.

If there were a "spirituality" beyond the "philosophical tradition of the West," Levinas thinks, it would have to be found beyond consciousness, that is, always beyond archic being. And that would be the place of anarchy—of a dangerous and adventurous anarchy that Western notions cannot offer. Anarchy is presented by Levinas as persecution and obsession. "The subject is affected without the source of the affection becoming a theme of representation": "Anarchy is persecution. Obsession is a persecution where the persecution does not make up the content of a consciousness gone mad; it designates the form in which the ego is affected, a form which is a defecting from consciousness. This inversion of consciousness is no doubt a passivity—but it is a passivity beneath all passivity."[7] Far from being a hypertrophy of consciousness, it hits us with irreparable and never-welcome damage. It comes from the outside. It is not domesticable, and it does not admit any reduction to principle. It is an absolute passion: "This passion is absolute in that it takes form without any a priori."[8] Do we want it or seek it? But that very question can only be a question for a consciousness ruled by the archic. Beyond consciousness we cannot resist the absolute passion, and for Levinas that is all that can be said. Anarchy is therefore for him the call to the unconditional that falls on us from the Other, from otherness, whatever it may be, forcing the dismantling of archic certainty, hence of the principle of consciousness or of consciousness as principle, but also of every ontology of command. What is it, specifically? Levinas calls it "a relation with a singularity."[9] It irrupts from a proximity that we cannot organize or measure, and it is a proximity beneath all distances (it "cannot be reduced to any modality of distance or geometrical contiguity"[10]). It is the "trace": "This way of passing, disturbing the present without allowing itself to be invested by the *arché* of consciousness, striating with its furrows the clarity of the ostensible, is what we have called a trace."[11] The trace is not reducible or tamable, and it does not submit to command. It exceeds or sub-cedes.

Schürmann invokes a "principle of anarchy" as a political response to times he considers of epochal or historical transition, times that he says are characterized by the absence of metaphysical principles of rule; so he tends to naturalize, hence deny, the persecutory aspect of me-ontological anarchy.[12] For him there would be nothing particularly painful in being thrown into an anarchic relation as an obligation and radical exigency. Subjective resources—the resources of the thinker—would be enough to maintain the dangerous adventure of anarchy under control. But this implies that the Schürmannian principle of anarchy could be no more than the still subjective, conscious reaction to the epochal dismantling of metaphysics. If that were the case, his principle of anarchy would emerge, purely and simply, as principle, and as principle of consciousness—in Levinasian terms, therefore, in a still radically modern, hence metaphysical mood. Schürmannian anarchy runs the counter-intentional risk of becoming just another form of principial mastery, or it would even be, as principle, the last form of mastery, the last form of subjective control. At the time of transition, posited as such by the hypothesis of metaphysical closure, metaphysics could still sell tickets for a show of radical consolation and attempted consolidation. But this is not good enough. Anarchy as principle is not an exposition but a counter-exposition. It is a reaction, a domestication, a re-enclosure, a capture and entrapment. And entrapment is, of course, not the way in which Muñoz thinks of it; nor does Agamben. I suspect that Schürmann would not have sponsored it if his early death had not prevented him from continuing his work. His and Muñoz's and Agamben's anarchic proposals do not wish to point to yet another principial or archic configuration. It seems to me that they seek to posit anarchy as a dimension at the limit of democratic politics, as a dimension of it that rejects any reduction to command, rejects any hegemonic capture, delegitimizes any ontology of rule always and in every case.

What about democracy, then? Jacques Rancière understands very well that the problem of a total or absolute democracy is far from being a matter of allowing for the triumph of the forces seeking total or absolute democracy. For him politics is always a polemical and unstable field where every achievement can be reversed and every defeat is temporary. Politics is always at the mercy of the police, even though the police can also suffer political defeat. In his essay "Should Democracy Come? Ethics and Politics in Derrida," Rancière makes it clear that the very concept of democracy is subjected to a radical instability, not because those who govern are sometimes scoundrels, even if they are, but rather because there is a difference inherent in democracy that makes it constitutively incapable of fully accomplishing itself as a form of government. To the very extent that democracy must be understood in every case as "an excess" regarding every form of government,[13] the positing of democracy as *imperium absolutum*, in Spinoza's formulation, makes no sense. But the senselessness of total democracy should not take us to its rejection in the name of some deluded ethical or political purity. In fact, the ethicization of democracy is Rancière's favorite warhorse and the source of most of his critical delegitimations. As a political term, *democracy* for Rancière must fall under exclusively political rationality, even though the latter is far from simple. The rejection of democratic politicity in the name of the ethical law, of some ethical law, is not only philosophically objectionable but even more objectionable from a political perspective. And this is what is ultimately at stake in his confrontation with Derrida. Rancière's fundamental question in that essay is whether deconstruction can come to define a political thought, that is, "a thought of the specificity of the political."[14] His answer is no. Rancière thinks that deconstruction, like Levinasian thought, is incapable of transcending an ethical structuration of existence. But what would happen if we posited, not an ethical structuration, but an anarchic structuration of existence, a fortiori an always irreducible anarchic dimension, always destituent and deconstituent, at the heart of every possible democracy?

For Rancière the very possibility of democracy implies before anything else the renunciation of the principle of legitimacy of government, which amounts to the rejection of any form of *arché*. A citizen in democracy, to the extent that it is defined as the citizen who can indifferently govern or be governed, cancels beforehand the logic of any principle of government. The *demos* in democracy refers fundamentally to an aprincipial principle of indifferentiation, an anarchic principle that dis-joins, that is, it disjunctively enjoins, power and the people. There is no political community without such tension: only an indifferentiation in the principle of power, which means that the only qualification to exercise power is to have no qualification at all, can produce politics, in a context where politics, in order to be politics and not principial domination, must be always already democratic. The part of those who have no part, to use the famous formulation in Rancière's *Disagreements*, is not the subaltern remainder, is not the victim or the disenfranchised or the oppressed; it is not, primarily, formed by any identitarian position; it is rather the very dissolution or indifferentiation of any principle of calculation, or count. We may call such an indifferentiation posthegemonic or anarchic (Rancière does not use those terms)—that is, the posthegemonic or anarchic dimension of democracy. Because it is an indifferentiation regarding any principle of calculation, it tends to be discounted as much as it discounts itself. The agent of discount is what Rancière calls "police." Against the police there stands, in every case, the undifferentiating affirmation, the negation of police negation. Such an affirmation in double negation is politics itself in its constitutive character. It is dissensus in the face of every social consensus, hence its always productively aesthetic character: it opens ever new sensoria, and it installs new regimes of the visible. Posthegemony always irrupts, when it irrupts, through an antagonism regarding every ontology of command, in destituent antagonism, as persecution and obsession. And it hits the structural heart of any hegemony.

For Rancière there is nothing in Derrida that would allow us to suppose that he also thought of politics as the power of the *demos*, as the power of the aprincipial principle of indifferentiation. Rancière says: "[Derrida's] democracy is a democracy without *demos*. What is absent from his perspective on politics is the idea of the political subject, of political capacity."[15] Rancière thinks that if democracy for Derrida is a democracy without a *demos*, it is because Derrida rejects or is incapable of thematizing the idea of a subject of politics. When Rancière condemns as a mere ethics the understanding or the rejection of politics in Derrida, such a condemnation is traceable to the alleged absence of a full subject of politics in Derrida, of a subject capable of taking upon itself the name of *demos* and of acting from such an (im)position, from such an "as if." The political subject in Rancière would be the one who says: I speak and I act as if I, qualified only by my dis-qualifications, were the very name of the people, the very embodiment of the constitutive principle of democratic action. According to Rancière, nothing in Derrida would authorize anybody, that is, any whoever, any nameless agent, to utter those words or to act as if they wanted to utter them. Which preempts the very process of counterhegemonic or posthegemonic convergence. The problem of deconstruction is that deconstruction names no subject of politics. But is Rancière right?

According to Rancière, Derrida cannot understand the demotic subject of politics because for him, as for many, given that it is a "widely accepted idea,"[16] "the essence of politics is sovereignty."[17] For Derrida the sovereign would be the other, that is, the guest who, by unconditionally imposing a law of otherness, the impossible law of unconditional hospitality, excludes from possibility an exigency of reciprocity, an exigency of radical substitutability, hence destroying any indifferentiating position essential for democratic politics. According to Rancière, the theory of sovereignty returns in Derrida as the sovereignty of the other. He substitutes aporia for dissensus, and "aporia means there can be no possibility of agreement in the practice of disagreement, there can be no substitution of the whole by the part and no subject can perform the equivalence of sameness and otherness."[18] Rancière thinks, then, that it is not just that Derrida and deconstruction have no concept of the specificity of politics; what matters even more is that deconstruction evacuates the very possibility of the political practice of democracy.

But if the sovereign is effectively the other, if anarchy is the persecution of the other (with pain resulting in the acquiescence to the other's demands), if we understand anarchy as a persecution and a rupture of the ontology of command in the indifferentiation of posthegemony, then Rancière may not have been sufficiently generous or has remained excessively caught up in his emphasis on subjective consciousness as the hegemonic principle of politics. From such an understanding, it would be possible to reinterpret or to correct—though it is not empirically necessary—the ostensible position in Levinas or Derrida or in other thinkers in the post-Heideggerian constellation and come to agree with what Agamben seems to suggest regarding an anarchic postulation at the very limit of democracy. Except that in democracy the limit is also the core.

APPENDIX 4

ALAIN BADIOU'S AGE OF THE POETS

> Who today would claim that he is equally at home in the essence of thinking and in the essence of poetry? —MARTIN HEIDEGGER

Is it true?[1] Badiou states: "Since Nietzsche, all philosophers claim to be poets, they all *envy* poets, they are all wishful poets or approximate poets, or acknowledged poets, as we see with Heidegger, but also with Derrida or Lacoue-Labarthe."[2] Badiou's provocation was the least of it because his main thesis was even more disturbing: "I maintain that the Age of Poets is *completed*",[3] "the fundamental criticism of Heidegger can only be the following one: the Age of Poets is completed, it is also necessary to de-suture philosophy from its poetic condition."[4] Philippe Lacoue-Labarthe responded gently but in a somewhat panicky tone:

> Should poetry cease to be of interest to philosophy? Must we—as a necessity or an imperative—sever the tie that for two centuries in Europe has united philosophy (or at least that philosophy that is astonished at its origin and anxious about its own possibility), and poetry (or at least that poetry that acknowledges a vocation toward thought and is also inhabited by an anxiety over its destination)? Must philosophy—by necessity or imperative—cease its longing for poetry, and conversely (for there is indeed reciprocity here), must poetry finally mourn every hope of proffering the true, and must it renounce? We would not be asking such a question, or we would be asking it differently, if Alain Badiou had not recently situated it at the very center of what is at stake today in philosophizing—in the very possibility of philosophizing.[5]

This discussion took place in the 1990s but is very much alive today, since we are on the verge of a new epoch of radical disorientation that, alas, has not been preempted by Badiou's conceptualization. "It is no longer required today," Badiou said in 1989, "that disobjectivation and disorientation be stated in the poetic metaphor. Disorientation can be *conceptualized*."[6] Let me anticipate that a full philosophical expression of both "disobjectivation" and "disorientation" remains for Badiou still today the task of a reflection that could not be passed on, without a radical loss of thought's potentiality, to any of the so-called conditions of philosophy—that is, neither to poetry (or art) nor to politics, mathematics (or science), or love. Indeed, the very attempt to solve the problems of the present, that is, of any given present, in exclusive or even overly dominant reference to any of the conditions that produce its truth, in Badiou's terms, is what results in what Badiou calls a "suture," whose undoing becomes then imperative for the sake of philosophy's own freedom. Philosophy does not produce truths because philosophy is not a truth procedure. It is, rather, a reflection on the truth procedures that define any specific age according to its conditions. Poetry, for instance, can produce its own truth, but poetic truth does not totalize or exhaust the possibility, or the necessity, of philosophy's task. Undoing the poetico-philosophical suture restores philosophy's freedom to think on the basis of its four conditions. Of course, the same should be said if the suture of philosophy under examination were politics or scientific procedure.

Badiou's work on modern poetry is extraordinary both in its rigor and in its capacity to abstract formal procedures from the poetic corpus under study. It is not to be considered literary criticism—it is something else. It is, precisely, the philosophical attempt to extract and explicitate a truth procedure from one of philosophy's conditions. But it has a polemical intent, which is what I will try to study and present in this essay. We could summarize it as an anti-Heideggerian intent—and what Badiou radically objects to is what he calls the "sacralization" of the poetic word that seals in Martin Heidegger the void of a historical situation. This becomes explicit, for instance, as we will see below, in Heidegger's essay on Rainer Maria Rilke's poetry, particularly on its introductory remarks on the poetry of Friedrich Hölderlin.[7] But I would like to proceed slowly and cautiously in my own argumentation and not offer conclusions prematurely, not without having allowed readers to see for themselves. This calls for a certain architectonics in my essay, which must rely heavily on Badiou's own statements. I will first offer a reading of what Badiou says about Fernando Pessoa, for Badiou one of the major poets who define "the age of the poets," because the presentation of Pessoa, or of Badiou on Pessoa, will lead directly to Badiou's self-identification with a "metaphysics without metaphysics," to be understood both as a corrective but also as a certain acceptance of the Heideggerian problematic vis-à-vis historical metaphysics. I think it is fair to say that the totality of Badiou's meditation on poetry, hence also his "scandalous" announcement of the necessary end of the age of the poets, is made from the position described as metaphysics without metaphysics. I will continue this with a short engagement with Badiou's essay "The Question of Being Today," where the notion that we must undo the Heideggerian notion of a "saving reversal" in thought leads directly to the rejection of Heidegger's sacralization of the poem, which is also the point where Badiou finds in Heidegger a disavowed metaphysics. The liberation of philosophy from metaphysics is another way of reading the necessary undoing of the poetico-philosophical suture. After those considerations I engage with the series of essays Badiou published on the age of the poets, collected in English in *The Age of the Poets*. The analysis of what Badiou's calls the "fourth relation," as a path that Heidegger could have taken but rejected, will be crucial to understanding Badiou's rupture with Heidegger on poetry. I will finish this appendix arguing that there is no end to the age of the poets except as an end concerning the poetico-philosophical suture at the service of a resacralization of existence. This is not a critique of Badiou's position—I only mean to make it explicit, even though, given that I end with the dangerous thought that Badiou might be considered a "left Heideggerian," my explicitness may have a bit of a bite. In any case, I can only hope that, by the end of this essay, for readers not necessarily familiar with Badiou's complex work, it will have become clear that a sustained attention to Badiou on poetry reveals not at all a dismissal of the truth dimensions of the poetic word, but rather its contemporary rescue—a rescue that I would not hesitate to call "antiphilosophical"—over against the particular mystique of a resacralizing thought that appropriates poetry's truth and places it at its service.

The annotations that follow take up Badiou's work after the precise articulation of his historical diagnosis on the completion of the age of the poets in *Manifesto for Philosophy*. They focus on the first four essays included in Badiou's *Que pense le poème?* (2016), which are also, in slightly altered order, the first four essays of Badiou's *The Age of the Poets* (2014), compiled and edited by Bruno Bosteels and Emily Apter and translated by Bosteels. They are essays from which criticism does not seem to have abstracted the necessary consequences, and which have also been insufficiently read.[8] Beyond achieving as precise as possible an understanding of what Badiou proposes concerning the poetico-philosophical suture and its dissolution, my interest is in determining how Badiou, by going beyond Heidegger and leaving behind what he considers "archi-metaphysical" (and therefore ontotheological, albeit disavowedly so) in Heidegger's metapoetics, enables a new presentation of the thought of the poem, now no longer beholden to the suture of philosophy and poetry.[9] I would not want to suggest that the four essays I seek to annotate exhaust the reach of Badiou's thinking on the age of the poets, roughly to be understood as the age after which we must reinvent the possibility of thought's freedom. Badiou has other things to say on this score and related matters, and he says many of them in his major works, starting with *Being and Event*, which has sections on Friedrich Hölderlin and Stéphane Mallarmé, but also in other works such as *Conditions*, *The Century*, and *Handbook of Inaesthetics*, and in his seminars. The subject has ramifications that extend well into Badiou's concern with "antiphilosophy" and what he calls sophistics. In *The Age of the Poets*, he comes to say that poetry is to the sophist what mathematics is to the philosopher.[10] But Badiou himself, on the basis of his own articulation of the historical specificity of the age of the poets, knows that such a statement is reductive and unsatisfying. After all, the poetry of the age of the poets is credited by him with having accomplished momentous developments in the history of thought. In *Manifesto for Philosophy*, he says: "If poetry has captured the obscurity of time in the obscure, it is because it has, whatever the diversity or even the irreconcilable dimension of its procedures, dismissed the subject-object 'objectifying' frame in which it was philosophically asserted, within the sutures, that the element of time was oriented. Poetic disorientation is first of all, by the law of a truth that makes holes in it, and obliterates all cognition, that an experience, simultaneously subtracted from objectivity and subjectivity, does exist."[11]

And he says: "Until today, Heidegger's thinking has owed its persuasive power to having been the only one to pick up what was at stake in the poem, namely the destitution of object fetishism, the opposition of truth and knowledge and lastly the essential disorientation of our epoch."[12] Declaring the completion of the age of the poets is to declare that Heidegger's thought must be left behind in the name of a new conceptualization that has solved all the impasses in Heidegger's thought.

That is easier said than done. Badiou's conceptualization, important as it is, does not have the power to kill what cannot be killed, which is not Heidegger's thought but rather the problems that Heidegger's thought attempted to confront.

One of the more interesting aspects of Badiou's philosophical self-positioning is precisely his acknowledgment that philosophy is endlessly and irreducibly contaminated by the singular experience of existence, which no scientific discursive thinking, that is, no *dianoia*, may capture. There are as many universalities out there as there are individuals. Poetic truth must be placed and understood in the context of an experience of life that cannot be disposed of by any kind of either deductive or apagogic reasoning. And poetry, together with art in general, is better positioned to express the singular than either science or politics. The present appendix is just a beginning of work on these issues, as it aims to establish a point from which to proceed, a succinct but accurate perspective. My intent is to show that, no matter how powerful Badiou's critique, the notion of the end of the age of the poets should be circumscribed to the precise end of the poetico-philosophical suture, that is, the paradoxical pretense that only poetry was a reasonable resource for thought. The age of the poets may have been completed, perhaps, but Lacoue-Labarthe should not have fretted so much about the severance of the tie between philosophy and poetry, not even in Badiou's own thinking, as I will try to show. Poetry is not the only reasonable resource for thought, but it is one such resource, and it remains an essential one. There has been no end to the poetic drive in philosophical thought, even if the suture itself—the stitching, sewing, tightening up of the borders of philosophy to the borders of poetry—must be given up.

Metaphysics without Metaphysics

Badiou came to know the work of the Portuguese poet Fernando Pessoa late in life. The encounter was enlightening and led Badiou to say that "philosophy is not—at least not *yet*—under the condition of Pessoa. Its thought is not yet *worthy of Pessoa*."[13] He explains his excitement by suggesting that Pessoa's "thought-poem inaugurates a path that manages to be neither Platonic nor anti-Platonic. Pessoa poetically defines a path for thinking that is truly *subtracted* from the unanimous slogan of the overturning of Platonism. To this day, philosophy has yet to comprehend the full extent of this gesture."[14] These are rather extraordinary words for a thinker who has long defined himself as Platonic, in addition to being an obvious disclaimer of his position, according to which "the Age of the Poets is *completed*." He adds a significant observation that might perhaps offer a clue to the simultaneous suspension and affirmation of Platonism in Pessoa's work, which Badiou endorses: "To be worthy of Pessoa would mean accepting the coextension of the sensible and of the Idea *but* conceding nothing to the transcendence of the One. To think that there is nothing but multiple singularities *but* not to draw from that tenet anything that would resemble empiricism."[15] Pessoa's "diagonal path"[16] becomes for Badiou expressive of a poetic truth that presents a condition for philosophical reflection, which must henceforth "follow the path that sets out . . . in the interval that the poet has opened up for us, a veritable philosophy of the multiple, of the void, of the infinite. A philosophy that will affirmatively do justice to this world that the gods have forever abandoned."[17] The latter, as we will see, is a disparaging observation concerning Heidegger's work. Badiou's intention to catch up with Pessoa's poetic truth already takes place in the path of a radical desacralization of thought.

In the same text, and in a manner consistent with the idea of Pessoa's double relation to Platonism, Badiou mentions the phrase "metaphysics without metaphysics,"[18] which he attributes to Judith Balso.[19] It is a phrase that Badiou has used several times, most recently in *L'immanence des vérités*, frequently in reference to Pessoa, but not always. In *L'immanence des vérités*, he goes so far as to say that the only difference between Pessoa and himself is that "Caeiro, inscribing himself . . . into what I have called 'the age of the poets,' writes his metaphysics without metaphysics in the form of short poems and not of long treatises."[20] But "metaphysics without metaphysics" also appears, without a reference to Pessoa, in the final paragraph of a not very well known but significant essay, namely, "Metaphysics and the Critique of Metaphysics."[21] The quote is long but it deserves the space:

> A contemporary metaphysics would deserve the name of metaphysics to the degree that it both rejected archi-metaphysical critique and upheld, in the Hegelian style, the absoluteness of the concept. On the contrary, it would not deserve this name if, elucidating from the beginning the

infinity of being as mathematizable multiplicity, it would lack any reason whatsoever to postulate the undetermined. Doubtless this would no longer properly speaking be a dialectical metaphysics, if it is indeed the case that it would no longer need to have recourse to the theme of a historical auto-determination of the undetermined. Rather, it would affirm, in a Platonic style (and therefore metaphysically) albeit in a style bereft of any hyperbolic transcendence of the Good (and therefore outside of metaphysics) that for everything that is exposed to the thinkable there is an idea, and that to link this idea to thought it suffices to decide upon the appropriate axioms. This is why I could propose that such an enterprise should present itself under the paradoxical name of a metaphysics without metaphysics.[22]

It is worth pointing out that, in those sentences, as he will later do in *L'immanence des vérités*, Badiou defines his own thought in a way that is strictly parallel to his observations regarding Pessoa's work. Yes, the concept is absolute, as the power of the idea is always able to capture the totality of the real. Thinking is being, axiomatically so.[23] But being is not the One: it is multiple, infinite (it is an infinite multiplicity), and atheistic. Badiou's own work, and not just Pessoa's, should be thought of as a "metaphysics without metaphysics." In what follows, I would like to take my own "diagonal path" into Badiou's work to point out the significance he assigns to poetic truth in the context of his own philosophical production, and therefore of his understanding of metaphysics.

Heidegger's Question of Being and Thought's Freedom

In "The Question of Being Today" (1988), Badiou attributes to Heidegger a commitment to a "saving reversal."[24] I think Heidegger's thought can be at least partially taken in a different direction, as Badiou himself does. Heidegger is after all the one who denounced metaphysics as "the commandeering of philosophy by the one,"[25] which is Badiou's starting point in that essay. This is his critique, however, in the form of a question that he tends to answer negatively: "can one undo this bond between being and the one, break with the one's metaphysical domination of being, without thereby ensnaring oneself in Heidegger's destinal apparatus, without handing thinking over to the unfounded promise of a saving reversal? For in Heidegger himself the characterization of metaphysics as history of being is inseparable from a proclamation whose ultimate expression ... is that 'only a God can save us.'"[26] But this is not entirely fair. The sentence from the posthumously published interview does not need to be taken literally, and there is in Heidegger no promise, no guarantee, of a saving reversal.[27] He repeatedly alluded to the possibility that the last epoch of metaphysics, in its very exhaustion, might show on its reverse side a way out. He quoted Hölderlin on "the saving power" that comes with danger, but it is a quotation, even if repeated, and its metaphorics do not strictly belong to Heidegger. Heidegger never said to my knowledge that there *was* a clear way out of the destitute or desolate world at the end of metaphysics (any more than he said that a god *would* save us), only that perhaps there could be one (although, it is true, he said it several times, and it was important to him to be able to say that). He also said, and it may not be all too different from what Badiou himself says, that poetic truth could and should show the way.[28]

After all, the *way out* is what Badiou himself is searching for. He thinks he can find it, for philosophy, in at least one of its conditions, namely, in mathematics in its Cantorian and post-Cantorian form, since mathematics offers the example of a pure "ontology" of the "multiple-without-oneness."[29] But he also finds it in art, politics, and love, to the extent that these truth procedures are in effect purveyors of truth. The task is then to pursue a philosophy based on the renunciation of the power of the one, on the renunciation of any hermeneutical *Versammlung*, not necessarily for the sake of "dissemination" in the Derridean sense, rather for the sake of getting rid of the "historical constraint of ontotheology."[30] And our task is to show how, according to Badiou, poetic truth might help.

Badiou's "The Question of Being Today" accepts the effects of ontotheological metaphysics as diagnosed by Heidegger in *Introduction to Metaphysics* (in his 1985–86 seminar on Heidegger, he actually linked them to the conclusions Karl Marx and Friedrich Engels reach in *The Communist Manifesto*),[31] namely, "the flight of the gods, the destruction of the Earth, the vulgarization of man, the preponderance of the mediocre."[32] Badiou finds in those very effects a "saving" power as well: "Thus the flight of the gods is also the beneficial event of men's taking-leave of them; the destruction of the Earth is also the conversion that renders it amenable to active thinking; the vulgarization of man is also the equalitarian irruption of the masses onto the stage of history; and the preponderance of the mediocre is also the dense luster of what Mallarmé called 'restrained action.'"[33] Philosophy's task, in order to produce whatever philosophy can produce in the way of "saving" or beneficial effects, goes for Badiou through thinking "the immemorial attempt to subtract being from the grip of the one."[34] One could say that this amounts to an announcement of a metaphysics of subtraction over against any metaphysics of presence, and that this is therefore a radically anti-Heideggerian project. But that claim would be wrong because mere subtraction does not found a metaphysics—it destroys it, instead—and because a final commitment to presence, or to the presentation of presence, is certainly not a conclusion one can comfortably derive from Heideggerian thought—not without considerable reservations.[35] It is possible to accept subtraction as an extremely effective way to embark on the destruction of any metaphysics of presence, always linked to the presenting of the one, and such a procedure of thought does not seem to me incompatible with a certain Heideggerian inheritance, or with a certain way of appropriating the Heideggerian inheritance.

Badiou's essay goes on to a reading of Plato's correction to Parmenides on the notion that only being *is*, that being is the one, and that the one can only be—the one is *not*, and what about it?—something he has also discussed in several of his seminars. He then proceeds to examine the impossibility of defining the multiple ("definition is the linguistic way of establishing the predominance of the entity"[36]), as testified to by Lucretius and then by axiomatic, mathematical thought. In mathematical ontology, which is not philosophy, only a condition of philosophy, Badiou finds the necessary resource to move away from destinal constraints toward a freedom of thought whose exercise is the task of philosophy in the present. Subtractive thought is primarily an-archic thought: "once ontology embraces . . . a thinking of pure inconsistent multiplicity, it has to abandon every appeal to principles. And conversely, . . . every attempt to establish a principle prevents the multiple from being exhibited exclusively in accordance with the immanence of its multiplicity."[37] An-archic thought has been linked to Heidegger by Reiner Schürmann and others.[38] Badiou is as committed as Heidegger to an a-principial thought away from hegemonic commonplaces, but he still thinks Heidegger is a thinker of a specifically salvific teleology. He says: "Thought—albeit at the price of the inexplicit or of the impotence of nominations—tears itself from everything that still ties it to the commonplace, to generality, which is the root of its own metaphysical temptation. And it is in this tearing away that I perceive thought's freedom with regard to its destinal constraint, what could be called its metaphysical tendency."[39]

A Mutual Liberation

Mathematics is not philosophy, only one of its conditions, in the same way that poetry is not philosophy, but philosophy must think poetic thought, it must bring poetry into its form of reflection, not being itself poetry. Any number of readers in our present are put off by Badiou's insistence on an ontology of the multiple-without-oneness derived from post-Cantorian mathematics, partly because they know no mathematics and feel disoriented by the appeal to it. Approximately the same number of readers are equally put off by what they assume to be Badiou's abjuration of poetry in his declaration of the notion that Paul Celan, confronted by the silence of the philosophical master, brought the age of the poets to its end, as if that meant that poetry is finished as a resource for thought and from now on we can only think politically or mathematically, or preferably mathematico-politically.[40] They fail to understand that what is meant by Badiou regarding the end of the age of the poets is at the same time a liberation of both poetry and philosophy into, respectively, their truth and their conditions. This is subtle, but not excessively subtle: the end of the age of the poets is an end to the "suture" of philosophy and poetry as an exclusive source of meaning, but it is not an end to the philosophical import of poetry or the poetic import of philosophy.

The point for Badiou, speaking as a philosopher and not as a poet, is that the end of the age of the poets liberates poetry from its suture to philosophy as much as it liberates philosophy from its suture to poetry. The suture itself was epochal, that is, historically contingent, and a derivation of a radical malaise in thought: given the fact that philosophy, in the guise of positivism and analytic philosophy on the one hand, and in the guise of Marxism and historical materialism on the other hand, found itself sutured to science and to politics, a dissenting faction emerged whose most eminent representative would prove to be

Friedrich Nietzsche. Nietzsche initiated, on the philosophical side, and through procedures that Badiou would later name antiphilosophical, a suture of thought to art, initially through his engagement with Richard Wagner's work and orientation.[41] Heidegger is the second great name of philosophy in the age of the poets, which is why Heidegger's failure to respond to Celan's demand concerning the Nazi Holocaust destroys the suture and opens a new path, registered as imperative, both for philosophy to respond to poetry's demands and for poetry to persist in its own specific register, now liberated from the need to account for a sense of the world, and for a sense of sense. Far from establishing a new or renewed destitution of thought, the end of the philosophical age of the poets enables philosophical reflection by cutting the knot that sutured it to poetry and doomed it to think of itself as a producer of poetic truth—in the specific sense of sacred or auratic truth, as we will see below.

Philosophy must now think of poetry as one of its conditions. This is probably an even more demanding predicament: the task for philosophy regarding poetry may yet be more arduous today, hence even more important, than it was during the age of the poets. The same is the case for philosophy regarding political or scientific truth, or the truth of love. The stakes have gone up in and after the process of the necessary de-suturing of philosophy to its conditions. Badiou's work actually says nothing else. The liberation of philosophy from its suture to truth procedures rescues philosophy from its twentieth-century impasses and restores it to its position as the holder of the site of thought's freedom. The freedom of thought is a not-so-paradoxical consequence of the fact that philosophy is under no obligation to produce political truth, scientific truth, erotic truth, or poetic truth. It only inhabits their paths, and learns from them, and perhaps subverts them.

The Fourth Relation

In the third essay of the series I am concerned with, namely, "The Philosophical Status of the Poem after Heidegger," Badiou detects three historical "regimes"[42] for the link between poetry and philosophy in order to postulate a "fourth relation between philosophy and poetry."[43] Since this fourth relation is the relation that Heidegger himself failed to establish, in Badiou's assessment, it is at least plausible to think that it is the relation Badiou himself favors. If so, it is the relation that will determine the link between philosophy and poetry at the end of the age of the poets; more precisely, after its end. "What will the poem be after Heidegger—the poem after the age of the poets, the post-romantic poem? . . . This is something the poets will tell us, for unsuturing philosophy and poetry, taking leave of Heidegger without reverting to aesthetics, also means thinking otherwise the provenance of the poem, thinking it in its *operative distance*, and not in its myth."[44] Badiou proceeds to mention "two indications"[45] that amount, if not to a definition, at least to a naming of the task of poetry. We must take them to be proleptic indications, to the extent they were provided by poets of the age of the poets and not by poets after Heidegger. One of them comes from Mallarmé, and it concerns "the moment of the reflection of its pure present in itself or its present purity."[46] The poem, in the purity of its present, names "what is present only insofar as it no longer disposes of any link with reality to ensure its self-presence."[47] Poetry would then be "the thought of the presence of the present" insofar as the present would have transcended its reality as a form of eternity.[48] The second indication comes from Celan. Badiou glosses: "When the situation is saturated by its own norm, when the calculation of itself is inscribed in it without respite, when there is no more void between knowing and foreseeing, then one must *poetically* be ready to be outside of oneself."[49] The step outside of oneself is an event extracted from the void of sense, from a lack of signification: a leap. Badiou concludes his essay by saying, not that those two indications define the poem of the future, but rather that they define what a poem "liberated from philosophical poetizing" "will always have been:" "the presence of the present in the traversing of realities, and the name of the event in the leap outside of calculable interests."[50] We take this to be the conception of the poem in the fourth relation, according to Badiou. What are the first three, and how is this fourth relation post-Heideggerian?

In Parmenides's poem there is a tension between the sacredness of the mytheme, which is the structure of authority under which the poem declares its truth, and the truth the poem itself purports to convey, which we could sum up in the notion that only being is.[51] The second is, Badiou says, necessarily desacralizing. The desacralization of apagogic reasoning, which is what medieval philosophy called the *reductio ad ab-*

surdum, has no need to rely on anything but its own force of argumentation. "The matheme, here, is that which, making the speaker disappear, emptying its place of any and all mysterious validation, exposes the argumentation to the test of its autonomy, and thus to the critical or dialogical examination of its pertinence."[52] This is the regime of what Badiou calls *fusion*, where the power of the argument is subordinate to the sacral authority of the enunciation itself. In Plato a relation of *distance* obtains. Plato wants to expel the poets from the Republic, as he has understood that "philosophy cannot establish itself except in the contrast between poem and matheme, which are its primordial conditions (the poem, of which it must interrupt the authority, and the matheme, of which it must promote the dignity.")[53] The Aristotelian moment is a moment of *inclusion* in which the poem comes under the jurisdiction of philosophical knowledge, which it classifies as a regional discipline that will later be called aesthetics. The poem has now become an object and is to be treated as such. "In the first case, philosophy envies the poem; in the second it excludes it; and in the third it classifies it."[54]

And Badiou, who wants to take his own distance from Heidegger, wishes now to know what Heidegger's thinking is. And he says: "Heidegger has subtracted the poem from philosophical *knowledge*, in order to render it into *truth*."[55] Heidegger thoroughly ruins the aesthetic approach without, however, compromising with Platonic distance. As a philosopher of the age of the poets, Heidegger privileges the "*operations* by which the poem takes note of a truth of its time," which, for the Heideggerian period, becomes the destitution of the category of objectivity in ontological presentation, which is a radically anti-Platonic gesture.[56] This means—"unfortunately" (40), says Badiou—that what is left is either a return to the sacralization of the saying or the thinking out of a "*fourth relation*."[57] Heidegger opts for the former: "Heidegger prophesies in the void a reactivation of the sacred within the undecipherable coupling of the saying of the poets and the thinking of the thinkers."[58]

The *fourth relation*, which is the relation that opens up at the end of the age of the poets and as a condition of the renewal of a desutured link between philosophy and poetry, is therefore what needs to be thought out or understood beyond the "two indications" given above, which referred both to pure presentiality and to a leap into the void beyond all calculation. If we understand Badiou correctly, this means that pure presentiality and the need for a leap into the void beyond calculation become, not philosophical truths, but rather conditions of philosophy.

Let me now move to "L'âge des poètes" ("The Age of the Poets"), the essay published as the second chapter in *Que pense le poème?*—but placed as the first chapter in the English-language collection of Badiou's essays on twentieth-century poetry and prose. He is very clear: the "age of the poets" is neither a historicist nor an aesthetic category (it does not mean to put all poetry of the time under a periodizing category; it does not pass judgment on which poets, by belonging to the age, are therefore the greatest poets). It is rather a philosophical category: "the moment proper to the history of philosophy in which the latter is sutured" to poetry.[59] This applies to certain poets or to certain poems within the epoch's poetic production. They are poets who accept the suture, and its injunction, and respond to it. Among them Badiou mentions Arthur Rimbaud and Mallarmé, Georg Trakl, Pessoa and Osip Mandelstam, and Celan. In their work "the poetic saying not only constitutes a form of thought and instructs a truth, but also finds itself constrained *to think this thought.*"[60] Thinking the thought of poetry, which poetry in the age of the poets does, is already a move toward the poetico-philosophical suture. It enables it without constituting it.

Take the poems of Alberto Caeiro, one of Pessoa's heteronyms. "For Caeiro, the essence of thought is to abolish thought."[61] In Caeiro's poetry, "being does not give itself in the thought of being, for all thinking of being is in reality only the thinking of a thought."[62] Caeiro abolishes the *cogito* in order to liberate being to a radical exteriority no longer constrained by modern subjectivism: "I try to say what I feel/Without thinking about things I feel."[63] Conscious reflection is an obstacle to the purity of presence, and it must be abolished so that being may come into its own. Caeiro's operation is an example. Other operations configure the truths of the poem in the age of the poetico-philosophical suture. Badiou names three, and I propose that they be added to the "two indications" in the *fourth relation* of poetry and philosophy. The first is "counter-romanticism," which subtracts the poem from the image and the dream in favor of the presentation of a counter-image in the form of a "tacit concept."[64] In the age of the poets there is a prohibition of the image in the thought of the poem. The second one is "detotalization."[65] There is a "separate, irreconcilable multiplicity" that is also inconsistent.[66] And the third one is "the diagonal,"[67] which is the attempt or the wager "that a nomination may come and interrupt signification."⁶⁸ Take, for example, Trakl's verse: "It is a light, which the wind has blown out."⁶⁹ But if the wind has blown out the light, then the light does not appear—or appears only poetically. "The poetic diagonal declares that a faithful thought, thus capable of truth, makes a hole in whatever knowledge is concentrated in significations. It cuts the threads, for another circulation of the current of thought."⁷⁰ This involves, Badiou points out, an endeavor of deobjectification, insofar as the object is "what disposes the multiple of being in relation to meaning or signification."⁷¹ And it also involves a "disorientation in thought,"⁷² since the sum of those operations "put[s] under erasure the presumption of a sense that gives meaning and orientation to History."⁷³

We have, then, as preliminary conditions of the *fourth relation*, pure presentiality and a leap into the incalculable, the thinking of the abolition of thinking within the poem, the prohibition of the image, the affirmation of an irreconcilable and inconsistent multiplicity, the active production of holes in signification, and the abjuration of a sense of history. Through its operations, the poetry of the age of the poets dismantles the pretensions of both the scientific and the political sutures of philosophy. And it "bequeaths to us, in order to liberate philosophy, the imperative of a clarification without totality, a thinking of what is at once dispersed and unseparated, an inhospitable and cold reason, for want of either object or orientation."⁷⁴ Badiou's question is whether philosophy can be faithful to that legacy, and his claim is that Heidegger failed to be so for the sake of engaging in a faux resacralization that betrayed the philosophical mission that already the Greek first beginning had determined to be the task of philosophy proper. This is intricate, for sure. But in the final analysis it amounts to positing that not just poetry in general but the very poetry of the age of the poets must be subjected to a de-sacralizing operation in order to liberate both poetry to itself and philosophy to its multiple conditions. Poetry is not the end goal of philosophical reflection—no more than politics or love or indeed scientific knowledge. A liberation of philosophy onto itself is therefore to be understood as the interruption of any one suture of philosophy to any one of its conditions—in our case, the interruption of the resacralizing suture of philosophy to poetry. To the extent that the poetry of the age of the poets had itself already renounced the work of sacralization, the announcement of the end of the age of the poets is really the unconcealment of Heidegger's operation of faux resacralization, conditioned by a disavowed ontology of the one. It is also the liberation of poetry from what we have to consider a Heideggerian sequestering of it.

Plato's Restitution

Before going on to the other two essays in the series I want to dwell for a moment on a difficulty that the reader may already have sensed: the poetic truth that Badiou's extraordinary analysis unveils is established by the constellation of poets that configure the age of the poets. Badiou's claim is that poetic truth conditions philosophical reflection, which must be commensurate with—that is, it must measure up to—the rigor of poetic discovery. Even if poetry is only one of its conditions, philosophy cannot be oblivious to it, but must let itself be determined by poetic saying. The fourth relation, in other words, constrains philosophy, which must find its freedom not in a refusal to meet the truths of its conditions, poetic or otherwise, once they are analytically determined, but rather in what can only be understood as a consistency with them. The fourth relation establishes a rule of consistency for philosophical reflection. This is nothing less than a paradox, since at the core of the poetic analysis we find "an irreconcilable and inconsistent multiplicity." The paradox is compounded, to my mind, by the fact that it is the poetic truth of the age of the poets that issues a rule of consistency to philosophy in the fourth relation, which can only be thought of as the relation that obtains at the end or after the end of the age of the poets, when the suture of philosophy to poetry has been arguably dissolved. I will come back to this. Let me now annotate the second essay in the English-language compilation, which is the first in the French volume, namely, "What Does the Poem Think?"

Faithful to the poetic truth of Alberto Caeiro's work, and in fact to the other truths he has delimited in the constellation of the age of the poets, Badiou insists that the poem is a form of thought and not of knowledge: "Not only does the poem have no object, but a large part of its *operation* aims precisely to deny the object, to ensure that thought no longer stands in a relation to the object. The poem aims for thought to declare what there is by *deposing* every supposed object. Such is the core of the poetic experience as an experience of thought: to give access to an affirmation of being that is not arranged as the apprehension of an object."⁷⁵ Through "subtraction" and "dissemination"⁷⁶ the poem "disconcerts" philosophy, that is, traditional philosophy, because "at the furthest remove from knowledge, the poem is exemplarily a thought that is obtained in the retreat, or the defection, of everything that supports the faculty to know."⁷⁷ This is the reason why the poem, or rather, the poem that is consistent with the inconsistent multiplicity of an affirmation of being that radically subtracts from knowledge, is "haunted by a central silence," and it is from there, from the point of that void in the situation, that it prepares its leap into the incalculable: "A pure silence, devoid of anything sacred, it interrupts the general racket. It lodges silence in the central framework of language and, from there, skews it towards an unprecedented affirmation. This silence is an operation. And the poem, in this sense, says the opposite of Wittgenstein. It says: I create silence in order to say that which is impossible to say in the shared language of consensus, to separate it from the world so that it may be said, and always re-said for the first time."⁷⁸

It is a silence with a bite: it ruins discursivity. It is radically antiphilosophical. It ignores *dianoia* (discursive thinking) and every kind of philosophical argumentation. It is "incalculable thought."⁷⁹ If *dianoia* is philosophical procedure, and if it is to be understood as "the thought that passes through, the thought that is the traversing of the thinkable,"⁸⁰ the poem targets the insufficiency of *dianoia*, which is also philosophy's insufficiency. At the end of *dianoia*, *epekeina tes ousias* (beyond substance), beyond every possible knowledge of the entity, Badiou says, "the poem is a thought in its very act, which therefore has no need to be also the thought of thought."⁸¹ This is what makes the ancient dispute between philosophy and poetry necessary, which Plato evoked: *palaia tis diaphora philosophia te kai poietike*—the ancient discord that the suture of philosophy and poetry had dreamed of suspending or reconciling.⁸² We can perhaps now better understand the implications of Badiou's definition of the poetry of the age of the poets in the first essay I examined: "The poems of the age of the poets are those in which the poetic saying not only constitutes a form of thought and instructs a truth, but also finds itself constrained to *think this thought*."⁸³ The intrusion in poetry of the thought of thought echoes the intrusion in philosophy of the strange and inconspicuous "light, which the wind has blown out": the ancient dark light of withdrawing being. We are back to the unheard-of meditation of Alberto Caeiro, according to which "being does not give itself in the thought of being, for all thinking of being is in reality only the thinking of a thought."[84]

It is now possible to understand that the posited rupture of the poetico-philosophical suture is far from being an abjuration of poetry, and that there was no need for Lacoue-Labarthe to worry. Poetic truth persists at the end of *dianoia* without being claimed by it. And yet *dianoia* must not ban it. But Plato did. The core of the fourth essay I wish to examine concerns the insufficiency of the Platonic gesture of violence against the poets in *The Republic* for the configuration of philosophy in our present. The fourth relation determines thought's freedom not through the abjuration of poetic truth but rather through the opening of thought to the determinations of poetic truth in the age of the poets. The consistency of philosophy must thus be understood as an acceptance of the radical inconsistency of objectless being. Heidegger is said to have recoiled in the face of it, toward the sacred of the first regime of the link between poetry and philosophy. Badiou persists in philosophical de-sacralization while remaining faithful to poetic operations. This is, I believe, the extent of the difference Badiou claims from Heidegger, which still retains Badiou in the Heideggerian wake and enables us to understand why the end of the age of the poets is a limited or restrained end, itself a philosophical operation through which philosophy opens itself again to its political and scientific and erotic conditions. I think the fourth essay in the series, "Philosophy and Poetry from the Vantage Point of the Unnameable," which is the last one I am commenting on here, points out the stakes for the futures of philosophy after the Heideggerian suture.

The Incalculable Wager

Let me recapitulate the list of poetic truths in the age of the poets, which forms a non-totalizing but epochal account of poetic destiny after the twentieth century: pure objectless presentiality and a leap into the incalculable; the thought of the abolition of thinking within the poem for the sake of a liberation of exteriority; the prohibition of the image, which always hides more than it reveals; the affirmation of an irreconcilable and inconsistent multiplicity as unnameable being; the active production of holes in signification, which amounts to a liberation of language from the constraints of inscription; and the surrender of a sense of oriented history. If reflection on what is imperative about those truths determines philosophy, the ensuing philosophical reflection will be opposed to any kind of archeo-teleo-onto-theology. It will be an an-archic philosophy without principles; it will suspend any positing of ends; it will understand being as the very void of ground; and it will not submit to any paternal sacredness or indeed to sacredness of any kind. Beyond that, it will only affirm thought's freedom to proceed to an order of singular, contingent, existential nomination. Is that Badiou's philosophy? I believe it is, in spite of everything.

Poetry bothers and disconcerts philosophy not simply because philosophy, a dianoetic process that believes in the transparency of the matheme and wants to get as close to it as possible, abhors "the metaphorical obscurity of the poem."[85] In particular, the poetry of the time of the poetico-philosophical suture, as we have seen and Badiou now repeats, "identifies itself as thought. It is not only the effectiveness of a form of thinking proffered in the flesh of words; it is also the set of operations by which this thinking thinks itself."[86] The poetry of the age of the poets has therefore usurped some of the functions of philosophy (since "philosophy . . . has no other stakes but to think thinking, to identify thought as the thinking of thinking"[87]). Double jeopardy: if poetry is also the thought of thought, then philosophy must include poetry in its purview, because philosophy is the thinking of thinking, therefore also the thinking of the thinking of thinking. Poetry has lodged deep into philosophy, in ways that are now more pervasive than they presumably were in Platonic times, and even in Heideggerian times. Philosophy has no choice but to deal with it, short of merely disavowing it as a condition of itself, thus betraying itself.

But there is another problem: mathematics, the model science, the paradigm of philosophy's dianoetic method, has evolved into an erratic situation, has been traversed, after Georg Cantor, Kurt Gödel, and Paul Cohen, by a principle of errancy "on which it cannot put a measure."[88] Mathematics and poetry have begun to move toward each other, very much against the Platonic injunction of radical distance. "At the same time that the poem arrives at the poetic thought of the thinking that it is, the matheme organizes itself around a point of flight in which the real appears as the impasse of all formalization."[89] Both poetry and mathematics, as conditions of philosophy, find their contemporary abyssal ground, are de-grounded, by a point of unnameability that is at the same time their power and their powerlessness: "Any truth stumbles upon the rock of its own singularity, and only there can it be announced, as powerlessness, that *there is* a truth."[90] This stumbling block is for Badiou to be named as *the unnameable*,[91] since truth can, neither in poetry nor in mathematics, force its nomination. The mathematical unnameable is consistency, just as the poetic unnameable is power. Both are simultaneously done and undone in unnameability as nomination. And this is Badiou's move: "Philosophy will place itself under the double condition of the poem and the matheme, both from the side of their power of veridiction and from the side of their powerlessness, or their unnameability."[92] Finally, against Plato, Badiou must choose, and paradoxically as the very condition of his exit from the age of the poets, to "welcome the poem in our midst, because it keeps us from supposing that the singularity of a thought can be replaced by the thought of this thought."[93] If so, then the task of poetry from the perspective of philosophy is far from having been completed. This final appeal to the singularity, contingency, and inconsistency of thought, from which alone a word, in the form of a wager, can be issued toward the incalculable, means, for me, that philosophy has now become open to thought's freedom, which is the rare freedom of existence.[94]

How to Live

The essay titled "The Age of the Poets," we are told, "was first published in French as part of the seminar at the Collège International de Philosophie organized and subsequently edited by Jacques Rancière under the title *La politique des poètes: Pourquoi des poètes en temps de détresse?*[95] The question in Rancière's title quotes first of all Hölderlin's "Bread and Wine" elegy, but secondarily it is a reference to a great and controversial lecture delivered on the occasion of the twentieth anniversary of Rainer Maria Rilke's death in 1946. Heidegger's "Why Poets?" lecture opens in immediate reference to Hölderlin's elegy and quotes the words omitted in the lecture's title: "in a desolate time."[96] Most of "Why Poets?" focuses on Rilke's later poetry, from the *Duino Elegies* and the *Sonnets to Orpheus* to even later texts and some of his letters, but I would like to concentrate, in order to move toward my conclusion, on the first few paragraphs of it, which have to do not just with Hölderlin but also with the Heideggerian determination of the historical time between Hölderlin and himself as an age of poetry or an age of the poets. Our "desolate" time is presented by Heidegger as the time of the death of God and the death of divinity. Heidegger says: "In the default of God notice is given of something even worse. Not only have the gods and God fled, but the radiance of divinity is extinguished in world-history. The time of the world's night is the desolate time because the desolation grows continually greater. The time has already become so desolate that it is no longer able to see the default of God as a default."[97] The age of the world's night is the age of the poets because "the abyss of the world must be experienced and must be endured. However, for this it is necessary that there are those who reach into the abyss."[98] When poets reach into the abyss they find "the tracks of the fugitive gods."[99] This has consequences: the "aether," as it shelters the tracks of the fugitive gods, is "the sacred."[100] "Yet who is capable of tracing such tracks? Tracks are often inconspicuous, and they are always the legacy of instruction scarcely divined. This is why the poet, at the time of the world's night, utters the sacred. This is the reason that the world's night, in Hölderlin's language, is the sacred night."[101] The world's night is the time of desolation. At such a time, "the condition and vocation of the poet have first become poetic questions for them. That is why 'poets in a desolate time' must specifically speak the essence of poetry in their poems."[102] The essence of poetry is to dwell in the sacred but empty night of the death of God. The death of God is the final accomplishment of the metaphysical destiny of Western humanity, which, in Hölderlin, Heidegger tells us, manifests itself "more intimately" than in any other poet of his time.[103] Because Hölderlin's poetry dwells in an essential "manifestness of being within the fulfillment of metaphysics" and at the same time dwells in and experiences "the extreme oblivion of being,"[104] it forces philosophy into a particular necessity: "by thinking soberly in what is said in his poetry, to experience what is unsaid. If we enter upon this course, it brings thinking and poetry together in a dialogue engaged with the history of being."[105]

The last sentence perhaps organizes for twentieth-century thought the (contested) age of the poets as the age of the poetico-philosophical suture. If philosophy takes its word for it, without critique, through a submission to a principle of poetic authority, the poetico-philosophical suture is consummated. This is essentially what Badiou means to undo.

In Heidegger, philosophy takes its word for it in the name not directly of the sacred but of an active search for the tracks of the sacred, which at the time of the consummation of metaphysics tracks the flight of the gods but also awaits "the advent of the fugitive gods," that is, their possible return.[106] In the context of such powerful imagery, it might seem superfluous to point out that Heidegger, in the rest of the essay, where he is no longer glossing Hölderlin, is concerned with an analysis of Rilke's poetry as still under the sway of metaphysics, concretely under the sway of a Nietzschean interpretation of being as will to power. But his conclusion reintroduces the theme of the return of the sacred. In the translation that follows *das Heile* is translated as "the whole" and *heil-los* as "the unwhole": "Because they experience unwholeness as such, poets of this kind who risk more are underway on the track of the holy . . . The unwhole, as the unwhole, traces for us what is whole. What is whole beckons and calls to the holy [*das Heilige*]. The holy binds the divine. The divine brings God closer."[107] The poets "of what is whole" are "poets in a desolate time" for whom "Hölderlin is the forerunner."[108] The poets of the age of the poets, who organize and even direct the dialogue between poetry and philosophy with the history of being, are poets of the holy, poets of the sacred, poets concerned with the flight and the return of the gods. This is something that Badiou cannot bear, and the very motor of his position.

It is no doubt the reason why Badiou's "The Philosophical Status of the Poem after Heidegger" is explicit in his denial: "Now philosophy cannot begin except by a desacralization: it installs a discursive regime that is its own, purely earthly legitimation. Philosophy demands that the mysterious and sacred authority of proffered profundity be interrupted by the secularism of argumentation."[109] There is to be no dialogue between poetry and philosophy in the name or under the yoke of the sacred. Only a *fusion* regime, such as the Parmenidean one, would tolerate the contrary state of affairs. The development of a *fourth relation* in the link between poetry and philosophy, which establishes poetry as truth procedure as a condition of philosophy, also at the same time subjects poetry to a philosophical and philosophically de-sacralizing critique. Let us remember the minimal definition of the fourth relation: poetry is "the presence of the present in the traversing of realities, and the name of the event in the leap outside of calculable interests." The sacred appears as a "calculable interest." This is the real rupture away from the age of the poets, which is not the end of the philosophical efficacy of poetry; it is simply a reorientation of purpose.

In the "Art and Poetry" chapter of his study of Badiou, Peter Hallward highlights points made in Badiou's *Handbook of Inaesthetics*: "Whereas mathematics composes the truth of 'the pure multiple as the primordial inconsistency of being as being,' being evacuated of all material presence or sensual intensity, 'poetry makes truth of the multiple as presence come to the limits of language. It is the song of language insofar as it presents the pure notion of *there is* in the very erasure of its empirical objectivity.'"[110] This is consistent with the first part of the minimal definition of the fourth relation that organizes the post-sutural link of poetry and philosophy. Why then is Hallward so resolute in declaring that "during the true age of poetry (roughly, from Rimbaud to Celan), poetry rightly took on some of the functions abandoned by a philosophy temporarily preoccupied with the sterile hypotheses of scientific positivism and historical materialism. This age, however, has now passed. The poem is simply incapable of a genuinely philosophical self-awareness. The poem declares the Idea, but not the truth of the Idea. The poem can aspire to condition philosophy, not to replace it."[111] It is one thing to give up on the understanding of the relationship between poetry and philosophy as a relationship bound to the silence of the divine, but a poetry that no longer dwells "in the sacred night of the death of God" may still maintain, in Badiou's concrete determination, "a genuinely philosophical self-awareness." Hallward is wrong. Badiou himself has shown, we have seen it, that poetry cannot be reduced to its Heideggerian definition for the age of the poets. This is why I think that Badiou's declaration of the end of age of the poets is a liberation of poetry from philosophy as much as it is a liberation of philosophy from poetry. But it is the kind of liberation that makes a better encounter possible or even necessary.

We may now come back to Badiou's "Metaphysics and the Critique of Metaphysics" and to his definition of philosophy. Badiou says: "Not only, and contrary to what Hamlet declares, is there nothing in the world which exceeds our philosophical capacity, but there is nothing in our philosophical capacity which could not come to be in the reality of the world. It is this coextensivity *in actu* of conceptual invention and of a reality-effect that is called the absolute, and it is this that is the sole stake of philosophy."[112] Philosophy thinks the absolute, because it thinks and is able to think not only poetic truth in the guise of the invention of presence (reality-effect) at the limit of language but also because it is prepared to offer to name the event in the leap outside of calculable interests, which is the only possible name of conceptual invention. In the conclusion of *Logics of Worlds,* titled "What Is It to Live?," Badiou says: "I am sometimes told that I see in philosophy only a means to reestablish, against the contemporary apologia of the futile and the everyday, the rights of heroism. Why not? Having said that, ancient heroism claimed to justify life through sacrifice. My wish is to make heroism exist through the affirmative joy which is universally generated by following consequences through. We could say that the epic heroism of the one who gives his life is supplanted by the mathematical heroism of the one who creates life, point by point."[113] But then there is also a poetic heroism that takes poetic truth beyond the minimal conditions of the fourth relation, and expands them to include a liberation of exteriority, the active production of holes in signification, which amounts to a liberation of language from the constraints of inscription, and the surrender of a sense of oriented history. Does this not, however, lead to a certain derangement of old metaphysical presuppositions while still holding well back from any archi-metaphysical projection (which is Badiou's objection to Heidegger)? Persisting on it, on the derangement as such, would be the inconsistent consistency of the poet.

There is no end to the age of the poets except as an end concerning the poetico-philosophical suture at the service of a resacralization of existence. The poets may continue to instruct in what is still essential: that the end of the metaphysical epoch in its ontotheological configuration imposes a displacement from the meaningfulness that was the privilege of metaphysical humanity; that the breakdown of expectations in the wake of the ontological event of the end of metaphysics brings along a destruction of hermeneutics to such an extent that the entry into any sort of fidelity to that event must be thought of as an appropriation into truth (in its full play of concealment and unconcealment) and not into meaning. In *Contributions to Philosophy* Heidegger says that a certain "restraint" (*Verhältnis*) is the appropriate mood and the style for existing at the end of metaphysical humanity.[114] I could rephrase it by saying that restraint, perhaps in the wake of the Mallarmean notion of "restricted action," is the faithful and guarded relation to the errant truth of our times, which becomes eternal truth in our "subjective fidelity." And memory, the poetic memory of our future implied in any commitment to the philosophical Idea, can only be a memory of disruption, the memory of a fundamental unknowability to be paired with Badiou's conceptual invention of the absolute. The immemorial is the breakdown of signification and the radical point of non-measure that organizes the mutual need, the mutual use, of being and thinking—of thinking by being and of being by thinking. This is learning how to live poetically, this is how I read Badiou on how to live poetically, which philosophy only thinks about. It might be too Heideggerian for Badiou; he may not like it. But I think he might like it even less if I were to call him, at the end of the day, the prince of the left Heideggerians.[115] In any case, poetry, in Badiou's sense, in the sense he favors, becomes another name for infrapolitical antiphilosophy.

NOTES

Uncanny Rest

1. I found these Quevedo verses in one of my texts for this week, in Álvaro Enrigue's novel *Sudden Death*, 142.
2. Poe, "Mask of the Red Death," 604–9.
3. Poe, "Mask of the Red Death," 609.
4. Or so I mostly remember it.
5. Badiou, *Parménide*, 109.
6. Badiou, *Parménide*, 111.
7. Badiou, *L'essence de la politique*, 156.
8. Galli, "Epidemia e sovranitá, 3."
9. Badiou, *L'essence de la politique*. Badiou is referring to Blanchot's *La communauté inavouable* (1984), Nancy's *La communauté désavouée* (1986), and Agamben's *La comunitá che viene* (1990).
10. Badiou, *Heidegger*, 291–92.
11. See Stiegler, *What Makes Life Worth Living*, 98: "The genuine question, for Europe as well as for the rest of the world, is whether it can invent—in dialogue with America and the new major industrialized nations—a *new way of life* where *economizing* means *taking care*."
12. Stiegler, *What Makes Life Worth Living*, 83.
13. See Papo Kling interview Jorge Alemán on YouTube at https://www.youtube.com/watch?v=aAle_yTJFmc and at https://www.youtube.com/watch?v=reCHq_7PTyg.
14. Nancy, *Birth to Presence*, 82–109.
15. Derrida, *Learning to Live Finally*, 22–26.
16. Alemán, *Soledad, común*.
17. Nancy, *Birth to Presence*, 174–75.
18. Graff Zivin, *Anarchaeologies*, 31–49.
19. Kierkegaard, *Fear and Trembling*, 85.
20. Kierkegaard, *Fear and Trembling*, 69–70.
21. Agamben, "Una domanda."
22. Tobit 2:8, quoted from *The New Oxford Annotated Bible*.
23. Tobit 4:3–4, quoted from *The New Oxford Annotated Bible*.
24. Heidegger, *Basic Writings*, 319–39.
25. Heidegger, *The Question concerning Technology*, 3–35.
26. Heidegger, *Pathmarks*, 90. The translators of the essay into Spanish, Hel-

ena Cortés and Arturo Leyte, propose the translation of *Nichtung* as "desisting," a term that I will use in what follows. "*Die Nichtung* and *nichten*, words in which *Nichts*, 'the void,' resonates, are interpretively translated as 'desisting' and 'to desist.' With this term we are not alluding to the habitual meaning of 'desisting from something,' but as a form of suspension inherent in being itself. We are avoiding the usage of the traditional term 'nihilate,' which, while having the phonetic fortune of preserving a play on words, nevertheless implies the negative meaning of annihilator, while also evoking a subjective state, and a marked transitivity which in no way corresponds to its meaning in the text" (Heidegger, ¿Qué es la metafísica?, 30n24).

27 Quoted in Heidegger, *Pathmarks*, 92–93.
28 Heidegger, *Pathmarks*, 93.
29 Heidegger, *Pathmarks*, 93.
30 Heidegger, *Pathmarks*, 96.
31 Villacañas, *Imperiofilia*, 161.
32 The quotation used as the epigraph for this part of the text is from Borges, "On Exactitude in Science," 325.
33 Tiqqun, *Cybernetic Hypothesis*, 10.
34 Tiqqun, *Cybernetic Hypothesis*, 27.
35 Tiqqun, *Cybernetic Hypothesis*, 43.
36 Tiqqun, *Cybernetic Hypothesis*, 55.
37 Quoted in Tiqqun, *Cybernetic Hypothesis*, 119.
38 Tiqqun, *Cybernetic Hypothesis*, 122.
39 Tiqqun, *Cybernetic Hypothesis*, 123.
40 Tiqqun, *Cybernetic Hypothesis*, 125.
41 Tiqqun, *Cybernetic Hypothesis*, 160.
42 Tiqqun, *Cybernetic Hypothesis*, 161.
43 Derrida uses the term in order to introduce the Heideggerianism *unumgänglich*. See Derrida, *Théorie et pratique*, 128.
44 The epigraphs taken from *Deseo de ser piel roja* appear on pp. 54 and 146 of the book.
45 Morey, *Deseo de ser piel roja*, 47.
46 Morey, *Deseo de ser piel roja*, 87.
47 Morey, *Deseo de ser piel roja*, 13.
48 Morey, *Deseo de ser piel roja*, 15.
49 Morey, *Deseo de ser piel roja*, 22.
50 Morey, *Deseo de ser piel roja*, 36.
51 Morey, *Deseo de ser piel roja*, 45.
52 Morey, *Deseo de ser piel roja*, 49.
53 Morey, *Deseo de ser piel roja*, 75.
54 Morey, *Deseo de ser piel roja*, 70.

55	Morey, *Deseo de ser piel roja*, 163.
56	Morey, *Deseo de ser piel roja*, 199.
57	Morey, *Deseo de ser piel roja*, 169.
58	Saer, *La pesquisa*, Kindle location 944–46.
59	Agamben, *Creation and Anarchy*, 50.
60	Tiqqun, *Theory of Bloom*.
61	Tiqqun, *Theory of Bloom*, 70.
62	Tiqqun, *Theory of Bloom*, 69.
63	Tiqqun, *Theory of Bloom*, 69.
64	Tiqqun, *Theory of Bloom*, 69.
65	Benveniste, *Dictionary of Indo-European Concepts and Society*, 88.
66	Benveniste, *Dictionary of Indo-European Concepts and Society*, 90.
67	Gramsci, *Pre-Prison Writings*, 72.
68	Benveniste, *Dictionary of Indo-European Concepts and Society*, 83.
69	Nietzsche, *Selected Letters*, 169.
70	Morey, *Vidas de Nietzsche*, 231.
71	D'Iorio, *Nietzsche's Journey to Sorrento*, 75.
72	D'Iorio, *Nietzsche's Journey to Sorrento*, 75
73	D'Iorio, *Nietzsche's Journey to Sorrento*, 76.
74	D'Iorio, *Nietzsche's Journey to Sorrento*, 75.
75	Nietzsche, *Human, All Too Human*, 186–87.
76	Nietzsche, *Human, All Too Human*, 193–94.
77	See Pindar, Pythian Ode 2, verse 72. Anthony Verity translates this as "You have learned what type of man you are: now be that man." But the *genoi, oios essi mathon* would probably allow for another, more Pythian rendition: "Having learned who you are, be that." In the Loeb Classical Library, William Race translates: "Become such as you are, having learned what that is" (Pindar, *Olympian Odes*, 245).
78	Please see note 1 of appendix 1, p. 172.
79	Gramsci, *Pre-Prison Writings*, 9–10.
80	Gramsci, *Pre-Prison Writings*, 13.
81	Gramsci, *Pre-Prison Writings*, 15.
82	Gramsci, *Pre-Prison Writings*, 16.
83	Gramsci, *Pre-Prison Writings*, 90.
84	Gramsci, *Pre-Prison Writings*, 99.
85	Gramsci, *Pre-Prison Writings*, 48.
86	Gramsci, *Pre-Prison Writings*, 50.
87	Gramsci, *Pre-Prison Writings*, 56.
88	Gramsci, *Pre-Prison Writings*, 56.
89	Gramsci, *Pre-Prison Writings*, 57.
90	Gramsci, *Pre-Prison Writings*, 62.
91	Gramsci, *Pre-Prison Writings*, 72.

92	Gramsci, *Pre-Prison Writings*, 88–89.
93	Gramsci, *Pre-Prison Writings*, 99.
94	Gramsci, *Pre-Prison Writings*, 26.
95	Gramsci, *Pre-Prison Writings*, 52.
96	Agamben, *Creation and Anarchy*, 1–13.
97	Agamben, *Creation and Anarchy*, 3.
98	Agamben, *Creation and Anarchy*, 13.
99	Agamben, *Creation and Anarchy*, 28.
100	The essential article by Thomas Sheehan to this effect, which summarizes and specifies other texts of his, is "But What Comes before the 'After'?" The mention of "the asymptotic condition of existence" tied to *ankhibasie* is on p. 50. Heidegger uses this Greek word for the first time late, invoking Heraclitus's fragment 122, in *Country Path Conversations*, 1. The volume contains manuscripts from 1944–45, the first of which is titled "*Ankhibasie*: A Triadic Conversation on a Country Path between a Scientist, a Scholar, and a Guide."
101	*The Logic of Sense* begins by exploring that paradox of time: "when I say 'Alice becomes larger,' I mean that she becomes larger than she was. By the same token, however, she becomes smaller than she is now." Deleuze, *Logic of Sense*, 1; see also 76–78.
102	Nancy, *Banality of Heidegger*, 59.
103	Gramsci, *Pre-Prison Writings*, 48.
104	"Both [history and *Phenomenology*] taken conjointly, and, therefore, history understood or history brought into concept, constitute memory and the Calvary of the absolute Spirit, the reality, truth and certainty of its throne, without which that absolute Spirit would be nothing but the solitary void of life; since only from the *chalice of this realm of spirits/foams forth for Him [for the absolute Spirit] his own infinitude*." Hegel, *Phenomenology of Spirit*, 914.
105	Derrida, *Of Spirit*, 40.
106	Derrida, Gadamer, and Lacoue-Labarthe, *La Conférence de Heidelberg*, 80.
107	Derrida, Gadamer, and Lacoue-Labarthe, *La Conférence de Heidelberg*, 13.
108	Derrida, Gadamer, and Lacoue-Labarthe, *La Conférence de Heidelberg*, 64.
109	Derrida, Gadamer, and Lacoue-Labarthe, *La Conférence de Heidelberg*, 68.
110	Derrida, Gadamer, and Lacoue-Labarthe, *La Conférence de Heidelberg*, 124.
111	Derrida, Gadamer, and Lacoue-Labarthe, *La Conférence de Heidelberg*, 125.
112	Derrida, Gadamer, and Lacoue-Labarthe, *La Conférence de Heidelberg*, 126.
113	Geronimo, *My Life*, 68.
114	Geronimo, *My Life*, 66.
115	Kraniauskas, "Reflux of Money," 230.
116	Badiou, *Manifesto for Philosophy*, 142.
117	Badiou speaks of "metaphysics without metaphysics" for the first time

in *Que pense le poème?*, 10. Most of that text in English, with additional materials, is included in *The Age of the Poets and Other Writings on Twentieth Century Poetry and Prose*, a collection of Badiou's essays translated by Bruno Bosteels. Badiou links Fernando Pessoa's expression to antiphilosophy, saying "systemic metaphysics having been surpassed, devalued, finished, only the poem was the guardian of a thought for our times that was total, and at the same time untethered from philosophic pretension" (*Que pense le poème?*, 10–11). But in *L'immanence des verités*, Badiou takes this topic up again and seems to attribute to himself, to his own work, that quality of "metaphysics without metaphysics," and so then a necessarily antiphilosophical position, although, we can imagine, only in a certain partial sense. See his pages in that work dedicated to Caeiro, 191–96. The only difference, he says with a bit of lightness, is that Caeiro wrote short poems and he, Badiou, writes brutal treatises. Is Badiou, increasingly, an elective antiphilosopher? See appendix 4 for more on this.

118 Heidegger, *On Time and Being*, 57.
119 Heidegger, *On Time and Being*, 56.
120 Badiou, *Heidegger*.
121 Heidegger, *On Time and Being*, 55.
122 Badiou, *Lacan*, 217.
123 Badiou, *Lacan*, 184.
124 Badiou, *Lacan*, 35.
125 Laclau, *Emancipation(s)*, 123.
126 Laclau, *Emancipation(s)*, 123.
127 Badiou, *Age of the Poets*, 36–43.
128 Badiou, *Age of the Poets*, 38.
129 Badiou, *Age of the Poets*, 38.
130 Badiou, *Age of the Poets*, 54.
131 Badiou, *Age of the Poets*, 41.
132 Badiou, *Age of the Poets*, 20.
133 Badiou and Tusa, *End*, 44–45.
134 Badiou and Tusa, *End*, 24.
135 Laclau, *On Populist Reason*, 222.
136 Laclau, *On Populist Reason*, 116.
137 What is said in "The Turn" is prepared in "The Danger." This lecture prepares the ground for and anticipates what will be determined in the following one (they are two consecutive lectures presented at Bremen) as what I am calling an antiphilosophical experience. First, Heidegger carefully establishes a notion of being of beings (*to einai*) to which he opposes "the world." This is the key passage: "Being has to own its essence from the worlding of world . . . the worlding of world is an appropriating (*das Ereignen*) in a still-unexperienced sense of this word. When world first

properly takes place, then being, and along with it the nothing, vanish into worlding. Only when the nothing, in its essence from the truth of being, vanishes into this is nihilism overcome" (Heidegger, *Bremen and Freiburg Lectures*, 46–47). There is therefore an assertion that world and being are the same, but not equivalent: "They are the same in radical differentiation" (47). The essential experience of forgetfulness defines human thinking at this stage or epoch. It is the epoch of positionality (*Gestell*). It is the epoch of technology. The world refuses itself. There is only a "hint" that such refusal takes place. In positionality, the essence of technology, the forgetting of the essence of being completes itself (49). But there is a hint. This hint that positionality as the being of beings offers a refusal of world through which we may get some kind of access to the fact that there is world, and not just positionality, is a reformulation of the earlier Heideggerian experience of the ontico-ontological difference. There is a difference, or the trace of a difference, or the hint of a difference, mysterious, between world and positionality. The hint is also called "a ray from the distant arrival of world" (50). This comes through the refusal of world. In other words, in the experience of world refusal the possibility of other-than-positionality-as-being-of-beings opens up. In the meantime, the pursuit and requisitioning of positionality, regarding which we have no choice, as we are not masters of being, is "the danger." We must traverse it. Earlier, Heidegger tells us, he called the zone of the traversing "errancy." The danger conceals itself as the danger that it is. We experience perils and plights, indeed of horrifying kinds, but the danger remains concealed. There is immeasurable suffering and pain, but the essence of pain is concealed. (*Nota bene*: a strange "we" surfaces here, as Heidegger says that "we" are unpained, but it is not clear whether those whose flesh went into the Nazi "fabrication of corpses in annihilation camps" or the starving dead in China are equally unpained.) To experience the danger as danger is, however, a requisite—positionality must be traversed. There is a suffering of thought, a pain of thought, and Kant and Nietzsche are mentioned here as two thinkers who underwent it. In accomplished positionality we must traverse and experience the danger of presencing. Presencing is the basic trait of positionality, a human production based on the presencing of being. If *physis* gives us a rock, the human posits a stone staircase. Human positioning is production: the pursuit and requisition of presence as standing reserve. These thoughts are continued in "The Turn" in the following way: Heidegger announces that the accomplished essence of positionality prepares a "change in being" (65). There is to be a "conversion of positionality" that would signal "the arrival of another dispensation" (65). The human must prepare itself for it. How? In thinking. Thinking is the "authentic action." "By thinking we first learn to dwell in the realm in which the conversion of the dispensation of being, the conversion of positionality, takes place" (67). This is "the turn," or its possibility. From the forgetting of being to the guardianship of the essence of being. We are not masters of being. We cannot command it. We can only prepare in the course of waiting. We prepare for a favor, a grace. It will come to us, if it comes, as a "lightning flash," a "flashing entry" (71). It will give us insight (*Einsicht*) into that which is. This is *Ereignis*. Being would have unconcealed for us "its highest secret" within the dominance of positionality (72). The favor, the grace, the *Einkehr* turned *Einsicht*—all of this seems to me an appeal to antiphilosophy as thought. To thought as antiphilosophy. With it nihilism will have been overcome. And an other beginning will have taken place. The history of the world would have been split in two. Resources that are no longer philosophical, but existential, are activated therein. If you can muster them. And then . . . if you wait well enough. Is this not, finally, transformation, transfiguration?

138 Heidegger, *Bremen and Freiburg Lectures*, 67.
139 Rancière, *Ignorant Schoolmaster*.
140 Wilderson, *Afropessimism*, 220.
141 Wilderson, *Afropessimism*, ix.
142 Wilderson, *Afropessimism*, 226.
143 Wilderson, *Afropessimism*, 95.
144 Wilderson, *Afropessimism*, 209.
145 Wilderson, *Afropessimism*, 222.
146 Wilderson, *Afropessimism*, 226.
147 Wilderson, *Afropessimism*, 249.
148 Wilderson, *Afropessimism*, 328.
149 Hartman, *Wayward Lives, Beautiful Experiments*, 227.
150 Badiou, *Nietzsche* 11
151 Badiou, *Nietzsche*, 31.
152 Badiou, *Nietzsche*, 32.
153 Hartman, *Wayward Lives, Beautiful Experiments*, 228.
154 "Riverrun, past Eve and Adam's, from swerve of shore to bend of bay, brings us by a commodious vicus of recirculation back to Howth Castle and Environs." Joyce, *Finnegans Wake*, 3.
155 Derrida, *La vie la mort*.
156 Derrida, *La vie la mort*, 199.
157 Derrida, *La vie la mort*, 199.
158 Derrida, *La vie la mort*, 292.
159 Derrida, *La vie la mort*, 203.
160 Derrida, *La vie la mort*, 207.
161 Derrida, *La vie la mort*, 208.
162 Heidegger, "Who Is Nietzsche's Zarathustra?," 431.

163   Heidegger, "Who Is Nietzsche's Zarathustra?," 425.
164   Nietzsche, *Ecce Homo*, 104.
165   Heidegger, "Who Is Nietzsche's Zarathustra?," 426–27.
166   Heidegger, "Who Is Nietzsche's Zarathustra?," 427.
167   Quoted in Heidegger, "Who Is Nietzsche's Zarathustra?," 418.
168   Heidegger, "Who Is Nietzsche's Zarathustra?," 428.
169   Heidegger, "Who Is Nietzsche's Zarathustra?," 431.
170   Just to be clear, a little repetition: the point at which Heidegger discovers that Nietzsche is at the same time a thinker of metaphysics and a thinker of something that remains unthought and impenetrable for metaphysics is the point that Zarathustra cannot proceed beyond, and it is what makes Zarathustra a precursor. Nietzsche was preparing, in the weeks and days preceding his collapse, that step beyond, which is a step beyond the spirit of revenge, an overcoming of revenge that would not be a mere inversion of it, hence more of the same. The revenge of revenge is still inscribed within will to power. Going beyond it remained in Nietzsche, given his early collapse, as the unthought-to-be-thought, hence the legacy he left to the rest of us.
171   The pages that follow are a theoretical fiction, as will be noticed. But not everything in them is false. They should be read in conjunction with appendix 4 in particular.
172   For a concise presentation of Fernando Pessoa's heteronyms, the reader should consult the introduction in Fernando Pessoa's *A Little Larger Than the Entire Universe: Selected Poems*.
173   Bracketed material in this transcription/translation has been added by me, Alberto Moreiras, the author of this book—not by my grandfather—and is an addition to the transcribed text.
174   It is not clear whether this is a picture of Timoteo himself or whether it portrays Alberto Moreiras, Timoteo's brother. They had, of course, a similar look, since they were brothers only a few years apart.
175   Pessoa, *A Little Larger Than the Entire Universe*, 33.

Appendix 1

1   I am aware of the difficulty of this question. Lacan himself says: "What, then, does he who has passed through the experience of this opaque relation to the origin, to the drive, become? How can a subject who has traversed the radical phantasy experience the drive? This is the beyond of analysis, and has never been approached. Up to now, it has been approachable only at the level of the analyst, in as much as it would be required of

him to have specifically traversed the cycle of the analytic experience in its totality." Lacan, *Four Fundamental Concepts of Psychoanalysis,* 273–74.

Appendix 2

1 Derrida, *Learning to Live Finally.*
2 Derrida, *Learning to Live Finally,* 52.
3 Derrida, *Learning to Live Finally,* 52.
4 Derrida, *Learning to Live Finally,* 27.
5 Derrida, *Learning to Live Finally,* 27–28.
6 Derrida, *Learning to Live Finally,* 48.
7 Derrida, *Learning to Live Finally,* 49.

Appendix 3

1 Agamben, *Creation and Anarchy,* 61.
2 Agamben, *Creation and Anarchy,* 61.
3 Lacan, "Discours de Jacques Lacan."
4 Agamben, *Creation and Anarchy,* 54.
5 Agamben, *Creation and Anarchy,* 54–55.
6 Levinas, *Otherwise Than Being,* 99.
7 Levinas, *Otherwise Than Being,* 101.
8 Levinas, *Otherwise Than Being,* 102.
9 Levinas, *Otherwise Than Being,* 100.
10 Levinas, *Otherwise Than Being,* 100–01.
11 Levinas, *Otherwise Than Being,* 100.
12 See Schürmann's *Le principe de anarchie* (*Heidegger on Being and Acting: From Principles to Anarchy*), in which he only mentions Levinas twice in footnotes.
13 Rancière, "Should Democracy Come?," 275.
14 Rancière, "Should Democracy Come?," 274.
15 Rancière, *Disagreements,* 278.
16 Rancière, *Disagreements,* 279.
17 Rancière, *Disagreements,* 279.
18 Rancière, *Disagreements,* 282.

Appendix 4

1. For the epigraph from Heidegger, see "Why Poets?," 206.
2. Badiou, *Manifesto for Philosophy*, 70
3. Badiou, *Manifesto for Philosophy*, 71.
4. Badiou, *Manifesto for Philosophy*, 74.
5. Lacoue-Labarthe, *Heidegger and the Politics of Poetry*, 17.
6. Badiou, *Manifesto for Philosophy*, 74.
7. Heidegger, "Why Poets?"
8. See, for instance, Eyers's "Badiou among the Poets" or Christian Doumet's "La fin de 'L'âge des poètes,'" both of them failed essays in my opinion, informative as they are in their own ways, to the extent that they get lost in inessential considerations and neglect to focus on what is determinant for the philosophy/poetry relation in Badiou. Justin Clemens's "Eternity Is Coming: The Age of the Poets by Alain Badiou" also fails to focus on the most relevant philosophical contribution of the book it reviews. Bosteels and Apter's introduction to *The Age of the Poets* suffers from the same problem even though the authors' knowledge of Badiou is not in question. There is a tendency in some of these critics, particularly in Eyers and Bosteels and Apter, to concentrate their remarks on the second half of the book, which really concerns early attempts by Badiou to come to terms with Althusserian Marxism's notions of the relative autonomy of art, bypassing what is for me new and crucial in Badiou's theses on the end of the age of the poets and the legacies of that age for contemporary thought. Let me, however, take this opportunity to praise Tom Betteridge's enlightening essay "Alain Badiou's Anabasis: Rereading Paul Celan against Heidegger." This essay does not mention *The Age of the Poets*; it takes most of what Betteridge wants to comment on from Badiou's *The Century*. But it is an excellent introduction to the different ways in which Heidegger and Badiou relate to the notion of "homecoming," in reference to Hölderlin and Celan, respectively. Celan is, of course, one of the major references in Badiou's *Age of the Poets*.
9. Badiou's critique of the critique of metaphysics is not limited to Heidegger's hermeneutics, but extends to Kant's critical philosophy and to Comtian positivism. All three of them would revert, in Badiou's determination, to a disavowed metaphysics in the form of an "archi-metaphysics." He says: "Critique, positivism, and hermeneutics, even if we were to grant them that they diagnose metaphysics correctly, merely replace it with what we shall call an archi-metaphysics, that is, with the suspension of sense to an undetermined that is purely and simply left to the historial determination of its coming. Archi-metaphysics is the replacement of necessary undetermined with a contingent one, or: the established power of an unknown

master is opposed by the poetics and the prophetics of the to-come. This is the case with the mystical element in Wittgenstein, as with the metaphorical God in Heidegger or the positivist church in Comte." Badiou, "Metaphysics and the Critique," 181.

10 Badiou, *Age of the Poets*, 47. The question of antiphilosophy is a ticklish issue in Heidegger, for instance, as it would have to do with Heidegger's thought on "the other beginning" and the cryptic writings he developed starting with *Contributions to Philosophy* and continuing on through the mid-1940s, and which he never wanted to publish while he was alive. Those volumes are still coming out in the *Gesamtausgabe*, and most of them are as yet untranslated: they include *Mindfulness*, *History of Being*, *Metaphysik und Nihilismus*, and *Die Stege des Anfangs* (the last of these still unpublished). Badiou never discusses them explicitly, but the thought of a possible antiphilosophy in Heidegger is in the background of his *Heidegger* seminar, and later in the antiphilosophy project in contemporary thought, that is, after Friedrich Nietzsche. See Badiou's work on Wittgenstein (*Wittgenstein's Antiphilosophy*), Nietzsche (*Nietzsche: L'antiphilosophie 1*), and Lacan (*Lacan: Anti-philosophy 3*).

11 Badiou, *Manifesto for Philosophy*, 73.
12 Badiou, *Manifesto for Philosophy*, 74.
13 Badiou, *Handbook of Inaesthetics*, 36.
14 Badiou, *Handbook of Inaesthetics*, 38.
15 Badiou, *Handbook of Inaesthetics*, 44.
16 Badiou, *Handbook of Inaesthetics*, 39.
17 Badiou, *Handbook of Inaesthetics*, 45.
18 Badiou, *Handbook of Inaesthetics*, 42.
19 Balso, *Pessoa*, 54–61.
20 Badiou, *L'immanence des vérités*, 191. See also 191–96 on the poems of Alberto Caeiro.
21 The essay is also significant in terms of establishing Badiou's antipathy for any kind of hermeneutical approach to truth, including but not limited to the Heideggerian one. It is hard to find fault with Badiou's critique as far as it goes, although I would like to say that it is or would have been quite possible, perhaps also desirable, to take a more generous approach to Heidegger's notion of a destruction of metaphysics without necessarily reducing him to the condition of an "archi-metaphysical" thinker.
22 Badiou, "Metaphysics and the Critique," 190.
23 Badiou posits, following Hegel and for reasons that have to do with his endorsement of dialectics, that the identification of thinking and being is an axiomatic point of departure for philosophy: a "preliminary thesis," he calls it. The reason for it to be axiomatic is obviously that it is also highly debatable—and the axiom takes care of the debate, preempting it. This is

the key passage: "Dogmatic metaphysics defends the rights of indeterminacy only within the bounds of a preliminary thesis which affirms that thought and the thinkable are homogeneous to each other. As Hegel writes in the introduction to the *Science of Logic*: 'Ancient metaphysics had in this respect a higher conception of thinking than is common today . . . This metaphysics believed that thinking (and its determinations) is not anything alien to the object, but rather is its essential nature, . . . and that thinking in its immanent determinations and the true nature of things form one and the same content.'" Badiou, "Metaphysics and the Critique," 182.

24 Badiou, "Question of Being Today," 40.
25 Badiou, "Question of Being Today," 40.
26 Badiou, "Question of Being Today," 40.
27 Heidegger, "'Only a God Can Save Us.' The *Spiegel* Interview (1966)." The interview was done by *Der Spiegel* on September 23, 1966, but Heidegger requested that it be published only after his death. *Der Spiegel* published it on May 31, 1976. These are the more relevant passages: "*Spiegel*: Now the question naturally arises: Can the individual man in any way still influence this web of fateful circumstance? Or, indeed, can philosophy influence it? Or can both together influence it, insofar as philosophy guides the individual, or several individuals, to a determined action? *Heidegger:* If I may answer briefly, and perhaps clumsily, but after long reflection: philosophy will be unable to effect any immediate change in the current state of the world. This is true not only of philosophy but of all purely human reflection and endeavor. Only a god can save us. The only possibility available to us is that by thinking and poetizing we prepare a readiness for the appearance of a god, or for the absence of a god in [our] decline, insofar as in view of the absent god we are in a state of decline. *Spiegel*: Is there a correlation between your thinking and the emergence of this god? Is there here in your view a causal connection? Do you feel that we can bring a god forth by our thinking? *Heidegger:* We cannot bring him forth by our thinking. At best we can awaken a readiness to wait [for him]" (Heidegger, "Only a God Can Save Us," 57). It is obvious that Heidegger's emphasis has to do with the fact that no human action by itself can determine a change in historical conditions, and thought can only prepare a possible change of epoch. An emphasis on the arrival of the future and salvific god is perhaps legible in these words, but I tend to read them in quite the opposite way: if there is any possibility of retrieval of a non-destitute future for humanity, it will have to come from elsewhere. We are impotent concerning it. One can definitely think this is a bad or even untenable political position, but I do not see it as a particularly religious one. The "waiting" regarding an absence that may or may not find a solution is to be thought of as a posture

of thought that preempts nihilistic fatalism rather than as a manner of prayer.

28 Heidegger refers to the verses in Hölderlin's "Patmos" elegy in connection with the destiny of the world in the 1946 lecture "Why Poets?" As this connects with the previous note and with Badiou's insistence on Heidegger as a thinker of religious salvation, let me quote the extended paragraph: "The essence of technology is dawning only slowly. This day is the world's night made over as the purely technological day. It raises the threat of a single endless winter. Man now foregoes not only defense, but the unbroken entirety of beings remains in darkness. What is whole withdraws. The world is being emptied of what is whole and heals. As a result, not only does the holy remain hidden as the track to the godhead, but even what is whole, the track to the holy, appears to be extinguished. Unless there are still mortals capable of seeing what is unwhole and unhealing threaten *as* unwhole and unhealing. They would have to discern which is the danger that assails man. The danger consists in the menace that bears on the essence of man in his relationship to being itself, but not in accidental perils. The danger is *the* danger. It conceals itself in the abyss in its relation to all beings. In order to see and to expose the danger, there must be such who first reach into the abyss. 'But where the danger lies, there also grows that which saves' (Hölderlin, *Sämtliche Werke*, vol. IV, p. 190)" (Heidegger, "Why Poets?," 221–22). What saves is therefore not the godhead but poetic truth. Those who are able to discern the danger are, as the essay will make clear, "the poets in desolate time" (Heidegger, "Why Poets?," 240). The 1955 lecture "The Question concerning Technology" presents Hölderlin's verses along similar lines, talking about ancient Greece: "What, then, was art—perhaps only for that brief but magnificent time? Why did art bear the modest name *techne*? Because it was a revealing that brought forth and hither, and therefore belonged within *poiesis*. It was finally that revealing which holds complete sway in all the fine arts, in poetry, and in everything poetical that obtained *poiesis* as its proper name. The same poet from whom we heard the words 'But where danger is, grows the saving power also' says to us: 'poetically dwells man upon this earth.'" (Heidegger, *Question concerning Technology*, 34). The saving power is the art of poetic revealing, or poetic truth. It does not seem to me Heidegger says anything else, particularly not anything "theological."

29 Badiou, "Question of Being Today," 41.
30 Badiou, "Question of Being Today," 41.
31 The November 18, 1986, session of Badiou's seminar on Heidegger refers to the same passages from *Introduction to Metaphysics* (1935), and immediately associates them with the famous passages on the melting away of everything solid at the hands of the bourgeoisie in *The Communist Man-*

ifesto. Badiou then says: "La vigueur de ce texte est absolument intacte, ce qu'il décrit continue à se derouler sous nos yeux, et, dans sa substance, c'est bien ce que Heidegger décrit sous le nom de nihilisme. Comment penser cette différence entre la predication nihiliste et ce qui est décrit ici comme les effets inéluctables de la généralisation du capital? Tout est dans l'accent, l'orientation de la pensée, et non dans les termes." [The vigor of this text is absolutely intact, that which it describes continues to deploy for our eyes and, in its substance, it is what Heidegger describes under the name of nihilism. How should we think of this difference between nihilist predication and that which is described here as the ineluctable effects of the generalization of capital? Everything is in the accent, the orientation of thought, not in the terms.] (Badiou, *Heidegger*, 60) Badiou finds here what I believe is the kernel of his disagreement with Heidegger, which I would propose we understand as the generative site of everything Badiou says against Heidegger. Yes, it is a question of the orientation of thought within the general disorientation produced both by nihilism and the bourgeois revolution. This is the time of the age of the poets, as we will see. It is clear that Badiou prefers the Marxist position, according to which we are called forth to a "beginning that will not recommence anything, because there is nothing to recommence." (Badiou, *Heidegger*, 61) The general dissolution of the old social links is for Marx "the condition of a production of truth" (Badiou, *Heidegger*, 61), while for Heidegger they would be the site of "a nostalgia for a return of categories whose loss of sense is deplorable. He aspires to the re-sacralization of existence, to the reappropriation of the site." (Badiou, *Heidegger*, 60) For Marx, instead, the real question is different: "There where Heidegger convokes us to the return of the sacred, Marx says to us: Is it possible to continue the dissolution of the images through a means other than Capital?" (Badiou, *Heidegger*, 61) Can we move to a new production of truth not based on a return of the old? Ultimately, Heidegger's "other beginning" probably has nothing to do with any return of the old sacred; it is also a new production of truth. There are clichés being used here. But we must agree with Badiou that there are some rhetorical configurations in Heidegger's text that project a reactionary politicity Badiou finds abhorrent and counterproductive.

32   Badiou, "Question of Being Today," 40.
33   Badiou, "Question of Being Today," 40.
34   Badiou, "Question of Being Today," 40.
35   See on this Jacques Derrida's "*Ousia* and *Gramme*: Note on a Note to *Being and Time*," in particular pp. 63–67. Talking about Heidegger's "The Anaximander Fragment," Derrida says that, on the one hand, Heidegger thinks or makes an attempt to think of modalities of presence and that, on the other hand, he seeks to call all modalities of presence in general "*the*

Greco-Western-philosophical closure" (Derrida, "*Ousia* and *Gramme*," 65). Derrida states that all the arduous fundamental meditations by Heidegger on presence, including the text on Anaximander, are *intra*-metaphysical meditations, but he also says that Heidegger is aware of it and that in such an awareness he prepares another gesture, "the more difficult, more unheard-of, more questioning gesture, the one for which we are least prepared" (Derrida, "*Ousia* and *Gramme*," 65). This would be a gesture that "only permits itself to be sketched, announcing itself in certain calculated fissures of the metaphysical text" (Derrida, "*Ousia* and *Gramme*," 65).
36 Badiou, "Question of Being Today," 43.
37 Badiou, "Question of Being Today," 45.
38 See Schürmann, *Heidegger on Being and Acting*. See also Moreiras ed., "On Reiner Schürmann."
39 Badiou, "Question of Being Today," 44–45.
40 See Lyons's *Paul Celan and Martin Heidegger* for a careful and fairly complete account of the relationship between the poet and the philosopher. See also Charles Bambach's *Thinking the Poetic Measure of Justice*. For Badiou's considerations on the (mis)encounter, see his *Manifesto for Philosophy*, 85–89.
41 Badiou makes a big deal of the importance of Nietzsche's relationship with Wagner in shaping Nietzsche's process of philosophical production and existential reflection. In fact, for Badiou the impossibility of saving the Wagner relation made Nietzsche's antiphilosophical trip rather desperate and led to a particular kind of impasse. Badiou, *Nietzsche*, particularly 233–311.
42 Badiou, *Age of the Poets*, 38.
43 Badiou, *Age of the Poets*, 41.
44 Badiou, *Age of the Poets*, 41–42.
45 Badiou, *Age of the Poets*, 42.
46 Badiou, *Age of the Poets*, 42.
47 Badiou, *Age of the Poets*, 42.
48 Badiou, *Age of the Poets*, 42.
49 Badiou, *Age of the Poets*, 43.
50 Badiou, *Age of the Poets*, 43.
51 On the "mytheme," see Lacoue-Labarthe, *Heidegger and the Politics of Poetry*, in particular "Prologue: Heidegger's Onto-Mythology" and "Poetry, Philosophy, Politics," where Lacoue-Labarthe engages Badiou's notion of the poetico-philosophical suture. Badiou also engages with the Parmenidean poem and with Plato's *Parmenides* in a number of seminars, but let me refer in particular to the 1986–87 seminar on Heidegger, where Badiou also discusses at length Heidegger's relationship to poetry and rehearses his own notion of the poetico-philosophical suture. See, in particular, his remarks on Parmenidean issues and the exit from Parmenides's apagogic

reasoning, *Heidegger*, 179–216. See also, of course, Badiou's 1985–86 seminar on Parmenides, *Parménide*.

52 Badiou, *Age of the Poets*, 37.
53 Badiou, *Age of the Poets*, 38–39.
54 Badiou, *Age of the Poets*, 39.
55 Badiou, *Age of the Poets*, 39.
56 Badiou, *Age of the Poets*, 40.
57 Badiou, *Age of the Poets*, 41.
58 Badiou, *Age of the Poets*, 41.
59 Badiou, *Age of the Poets*, 4.
60 Badiou, *Age of the Poets*, 5.
61 Badiou, *Age of the Poets*, 7.
62 Badiou, *Age of the Poets*, 8.
63 Badiou, *Age of the Poets*, 8.
64 Badiou, *Age of the Poets*, 13.
65 Badiou, *Age of the Poets*, 13.
66 Badiou, *Age of the Poets*, 14.
67 Badiou, *Age of the Poets*, 13.
68 Badiou, *Age of the Poets*, 15.
69 Badiou, *Age of the Poets*, 15. The poem is Trakl's "Psalm."
70 Badiou, *Age of the Poets*, 16.
71 Badiou, *Age of the Poets*, 16.
72 Badiou, *Age of the Poets*, 18.
73 Badiou, *Age of the Poets*, 18.
74 Badiou, *Age of the Poets*, 20.
75 Badiou, *Age of the Poets*, 28–29.
76 Badiou, *Age of the Poets*, 29.
77 Badiou, *Age of the Poets*, 31.
78 Badiou, *Age of the Poets*, 24–25.
79 Badiou, *Age of the Poets*, 33.
80 Badiou, *Age of the Poets*, 33.
81 Badiou, *Age of the Poets*, 34.
82 Badiou, *Age of the Poets*, 32.
83 Badiou, *Age of the Poets*, 5.
84 Badiou, *Age of the Poets*, 8. See, on this, the literary hoax or semi-hoax perpetrated by Yoandy Cabrera, Rodolfo Ortiz, and myself, which nevertheless includes earnest reflection on Alberto Caeiro's poetry and profile: Caeiro and Moreira's *Infracendencia*. See also Caeiro, *Obra Completa de Alberto Caeiro*. The more relevant pages have already been read by the patient reader of this book, as they constitute Remark 7 of it. Their function was to bring the main text of this book to a close, in a somewhat contradictory manner—but then Caeiro's poetry is itself a radical decision of

existence—so not so contradictory. The function of this note is to offer an example of what is meant by poetico-philosophical suture in Badiou—as you may conclude, it is not entirely dead. Or perhaps it is, since it is antiphilosophy that is at play here.

85 Badiou, *Age of the Poets*, 48.
86 Badiou, *Age of the Poets*, 49.
87 Badiou, *Age of the Poets*, 48.
88 Badiou, *Age of the Poets*, 50.
89 Badiou, *Age of the Poets*, 50.
90 Badiou, *Age of the Poets*, 54.
91 Badiou, *Age of the Poets*, 54.
92 Badiou, *Age of the Poets*, 57.
93 Badiou, *Age of the Poets*, 58.
94 I have tried to reflect on these issues in my book *Infrapolítica*.
95 Badiou, *Age of the Poets*, 206.
96 Heidegger, "Why Poets?," 200.
97 Heidegger, "Why Poets?," 200.
98 Heidegger, "Why Poets?," 201.
99 Heidegger, "Why Poets?," 202.
100 Heidegger, "Why Poets?," 202.
101 Heidegger, "Why Poets?," 202.
102 Heidegger, "Why Poets?," 203.
103 Heidegger, "Why Poets?," 203.
104 Heidegger, "Why Poets?," 204.
105 Heidegger, "Why Poets?," 204.
106 Heidegger, "Why Poets?," 202.
107 Heidegger, "Why Poets?," 240.
108 Heidegger, "Why Poets?," 240.
109 Badiou, *Age of the Poets*, 36.
110 Hallward, *Badiou*, 196–97.
111 Hallward, *Badiou*, 200.
112 Badiou, "Metaphysics and the Critique," 189.
113 Badiou, *Logic of Worlds*, 514.
114 "Restraint is the style of inceptual thinking only because it must become the style of future humanity grounded in Da-sein, i.e., only because it bears this grounding and is its pervasive disposition. Restraint, as style: the self-certainty of the grounding measure and of the sustained wrath of Da-sein. It determines and disposes the style, because it is *the basic disposition*" (Heidegger, *Contributions to Philosophy*, 28).
115 The 2015 foreword to Badiou's 1992–93 seminar on Nietzsche concludes with the following words: "On verra comment, gouverné par cette profonde sympathie, le commentaire en detail et l'admirant sans avoir pour autant à

lui concéder quoi que ce soit, j'ai pu décerner à Nietzsche, en mon seul nom, le titre suivant: prince pauvre et définitif de l'antiphilosophie." [It will be seen how, governed by this deep sympathy, commenting him in details and admiring him without however having to concede anything to him, I have been able to discern in Nietzsche, in my sole name, the following title: poor and decisive prince of antiphilosophy.] (Badiou, *Nietzsche*, 11).

BIBLIOGRAPHY

Agamben, Giorgio. *Creation and Anarchy: The Work of Art and the Religion of Capitalism*. Translated by Adam Kotsko. Stanford, CA: Stanford University Press, 2019.
Agamben, Giorgio. "Una domanda." *Quodlibet*, April 13, 2020, https://www.quodlibet.it/giorgio-agamben-una-domanda.
Alemán, Jorge. *Soledad, común: Políticas en Lacan*. Madrid: Clave intelectual, 2012.
Badiou, Alain. *The Age of the Poets and Other Writings on Twentieth-Century Poetry and Prose*. Translated by Bruno Bosteels, with an introduction by Emily Apter and Bruno Bosteels. London: Verso, 2014.
Badiou, Alain. *Being and Event*. Translated by Oliver Feltham. London: Continuum, 2005.
Badiou, Alain. *The Century*. Translated by Alberto Toscano. London: Polity, 2007.
Badiou, Alain. *Conditions*. Translated by Steven Corcoran. London: Continuum, 2008.
Badiou, Alain. *Handbook of Inaesthetics*. Translated by Alberto Toscano. Stanford, CA: Stanford University Press, 2005.
Badiou, Alain. *Heidegger: L'être 3, figure du retrait, 1986–1987*. Paris: Fayard, 2015.
Badiou, Alain. *Lacan: Anti-philosophy 3*. Translated by Kenneth Reinhard and Susan Spitzer. New York: Columbia University Press, 2018.
Badiou, Alain. *L'essence de la politique (1991–92)*. Paris: Fayard, 2018.
Badiou, Alain. *L'immanence des verités: L'être et l'événement III*. Paris: Fayard, 2019.
Badiou, Alain. *Logic of Worlds: Being and Event II*. Translated by Alberto Toscano. London: Continuum, 2009.
Badiou, Alain. *Manifesto for Philosophy*. Edited and translated by Norman Madarasz. Albany: State University of New York Press, 1992.
Badiou, Alain. "Metaphysics and the Critique of Metaphysics." *Pli* 10 (2000): 174–90.
Badiou, Alain. *Nietzsche: L'antiphilosophie 1 (1992–93)*. Paris: Fayard, 2015.
Badiou, Alain. *Parménide: L'être 1, figure ontologique, 1985–1986*. Paris: Fayard, 2014.
Badiou, Alain. *Que pense le poème?* Caen, France: NOUS, 2016.
Badiou, Alain. "The Question of Being Today." In *Theoretical Writings*, edited and translated by Ray Brassier and Alberto Toscano, 39–48. London: Continuum, 2004.
Badiou, Alain. *Wittgenstein's Antiphilosophy*. Translated by Bruno Bosteels. London: Verso, 2011
Badiou, Alain, and Giovanbattista Tusa. *The End: A Conversation*. London: Polity, 2019.

Balso, Judith. *Pessoa, le passeur métaphysique*. Paris: Seuil, 2006.

Bambach, Charles. *Thinking the Poetic Measure of Justice: Hölderlin-Heidegger-Celan*. Albany: SUNY University Press, 2013.

Benet, Juan. *El ángel del Señor abandona a Tobias*. Barcelona: La Gaya Ciencia, 1976.

Benveniste, Emile. *Dictionary of Indo-European Concepts and Society*. Chicago: Hau Books, 2016.

Betteridge, Tom. "Alain Badiou's Anabasis: Rereading Paul Celan against Heidegger." *Textual Practice* 30, no. 1 (2015): 45–68.

Borges, Jorge Luis. "On Exactitude in Science." In *Collected Fictions*, translated by Andrew Hurley, 325. New York: Penguin, 1988.

Caeiro, Alberto, and Timoteo Moreira. *Infracendencia: Inéditos del entorno (¿póstumo?) de Fernando Pessoa*. Transcription and notes by Alberto Moreiras, with an introduction by Rodolfo Ortiz and a postface and notes by Yoandy Cabrera. Vancouver: La Mariposa Mundial, 2020.

Caeiro, Fernando Pessoa. *Obra completa de Alberto Caeiro*. Edited by Jerónimo Pizarro and Patricio Ferrari. Lisbon: Tinta da China, 2019.

Capizzi, Antonio. *Introduzione a Parmenide*. Roma-Bari: Laterza, 1975.

Clemens, Justin. "Eternity Is Coming: The Age of the Poets by Alain Badiou." *Sydney Review of Books,* February 19, 2015, 1–10.

Deleuze, Gilles. *The Logic of Sense*. Translated by Mark Lester. New York: Columbia University Press, 1990.

Derrida, Jacques. *Learning to Live Finally: The Last Interview*. Translated by Pascale-Anne Brault and Michael Naas. Hoboken, NJ: Melville House, 2007.

Derrida, Jacques. *Of Spirit: Heidegger and the Question*. Translated by Geoffrey Bennington and Rachel Bowlby. Chicago: University of Chicago Press, 1991.

Derrida, Jacques. "*Ousia* and *Gramme*: Note on a Note to *Being and Time*." In *Margins of Philosophy,* translated by Alan Bass, 29–68. Chicago: Harvester Press, 1982.

Derrida, Jacques. *Théorie et pratique: Cours de L'ENS-Ulm 1975–76*. Paris: Galilée, 2017.

Derrida, Jacques. *La vie la mort: Séminaire (1975–76)*. Edited by Pascale-Anne Brault and Peggy Kamuf. Paris: Seuil, 2019.

Derrida, Jacques, Hans-Georg Gadamer, and Philippe Lacoue-Labarthe. *La Conférence de Heidelberg: Heidegger, portée philosophique et politique de sa pensée*. Introduction by Mireille Calle-Gruber, note by Jean-Luc Nancy. Abbaye d'Ardenne: IMEC, 2014.

Didi-Huberman, Georges. *Survival of the Fireflies*. Translated by Lia Swope Mitchell. Minneapolis: University of Minnesota Press, 2018.

D'Iorio, Paolo. *Nietzsche's Journey to Sorrento: Genesis of the Philosophy of the Free Spirit*. Chicago: University of Chicago Press, 2016.

Doumet, Christian. "La fin de 'L'âge des poètes.' Remarques sur un philosophème." *Litttérature* 156 (December 2009): 42–54.

Enrigue, Álvaro. *Sudden Death*. Translated by Natasha Wimmer. New York: Riverhead Books, 2016.

Eyers, Tom. "Badiou among the Poets." *Boundary 2* 43, no. 2 (2016): 141–61.

Galli, Carlo. "Epidemia e sovranitá." *Ragioni politiche di Carlo Galli*, April 7, 2020, https://ragionipolitiche.wordpress.com/2020/03/27/epidemia-e-sovranita/.

Geronimo. *My Life: As Told to S. M. Barrett*. Mineola, NY: Dover, 2019.

Graff Zivin, Erin. *Anarchaeologies: Reading as Misreading*. New York: Fordham, 2020.

Gramsci, Antonio. *Pre-Prison Writings*. Translated by Richard Bellamy. Cambridge: Cambridge University Press, 1994.

Hallward, Peter. *Badiou: A Subject to Truth*. Minneapolis: University of Minnesota Press, 2003.

Hartman, Saidiya. *Wayward Lives, Beautiful Experiments*. New York: Norton, 2019.

Hegel, Georg Wilhelm Friedrich. *Phenomenology of Spirit*. Translated by A. V. Miller. Oxford: Oxford University Press, 1977.

Heidegger, Martin. *Basic Writings: From "Being and Time" (1927) to "The Task of Thinking" (1964)*. Edited and translated by David Farrell Krell. New York: Harper and Row, 1977.

Heidegger, Martin. *Being and Time*. Translated by Joan Stambaugh. Albany: State University of New York Press, 1996.

Heidegger, Martin. *Bremen and Freiburg Lectures: Insight into That Which Is and Basic Principles of Thinking*. Translated by Andrew J. Mitchell. Bloomington: Indiana University Press, 2012.

Heidegger, Martin. *Contributions to Philosophy (Of the Event)*. Translated by Richard Rojcewicz and Daniela Vallega-Neu. Bloomington: Indiana University Press, 2012.

Heidegger, Martin. "'Only a God Can Save Us.' The *Spiegel* Interview (1966)." In *Heidegger: The Man and the Thinker*, edited and translated by Thomas Sheehan, 45–67. New Brunswick, NJ: Transaction, 2010.

Heidegger, Martin. *On Time and Being*. Translated by Joan Stambaugh. New York: Harper and Row, 1972.

Heidegger, Martin. *Pathmarks*. Edited and translated by William McNeill. Cambridge: Cambridge University Press, 1998.

Heidegger, Martin. *¿Qué es metafísica? Seguido de epílogo a ¿Qué es metafísica? e introducción a ¿Qué es metafísica?* Translated by Helena Cortés and Arturo Leyte. Madrid: Alianza Editorial, 2003.

Heidegger, Martin. *The Question concerning Technology and Other Essays*. Translated by William Lovitt. New York: Harper and Row, 1977.

Heidegger, Martin. "Who Is Nietzsche's Zarathustra?" Translated by Bernd Magnus. *Review of Metaphysics* 20, no. 3 (1967): 411–31.

Heidegger, Martin. "Why Poets?" In *Off the Beaten Track*, edited and translated by Julian Young and Kenneth Haynes, 200–41. Cambridge: Cambridge University Press, 2002.

Heidegger, Martin. *Country Path Conversations*. Translated by Bret W. Davis. Bloomington: Indiana University Press, 2010.

Joyce, James. *Finnegans Wake*. New York: Penguin, 1999.

Kafka, Franz. "The Wish to Be a Red Indian." In *The Complete Stories of Franz Kafka*, edited by Nahum N. Glatzer, 390. New York: Schocken, 1971.

Kierkegaard, Søren. *Fear and Trembling: Dialectical Lyric by Johannes de Silentio*. Translated by Alastair Hannay. New York: Penguin, 1985.

Klein, Naomi. "Screen New Deal: Under Cover of Mass Death, Andrew Cuomo Calls in the Billionaires to Build a High-Tech Dystopia." *The Intercept*, May 8, 2020, https://theintercept.com/2020/05/08/andrew-cuomo-eric-schmidt-coronavirus-tech-shock-doctrine/.

Kraniauskas, John. "The Reflux of Money: Outlaw Accumulation and Territorialization in *Breaking Bad*." In *Aspects of Marx's* Capital *Today*. Edited by Peter Osborne, Eric Alliez, and Eric-John Roberts, 208–33. London: CRMEP Books, 2019.

La Boétie, Etienne de. *The Politics of Obedience: The Discourse of Voluntary Servitude*. Translated by Harry Kurz. Auburn, AL: Ludwig von Mises Institute, 2008.

Lacan, Jacques. "Discours de Jacques Lacan à l'Université de Milan le 12 mai 1972, paru dans l'ouvrage bilingue." In *Lacan in Italia 1953–1978*, 32–55. Milan: La Salmandra, 1978.

Lacan, Jacques. *The Four Fundamental Concepts of Psychoanalysis*. Vol. 11 of *The Seminar of Jacques Lacan*. Edited by Jacques-Alain Miller, translated by Alan Sheridan. New York: W. W. Norton, 1998.

Laclau, Ernesto. *Emancipation(s)*. New York: Verso, 1996.

Laclau, Ernesto. *On Populist Reason*. London: Verso, 2015.

Lacoue-Labarthe, Philippe. *Heidegger and the Politics of Poetry*. Translated by Jeff Fort. Chicago: University of Chicago Press, 2007.

Levinas Emmanuel. *Otherwise Than Being, or Beyond Essence*. Translated by Alphonso Lingis. Boston: Kluwer, 1991.

Lyons, James K. *Paul Celan and Martin Heidegger: An Unresolved Conversation, 1951–1970*. Baltimore, MD: Johns Hopkins University Press, 2006.

Marías, Javier. *Thus Bad Begins*. Translated by Margaret Jull Costa. New York: Knopf, 2016.

Mazzolini, Samuele. "Populism Is Not Hegemony: Towards a Re-Gramscianization of Ernesto Laclau." *Theory and Event* 23, no. 3 (2020): 765–86.

Moreiras, Alberto, ed. "On Reiner Schürmann." Special issue, *Política común* 11 (2017).

Moreiras, Alberto. *Infrapolítica.: Instrucciones de uso*. Madrid: La Oficina, 2020.

Moreiras, Alberto. *Infrapolitics: A Handbook*. New York: Fordham University Press, 2021.

Moreiras, Alberto. *Sosiego siniestro*. Madrid: Guillermo Escolar, 2020.

Morey, Miguel. *Deseo de ser piel roja*. Barcelona: Anagrama, 1994.

Morey, Miguel. *Vidas de Nietzsche*. Madrid: Alianza Editorial, 2018.
Muñoz, Gerardo. "¿Democracia o anarquía?" *Infrapolitical Deconstruction (and Other Issues Related and Unrelated)* (blog), May 28, 2020, https://infrapolitica.com/2020/05/28/democracia-o-anarquia-por-gerardo-munoz/.
Nancy, Jean-Luc. *The Banality of Heidegger*. Translated by Jeff Fort. New York: Fordham University Press, 2017.
Nancy, Jean-Luc. *The Birth to Presence*. Translated by Brian Holmes and others. Stanford, CA: Stanford University Press, 1993.
The New Oxford Annotated Bible: New Revised Standard Version with the Apocrypha. Edited by Michael D. Coogan. New York: Oxford University Press, 2001.
Nietzsche, Friedrich Wilhelm. *"The Anti-Christ," "Ecce Homo," "Twilight of the Idols," and Other Writings*. Edited by Aaron Ridley, translated by Judith Norman. New York: Cambridge University Press, 2005.
Nietzsche, Friedrich Wilhelm. *Ecce Homo: How One Becomes What One Is*. Translated by R. J. Hollingdale. New York: Penguin, 1992.
Nietzsche, Friedrich Wilhelm. *The Gay Science*. Translated by Walter Kaufmann. New York: Vintage Books, 1974.
Nietzsche, Friedrich Wilhelm. *Human, All Too Human. A Book for Free Spirits*. Translated by Gary Handwerk. Stanford, CA: Stanford University Press, 1995.
Nietzsche, Friedrich Wilhelm. *Selected Letters of Friedrich Nietzsche*. Edited and translated by Christopher Middleton. Indianapolis, IN: Hackett, 1996.
Nietzsche, Friedrich Wilhelm. *Thus Spoke Zarathustra: A Book for All and None*. Translated by Walter Kaufmann. New York: Viking Press, 1966.
Parmenides. *Parmenide: Testimonianze e frammenti*. Translated and Edited by Mario Untersteiner. Florence: La Nuova Italia Editrice, 1958.
Pessoa, Fernando. *A Little Larger Than the Entire Universe: Selected Poems*. Edited and translated by Richard Zenith. London: Penguin, 2006.
Pindar. *The Complete Odes*. Translated by Anthony Verity. Oxford: Oxford University Press, 2007.
Pindar. *Olympian Odes, Pythian Odes*. Translated and edited by William H. Race. Cambridge, MA: Harvard University Press, 1997.
Poe, Edgar Allan. "The Mask of the Red Death." In *The Complete Stories*, 604–9. New York: Alfred A. Knopf, 1992.
Ranciére, Jacques. *Disagreements: Politics and Philosophy*. Translated by Julie Rose. Minneapolis: University of Minnesota Press, 1999.
Rancière, Jacques. *The Ignorant Schoolmaster: Five Lessons in Intellectual Emancipation*. Translated by Kristin Ross. Stanford, CA: Stanford University Press, 1991.
Rancière, Jacques. "Should Democracy Come? Ethics and Politics in Derrida." In *Derrida and the Time of the Political*. Edited by Phen Chea and Suzanne Guerlac, 274–88. Durham, NC: Duke University Press, 2009.
Saer, Juan José. *La pesquisa*. Buenos Aires: Rayo Verde, 2012.

Schürmann, Reiner. *Heidegger on Being and Acting: From Principles to Anarchy*. Translated by Christine-Marie Gros and Reiner Schürmann. Bloomington: Indiana University Press.

Schürmann, Reiner. *Le principe d'anarchie*. Paris: Seuil, 1982.

Sheehan, Thomas. "But What Comes before the 'After'?" In *After Heidegger*, edited by Gregory Fried and Richard Polt, 41–55. London: Rowman and Littlefield, 2018.

Sheehan, Thomas. "Heidegger's Interpretation of Aristotle: *Dynamis* and *Ereignis*." *Philosophy Research Archives* 4, no. 1258 (1978): 1–33.

Stiegler, Bernard. *What Makes Life Worth Living? On Pharmacology*. Translated by Daniel Ross. Cambridge, UK: Polity, 2013.

Thoreau, Henry David. *Walden*. In *The Portable Thoreau*, edited by Jeffrey S. Cramer, 197–468. New York: Penguin, 2012.

Tiqqun. *The Cybernetic Hypothesis*. Translated by Robert Hurley. Pasadena, CA: Semiotext(e), 2020.

Tiqqun. *Theory of Bloom*. Translated by Robert Hurley. Berkeley, CA: LBC Books, 2012.

Villacañas, José Luis. *El neoliberalismo como teología política*. Madrid: Ned, 2020.

Villacañas, José Luis. *Imperiofilia y el populismo nacional-católico: Otra historia del imperio español*. Madrid: Lengua de trapo, 2019.

Wilderson, Frank. *Afropessimism*. New York: Liveright, 2020.

INDEX

Afropessimism, 101, 102, 103, 104
Agamben, Giorgio, 10, 28, 29, 35, 37–38, 44, 45, 63, 69, 71, 74, 125, 131, 132, 134, 137
Alemán, Jorge, 15–16, 57–60, 123–24
Anarchy, 132, 133, 134, 137,
Ankhibasie, 71–3, 107
antagonism, 34, 136
Antigone, 29
Antiphilosophy, xi, 25, 26, 44, 45, 55, 63, 68–70, 72, 73–75, 79, 87, 89, 90–94, 97, 98, 105, 106, 124, 141, 149, 163
Apache, 42, 43, 84, 85, 89
Archipolitics, 103, 104, 106
Aristotle, 44, 61, 62–4, 66, 74–76, 94, 95, 151

Badiou, Alain, 6, 8, 10–3, 89–97, 102, 105, 118, 138–62
Barrett, S. M., 84
Bascuñán, Matías, 75–78
Bataille, Georges, 28
Benjamin, Walter, 28
Birnbaum, Jean, 127
Blanchot, Maurice, 10
Borges, Jorge Luis, 39
Bosteels, Bruno, 140

Caeiro, Alberto, 91, 95, 112–22, 144, 152, 154, 155
Cantor, Georg, 156; Cantorian 146, 148
Capizzi, Antonio, 5
Carroll, Lewis, 78
Celan, Paul, 95, 118, 148, 149, 150, 151, 161, 174, 179
Cesarano, Giorgio, 40, 41

Dasein, 57, 62, 67, 71, 72, 75, 81, 83
death drive, 70, 72, 75, 77
decision of existence, xi, xii, 15, 57, 59–62, 68–72, 73–75, 76–79, 81, 82, 84–85, 89, 96, 107, 109–11, 124, 180–81
Deleuze, Gilles, 78, 128
Democracy, 8, 10, 83, 102, 131, 132, 134–7, 163
Derrida, Jacques, 15, 41, 59, 64, 74, 75, 81–4, 106, 107–10, 111, 127–9, 131, 132, 134, 136–7, 139, 145, 163
D'Iorio, Paolo, 53

Exodus, xi, 28, 44,

Foucault, Michel, 15, 128

Gadamer, Hans-Georg, 82
Galli, Carlo, 8, 10
Geronimo, 41, 84, 85, 89
Gramsci, Antonio, 40, 48, 64–66, 69, 77, 79, 80, 83, 99, 100

Hallward, Peter, 161
Hartman, Saidiya, 104, 106
Hegel, George Wilhelm Frederich, 64, 66, 79, 80, 83, 93, 144
Hegemony, 35, 47, 48, 59, 66, 80, 84, 90, 93, 96, 97, 99–101, 106, 132, 134, 136, 137, 147
Heidegger, Martin, 11–3, 17, 31, 34, 48, 57, 58, 60, 62, 63, 64, 67, 71, 75, 76, 78, 81–3, 91–5, 96, 98, 107, 108–10, 131, 137, 139–63
Heraclitus, 71, 93
Hill, Walter, 89

infracendence, 111, 113, 120

infrapolitics, xi, 26, 27, 28, 38, 43, 44, 49, 50, 72, 87, 88, 89, 90, 100, 102, 103, 106, 163

jouissance, 75, 78

Kafka, Franz, 38
Kant, Immanuel, 74, 76, 77, 83, 128, 170
Kierkegaard, Sören, 23, 24, 57–9, 62, 76, 93
kinesis, 61, 67
Klein, Naomi, 88
Kling, Papo, 16
Kofman, Sarah, 128
Kraniauskas, John, 89

Lacan, Jacques, 15, 36, 57, 58, 59, 60, 62, 91–3, 98, 105, 123, 124, 127
Laclau, Ernesto, 90, 92, 93, 96, 97, 99
Lacoue-Labarthe, Philippe, 82, 84, 139, 143, 156
Lea, Henry Charles, 36
Leibniz, Gottfried Wilhelm, 11, 12, 13, 25, 91
Levinas, Emmanuel, 81, 128, 131–34, 135, 137
Lucretius, 147
Lyotard, Jean-François, 128

Mallarmé, Stéphane, 104, 142, 147, 150, 152, 162
Mandelstam, Osip, 152
Marías, Javier, 85, 87, 88
marranos, 23, 24, 36, 37, 56, 57
Marx, Karl, 65, 66, 67, 91, 95, 102, 146, 147, 178
Mazzolini, Samuele, 99
metaphysics without metaphysics, 91, 94, 95, 112, 140, 141, 143, 144, 145

Milner, Jean-Claude, 92
Moreira, Alberto, 112, 113
Moreiras, Alberto (grandfather of author), 172
Moreiras, Timoteo, 111, 112, 114, 118, 120, 174
Morey, Miguel, 41, 42, 50
Muñoz, Gerardo, 15, 131, 134

Nancy, Jean-Luc, 10, 15, 19, 79, 80, 82, 84, 163
Nietzsche, Friedrich, 8, 12, 25, 26, 50, 52–58, 61, 62, 63, 67, 76, 91, 93, 98, 103, 105, 107–10, 123

ontotheology, 66, 82, 124, 146

pandemic, ix, x, xii, 7, 11, 13, 14, 27, 29, 32–8, 42, 43, 57–60, 103, 106, 124, 125
Parmenides, 5, 6, 25, 26, 93, 94, 95, 147, 150, 160
Pasolini, Pier Paolo, 28
Pessoa, Fernando, 91, 111, 112, 116, 118, 120, 140, 143, 144, 145, 152, 169, 172
Pindar, 67, 70, 71, 76, 123, 124, 163
Poe, Edgar Allan, 4
Posthegemony, 49, 50, 72, 80–82, 100, 101, 104, 105, 106, 135, 136, 137

Rancière, Jacques, 100, 131, 134–7, 158
Rilke, Rainer Maria, 140, 158, 160
Rodríguez Matos, Jaime, 15–17, 127

Saer, Juan José, 44
Schmitt, Carl, 79
Scholem, Gershom, 38
social death, 102, 103, 105
Schürmann, Reiner, 131–4, 147
Stiegler, Bernard, 13

Tiqqun, 39, 131
Tobias (biblical/apocryphal character), 26, 27, 29

Villacañas, José Luis, 35–7, 79

waywardness, 104–6
Williams, Gareth, 81
Wittgenstein, Ludwig, 91, 93, 98, 154

www.ingramcontent.com/pod-product-compliance
Lightning Source LLC
Chambersburg PA
CBHW051126160426
43195CB00014B/2355